Nailed

The Biography of Jimmy Nail

After gaining a sportsman's degree in English from Cardiff University, Geraint Jones set out on a career in journalism which led him, via Neen Savage, Hope Bagot and Birmingham, to a Fleet Street career on two national newspapers. He currently works as a freelance writer.

Jones was due to be a Christmas Day baby, but arrived late in the death throes of 1958. His life has been characterised by an increasingly unhealthy and long-distance passion for North Wales's finest football league team. To recuperate, he lives quietly in north London with his partner, Deborah and their son Nye. Two cats have assumed squatters' rights.

Nailed
The Biography of Jimmy Nail

HarperCollins*Publishers*

HarperCollins*Publishers*
77–85 Fulham Palace Road,
Hammersmith, London W6 8JB

A Paperback Original 1998
1 3 5 7 9 8 6 4 2

A catalogue record for this book is
available from the British Library

ISBN 0 00 653079 2

Text layout by Mick Sanders

Printed and bound in Great Britain by
Caledonian Book Manufacturing Ltd, Glasgow

CONTENTS

PROLOGUE

Newcastle-upon-Tyne, 1970. A chilly autumn evening, already quite dark. A crowd has gathered outside the famous Mayfair Dance Hall in the heart of the city. Nothing unusual about that. The Mayfair is one of the most popular venues for young people. Except that this crowd is not the normal collection of party-going animals eager to dance and drink the night away. A closer inspection reveals people of all ages. What is more, they do not want to go in. They have come to watch.

A man with a loud hailer shouts for quiet and the good-humoured hubbub dies down to attentive silence. All eyes are on the film camera and the director, Mike Hodges, who shouts out his orders. Then comes the moment everyone has been waiting for. The star, Michael Caine, walks to his position a few yards from the main entrance, ready for his cue. Hodges waits while the last few voices in the crowd die away and calls 'Action'. Caine, easy, exuding self confidence, begins his walk from his position to the dance hall doorway. When he reaches it the director shouts 'Cut'. The tension breaks. The crowd applauds.

The scene is a straightforward one. Caine is pursuing a man into the club and he just needs to walk to the doorway. As simple as that. Yet the scene is shot time and again until Hodges is convinced he has it as he wants it. There is a lot of hanging around, not much to watch, but no one leaves. This is too much of a novelty. Big time film makers and big stars coming to Newcastle to make a picture. It is unheard of.

1

In the crowd is a sixteen-year-old boy. Although he is young, he towers above most of the people around him. He is alone and has a sullen demeanour which, allied to his size, encourages other onlookers to give him a wide berth. He does not care. He is utterly transfixed by what is going on before him. He watches the director instructing those around him, he watches the camera crew in action, but most of all he watches the star, Michael Caine. He knows that Caine came from humble beginnings, that he used his talent and the force of his personality to become a big shot. He notices that although he is not conventionally good looking he has a quality that makes it difficult to take your eyes off him. He has charisma.

The following year the film, *Get Carter*, shot almost entirely on location in Newcastle, is released to huge critical acclaim. The boy, now seventeen, goes to see it in his local cinema. He marvels at the way his home city has been used to convey the film's bleak, uncompromising message. On his way back to the small council house he shares with his mother and father, his mind goes back to the night he saw this wonderful creation being put together. The boy may not look it, but he is bright, perceptive. He analyses Caine's performance. He realises that Caine did little more in that simple scene he witnessed than exude the force of his personality. By the time the bus has taken him the two miles up the Benton Road to his estate, he has decided. 'I can do that,' he says to himself. 'I can do that.'

1
MYTH AND REALITY

Separating myth from reality in the life of Jimmy Nail is no simple task. His sister, the actress Val McLane, summed it up wonderfully succinctly. 'His stories change,' she said.

His stories have always changed. Even before he became famous Jimmy Nail liked nothing better than to mythologise. It always seemed necessary for him to have a mask he could slip on when he needed it. Just as his extraordinary face never looks the same from one photograph to the next, so most of the events of his life have acquired different versions in the re-telling.

Let's begin with his name. Plain James Bradford appears on his birth certificate, although thirty-six years later, as the informant on his father's death certificate, he lodged his name as James Michael Bradford. Just for good measure 'Aloysius' was acquired at his confirmation. (St Aloysius was famed for his piety and charity.) The general effect became a rousing one for profile writers. James Michael Aloysius Bradford has a ring to it.

He was born 16 March 1954, the third child of James Bradford senior and his wife Laura (née Johnson). The Bradfords already had two daughters – Val, then aged ten, and seven-year-old Shelagh. Jimmy was the boy they longed for.

Ten days short of his fortieth birthday when his son was born, Jimmy senior was typical of many working men of the time whose lives were riven by World War II. He was born on 26 March 1914, in a small back-to-back terraced house on Caledonia Street, a quarter of a mile from the north bank of the river Tyne, in the Walker district of Newcastle. His father George Bradford, a coal hewer and mother Catherine (nee Boylen) were part of a large clan in Walker at the time. Most earned a living from the traditional heavy industries – the mines and the shipyards.

Although not particularly big, Jimmy's father had a reputation as a hard man, someone it was advisable not to mess with. He had a face that could have been hewn from an old Durham coalfield – lean, angular, more regular than his son's, with narrower eyes. But the nose is the same, although his father managed to prevent it becoming broken and misshapen. Whereas Jimmy junior's 'meanders all over his face', to quote one profile writer, his father's was symmetrical and jutted proudly out of a face that was strong enough not to be dominated by it.

The swashbuckling image was enhanced by his father's stories that as well as boxing for a living before the war he also played professional football for Huddersfield Town – then a major English First Division club. In a football-mad city like Newcastle this was enough to make him an heroic figure.

In many ways, James Bradford and Laura Johnson were a match of opposites. Laura, tall, big-boned with a gentle nature which belied her inner strength. Jimmy, wiry, energetic, aggressive, a man given to outbursts of temper and who never shied away from speaking his mind, especially in drink.

Whatever sporting ambitions he had were put paid to when war broke out and the twenty-five year old began service in the Royal Navy. Shrapnel injuries to his legs meant he needed leg irons for eight years after he limped back ashore in 1945 looking for work to support his young family.

The exact level of sporting potential which was thwarted by the war is not clear. Jimmy junior would naturally have been proud to tell his young friends that his father was an ex-boxer who played football for Huddersfield Town. A hard man who played soccer at the top level was a figure to be admired and gave the young boy a certain respect among his peers. The truth is not quite so clear. There is no record of Jimmy Bradford ever having been on Huddersfield Town's books. It is certain he never made a first team appearance although it is possible he was in their reserves as these records are incomplete. Similarly there is no record of him boxing, although this is even more of a grey area and it is quite possible he plied that trade in the thirties without any evidence remaining.

After the war things become clearer. Jimmy senior took a job as a painter at NEI Parsons, the turbine manufacturers in Newcastle, and settled down to family life.

Jimmy Nail has often described his early years as impoverished. On one occasion he explained his love of good shoes as a result of never having had decent ones to wear as a child. On another he told how his mother would often walk a couple of miles to return empty pop bottles and claim the tuppence or threepence that was on offer. He qualifies this by admitting he didn't realise how poor his family was until he got older. This may, of course be the hindsight of a man who is now a millionaire and who describes his early family life as like living on Mars. But was it truly as alien an upbringing as he makes out? Are the images of poverty he invites his audience to conjure really appropriate? The truth is, the more he exaggerates his impoverished beginnings, the more he proclaims his achievement in escaping from them.

Home was 10 Penfold Close, an end of terrace, red-brick council house, in one corner of the intimate, three-sided close. It is one of a series that appends Fairways Avenue in Longbenton, a working-class suburb about three miles north of Newcastle city centre. The Bradfords moved here after they married, attracted by the more modern, spacious houses on offer on the new estates, in which they could more comfortably raise a family.

Life in Penfold Close was close knit. It contained just twelve houses in three four-block terraces. Two terraces faced each other and the third joined them together. Number 10 was the end of this block on the right hand side, facing the close from Fairways Avenue. The Close is part of a cluster of council homes – too small to be called an estate – that line the streets between the main A188 route north, the A191 to Whitley Bay and Coach Lane. Although just a stone's throw away, they are very different in character from the homes of the main Longbenton estate north of the A191. The dwellings there come closer to most people's pre-conception of a run-down inner city district. There are derelict blocks with boarded windows and graffiti-covered walls, pubs which intimidate the stranger, and lots of middle-aged men with time on their hands.

But the Bradford enclave is altogether better-tended. The paintwork is fresher, the lawns are cared for, flower beds are weed-free. Everything smacks of pride in appearance, self-reliance and hard-won self-respect. Number 10 was a microcosm of this working-class respectability. By no stretch of the imagination could the Bradfords be described as well-off – even comfortable is a generous description – but they were not poor by the standards of the day.

Money was tight, but the children, unlike many others, never 'went without'. Jimmy certainly could not have been born into a more loving environment. The baby boy was the apple of his mother's eye. Val and Shelagh, who were old enough to 'mother' their baby brother, greeted his arrival joyously. His father was less of an influence in these early years as he spent his days at work and most of his evenings in the pub.

Margaret Allan, who still lives on Penfold Close, remembers the Bradfords well. 'They were like everybody else on the Close, not flush with money but not badly off. They were not poor,' she said.

Not poor, and highly aspirational. Val was bright and was encouraged to achieve from the outset. She studied English at Leeds University, took a postgraduate course in drama, worked as an English teacher for three years then as a broadcaster with the BBC. In between that she established herself as an actress of national standing. Almost eleven years older than Jimmy, she was the success story of the family when he was barely out of short trousers.

It was decided not to send Jimmy to any of the local state schools. Laura, especially, preferred for him to go to the Roman Catholic Infants School in their native Walker. This was not by any means the easiest option for her as it was an inconvenient bus ride away. But she decided she wanted Jimmy to have what she considered to be the best educational grounding and was prepared to put up with the inconvenience. Each morning she and Jimmy would catch the number nineteen bus for the twenty-minute ride to school. Because of the distance, there was no question of Jimmy going home for his dinner, but equally the family decided he would not have school meals like most of the other pupils. Instead it was arranged for him to go to his aunt's who lived close by.

Not going to the local school meant that Jimmy was set slightly apart from the other children on his estate. He didn't mix with them very much as that crucial social forum, the school playground, was denied him. Even at Walker RC he was whisked away at lunchtime which meant that socialising was confined to the short mid-morning and afternoon breaks.

One mother who knew both Jimmy senior and Laura from their teenage years in Walker found herself on that same number nineteen bus each morning. Her children went to Walker RC and she worked as a dinner lady there. She vividly remembers the shy boy who stayed close to Laura and refused to join the other schoolchildren who would congregate to talk, play games and make mischief. 'Jimmy was a very sullen, quiet boy. He never left his mam's side when they were on that bus, he never went and sat with the other boys and girls,' she said.

She is full of praise for Laura as a 'quiet, respectable' woman devoted to her children and determined they should get the best opportunities it was in her power to provide. 'She was devoted to her children. Jimmy was the light of her life, her only son. She adored him.'

The friend confirms the generally-held view of the Bradford's status in their community. 'The family weren't poor. They were always smartly dressed. There were a heck of a lot more poorer people than they were.'

When Jimmy finished at the infants' school in 1961, his parents decided to take him out of Walker RC and send him to Benton Park Junior School, a few minutes' walk from Penfold Close. Laura had found the daily journey to Walker a grind and as Jimmy got older he quite reasonably wanted to go to school with the estate children he was beginning to make friends with.

By now his eldest sister Val was a confident seventeen year old with her sights set on university and Shelagh was fourteen and doing well in school. Jimmy was also a bright boy who appeared to be following in their impressive footsteps. The local school had a good reputation and other mothers had spoken highly of it to Laura. Jimmy was now seven years old. Old enough to walk the short way to school with his growing group of new friends as long as he took care crossing the busy Benton Road. He was growing up, taking his first tentative steps out from under the shade offered by his mother's protective umbrella.

Val remembers him as a nervous, highly strung child, whose very intelligence gave him problems in the classroom. 'He was very wiry, very nervy, lived on his wits, had difficulty at school because he was very bright and consequently he suffered for that because he used to finish his work early and then he was punished. One particular teacher used to lock him in a cupboard to calm him down.'

The humiliation of being dragged from the class and the terror of being cooped up in the cupboard had an effect on Jimmy which was to affect him for the rest of his life. It left him with acute claustrophobia.

This early part of Jimmy's life had been heavily influenced by his mother and sisters. Now the balance was beginning to shift. He was growing up, finding his feet in the community. In a world where traditional masculine qualities were revered, Jimmy began to look to his father for guidance. The old man was not everything Laura may have wished for as a role model for her son, but he had plenty of attractive credentials for the young boy. He was a man's man, a rough-hewn Geordie. He worked hard, drank hard, and was not afraid to call a spade a spade. He was a 'real character', as men of a certain type are oft described in Newcastle. It is a term of admiration, of respect and no little awe. A 'real character' is someone – almost always a man – who goes his own way, who says what he thinks whatever the consequences. Generally an independent, strong-willed, occasionally bloody-minded so-and-so.

It also became clear that although Jimmy had inherited his mother's physique – tall, raw boned with big hands and feet – he began to show signs of his father's character. It was a dangerous combination.

There was nothing unusual about the roles adopted by husband and wife. He was the bread winner, she was the one who held the family together. That the young Jimmy saw little of his father, especially during the week, was not exceptional. Jimmy senior was up at 6.30 a.m. every day. His son remembers him 'coughing, coughing, coughing his guts up'; a spectacle which has left him with an abiding revulsion of smoking. After a day's work at Parsons, Jimmy senior would then do what he was conditioned to do – go to the pub. Very often by the time his father got home, Jimmy junior would be tucked up in bed by a mother ever mindful that he needed a good night's sleep to be fresh for school the next day.

While the women in the family created an atmosphere conducive to him working hard at school and aiming to 'better himself', in the popular jargon of the day, his father was very much the unreconstructed male. As with most boys, the older he got the more he looked up to the old man. The role model he provided – sporting hero, no-nonsense hard-man who did not shirk a hard day's work and then liked to let his hair down in the pub – was a powerful one.

These two influences developed side by side and exerted opposing pulls on the growing boy. He developed a taste for reading poetry, and even began reading the dictionary to improve his vocabulary. While he felt able to talk about these things with his mother and sisters, his father was not interested. Within the confines of working-class Newcastle, he was a successful, respected man. His peers listened to his stories of football and boxing and the rough life of the Navy with respect. He also brought these tales home to the fireside and enjoyed telling his son about his colourful earlier life, ignoring the tuts and shaking head of his wife. The old man also saw something of himself in the boy. He recognised the quick temper, the stubborn streak, the force of personality. A chip off the old block is young Jim, he would say with pride. Laura knew better.

The eleven-plus examination was the first big enigma of Jimmy's life. From the security of fame and wealth, the adult Nail is fond of talking about how the education system failed him, how it misunderstood boys like him and spewed them out to take their chances in the pit, the shipyards or the building sites. How loving the 'power, romance and escapism offered by written words' and nurturing dreams of being an English teacher were scant protection against the awful callousness of a system which judged him on appearances only.

It is from the eleven-plus that the adult Nail traces his disaffection with the establishment. He tells the story of how his heart sank when he was told he had failed and had to go to the technical school, describing it as 'just a borstal'. Years later, he says, his mother bumped into his old primary school headteacher, a Mr Turnbull, who told her young Jimmy had actually done brilliantly but boys like him were not wanted in the grammar school, so the two schools had conspired to thwart his ambitions.

Listening to the sleek, expensively dressed, successful man recounting this story leaves one with a sense of anger at the injustice and also admiration for the talent and determination that must have been required to get him from such a hopelessly disadvantaged background to the bright lights of stardom he basks in today.

It is only when the events are examined a little more closely that doubts as to the veracity of Nail's story creep in.

Nail recalls his headmaster as Mr Turnbull. Yet in the years he spent at Benton Park Primary – 1961–65 – the head was Mrs Hayes. There is no record of a Mr Turnbull at the school. Also Mr T. J. Laidler MSc, former head of Manor Park Technical School, would probably not take kindly to Jimmy's description of his school as 'just a borstal'. Nail's assertion that he was deprived of his eleven-plus pass and was therefore forced into a second-class education appears to confuse the terms 'Technical' and 'Secondary Modern'.

Mr Laidler was head of Manor Park Technical when it opened in 1961. In the programme for the official opening ceremony of 24 March it declared its intentions of offering 'a liberal education permeated with and inspired by twentieth century technology ... the same high standards as those gained by grammar schools will be aimed at, but by a different method of approach, working from the practical to the theoretical, from concrete facts to abstract concepts.'

Taking a total of 854 pupils from the 'entire east side of Newcastle', the school offered five year O-level courses and a sixth form for students taking A-levels. A spokeswoman from the present-day Manor Park School is adamant that the technical school of the sixties only admitted eleven-plus passes. Scholarship failures would have been sent to North Heaton Secondary Modern.

Jimmy was a bright boy from a background that encouraged him to do well at school. He was the kind of child who would be expected to pass his eleven-plus. To do so and win a place in a modern, ambitious secondary school, was nothing more than the next step in his education. Yet he subsequently insisted that he hadn't. It is possible that he has genuinely forgotten the events of that part of his life. It is also possible that he needs to keep people guessing, to present a misleading impression of an impoverished, disadvantaged working-class childhood and inferior education so that his subsequent achievements seem all the more impressive.

2
A TURNING POINT

Some tragedies can be predicted, prepared for even. Others strike out of the blue. When tragedy visited the Bradford family it came without warning.

Jimmy was thirteen, just a boy. His world was secure. He went to bed on the Friday night of 9 June 1967 content and looking forward to what fun the weekend might bring. He woke on Saturday and found that all the rules had changed. His sister Shelagh was dead. He did not understand how it had happened. He just knew that one of the pillars of his life – one of its certainties – had been wrenched away.

Despite his adult recollections to the contrary, there seems to have been little in Jimmy's life up until then to disturb him. He was doing well at secondary school and his fondness for the written word continued to develop. He even wrote some poetry, protesting against the Vietnam war. He was passionate about football and showed considerable promise as a centre half, much to the delight of his father. Home life was comfortable. Val and Shelagh had both left home and he missed them, but there was plenty to occupy his mind.

Shelagh was a student nurse at Newcastle General Hospital. After two years' training she was making good progress. A popular and respected figure amongst her fellow students, she entered wholeheartedly into the life of the hospital. She was chairman of the Student Nurses Association, a role that involved her in many duties on top of her arduous working hours on the wards. But, like her siblings, Shelagh was a forceful personality who enjoyed the extra responsibility the role offered. She was particularly looking forward to acting as one of the Association's delegates at a weekend conference in London later that month.

The Friday night was a special one in Shelagh Bradford's life. It was her twentieth birthday. A nurses' dance was already arranged for that evening so Shelagh decided to hold a party for her friends afterwards at her small ground floor flat at 24 Harley Terrace, Gosforth, a suburb to the north-west of the city centre no more than two miles away from the family home in Longbenton. The young woman did not balk at the prospect of a double celebration – dancing early in the evening, then a cosy gathering ready to carouse into the small hours. She appeared lively at the dance but everything changed dramatically once she got home. Her brother-in-law, Martin McLane found her in tears.

'I asked her what was the matter but she told me I would not understand if she told me,' he told the inquest into her death. 'She told my wife she was upset about a man called Mike.'

The McLanes did their best to comfort Shelagh and left at 2 a.m. with the party still going strong. Eventually the last of the forty guests drifted away and her neighbour, Hazel Curless, was about to go back to her own flat upstairs in the Victorian terrace when she found Shelagh unconscious. She dialled 999 and desperately tried to revive the girl with heart massage. It was all in vain, Shelagh was dead by the time the ambulance arrived.

A post mortem examination found traces of two drugs in her bloodstream. Sodium Amytal, a commonly prescribed barbiturate and dextropropoxyphene, a popular pain killer not much stronger than aspirin. At that time barbiturates were prescribed for two main purposes: as a sleeping pill and as tranquillisers, in the way Valium would be recommended today. Shelagh, according to her family, was using them as sleeping pills because of the disruptive effect shift work was having on her sleeping pattern. But there was a big problem with barbiturates which was only just being recognised in 1967 and which led to them being banned altogether by the mid-seventies. Doctors found that the drug was too easy to overdose on and was also being widely abused because it produced in patients a feeling of well-being similar to being mildly drunk.

In the late sixties one of the most common reasons for admission to the emergency department of a hospital was barbiturate overdose and, according to Professor Vincent Marks, a former vice president of the Royal College of Pathologists, very few were accidental. It was easily the commonest form of death by overdose.

'They were almost never accidental, they were suicidal,' said Professor Marks. 'Of course one didn't necessarily want to say that they were suicidal. If you could find any reason to avoid a suicide verdict you did so. If, therefore, there were two or more drugs present and there was no suicide note and there was no evidence of attempted suicide, you would describe it as accidental death.'

Thirty years ago there was not the same stringency about drug interaction as there is today. A person given barbiturates as sleeping tablets would not be warned to avoid alcohol, only that by drinking alcohol they would increase the effect of the drug. Despite that, it was rare to die as a result of a barbiturate/alcohol combination, said Professor Marks.

The one factor which a pathologist would look for to help a coroner reach a verdict in these cases was the concentration of barbiturates in the bloodstream. An abnormally high amount would point conclusively to suicide. But if the level was moderate it was often interpreted as accidental poisoning.

The coroner recorded a verdict of accidental death by sodium amytal and dextropropoxyphene poisoning. The impression the Bradford family carry from the inquest is that Shelagh may have been allergic to one of the drugs she took or that the combination of barbiturates, dextropropoxyphene and alcohol triggered a reaction which could not have been foreseen.

Ask any parent what is the worst thing that could happen to them and they will invariably tell you that it would be for their children to die before them. There is something unbearable about the prospect of surviving your offspring. But to lose a child in the prime of her life, in such mysterious and unforeseen circumstances makes the torment even more acute.

Although there is no incontrovertible evidence that Shelagh

Bradford deliberately took an overdose, the family would be less than human if the possibility had not gnawed at them from time to time. She was upset about a man, she was a nurse who would have been aware of the dangers of barbiturates from her experiences at the hospital. However many times they dismissed it from their minds, the uncertainties of that tragic night remain.

Laura Bradford never recovered. Normally a serene, gentle woman, she became hysterical when told the news. She began to scream uncontrollably. Her chestnut brown hair turned grey overnight. She has shed tears for her lost daughter every day of her life since. The effect on Jimmy was twofold. Not only did he have to cope with the loss of his sister at an extremely vulnerable age, he had to witness his beloved mother in torment. Suddenly the woman who had quietly taken care of him all his life was displaying a violence of emotion he had not experienced before. The woman who he had always turned to for the answers was now seeking them herself.

Jimmy has only spoken publicly about his sister's death twice.

In 1995 Jimmy Nail was interviewed by Melvyn Bragg for ITV's South Bank Show. Bragg asked him about Shelagh's death. It was a question that was certainly agreed beforehand. Even though he was prepared for it Nail's face suddenly sagged when Bragg reminded him of the effect it had on his mother. His jaw dropped, elongating his face, his big eyes bulged for a few seconds and stared into space before he collected himself. In the same interview he admitted that it was 'something I buried so deeply that I cannot even think back to what my reaction was'.

Three years earlier, he told Chrissy Iley in an interview published in the *Sunday Times* magazine: 'I was thirteen, it didn't affect me much at the time. My mum was in the street and a police car parked outside. Our door was open and I remember my mum screaming. I just closed down. But I remember the funeral. It was fucking ghastly.'

He quickly counters the 'fucking ghastly' comment with one designed to shore up emotion. 'It's no more and no less misery than most people have in their lives,' he says, deceiving himself that the macho Geordie should be able to deal with it.

Carol Johnson, ex-wife of AD/DC lead singer Brian Johnson, is one of Jimmy's closest friends and yet he only ever mentioned the tragedy to her once, and in the same clumsy way he talked about it on television. She insists he told her that Shelagh had killed herself after a row with a boyfriend. All he can come up with – or all he is prepared to come up with – are the undigested flashbacks from that time. There is no sign that he is able to offer any cogent explanation of how the tragedy affected him or how it has influenced his adult life.

He conceded to Bragg: 'My sister died when I was thirteen and I do not know whether that had anything to do with what happened to me, because I veered off a bit at that age.'

He was thirteen, an extremely vulnerable age. It is a time when boys experiment at being men, when they often become rebellious and scornful of authority and most of all of the family that reared them.

One characteristic which facilitated the transition from youth to young man more easily than any other was size. Suddenly the young Jimmy found he had plenty of it. He shot up in height almost overnight into a towering, gangly teenager with enormous hands and feet. Other boys looked up to him – literally as well as metaphorically – and he found he enjoyed the sense of power this gave him. He was a bright boy who had inherited his father's truculence. This combination added to the profound effects of his sister's death made him almost impossible to handle at school. At home it was a similar story. The invincibility of the family unit had been exposed as a myth. He had no faith in it anymore.

Val McLane has no doubts about the fundamental effect Shelagh's death had on her brother. She points out that while the other members of the family were adult, Jimmy was just a boy. Inevitably, while his mother, father and sister withdrew into themselves to grieve, Jimmy was left isolated. At the time he needed the support of his family the most, he found it wanting. She maintains this was the starting point of his troubled adolescence.

Shelagh's death, she said, 'has coloured the whole of his life since, it's certainly coloured the whole of my life. I think the problems that he has encountered have arisen from the terrible trauma of losing his sister when he was thirteen.

'The whole family was traumatised and nobody had any time particularly to give to Jimmy. He was left to recover from this on his own because we were suffering so much. Nobody received any kind of help in those days – we are talking about 1967 – and as a result of that I think he did go through a rebellious phase. Whenever he is faced with a problem, and he still does it now, he takes it within himself and tries to solve it himself.'

One particular episode reveals the turmoil and alienation the young Jimmy was suffering. His footballing ability – inherited from his father – had blossomed to the extent that he was offered a trial with Newcastle United, a rare honour.

Jimmy didn't turn up. He was offered a chance that hundreds of boys his age would have given their eye-teeth for and he didn't turn up.

His explanation, given years later, is extraordinary. He told a journalist in 1985, 'I had a trial arranged at Newcastle United when I was around thirteen. When the day arrived I looked out of my bedroom curtains and saw snow. I thought, "No thanks", and went back to bed. I was never allowed to play for the school team again.'

The outrage felt by teachers and pupils is understandable. Here was a talented boy given a much-coveted opportunity and he threw it away for no apparent reason. Jimmy went from a position where he was respected and admired to one in which he was ostracised. Less talented boys could not forgive him for throwing his chance away. Teachers who gave up their spare time to coach the school football team felt he did not merit their efforts.

This behaviour can surely only be explained by the dislocation he was feeling over his sister's death. His life had been turned upside down, the things he had put his trust in were shifting about, everything was warped. It was another example of a wasted opportunity at this crucial time in his life. More were to come.

About this time Manor Park School organised a series of careers meetings for pupils. Jimmy's detailed account of the encounter twenty-five years later is an indication of the effect it had on him.

The careers adviser, without looking up from his papers asked Jimmy what he would like to be. 'I said, well, I wouldn't mind being a policeman, actually, or an English teacher.'

The reply was devastating. 'He said, "Son, there are three options for kids like you: the shipyards, the pit or the building site." That was the limit of my future as far as the establishment was concerned, or so I felt. I thought, If that's what they are offering me, well fuck it.'

Things went downhill at school from then on. The boy who once read poetry and the dictionary and wrote his own verse organised a book-burning session among fellow-pupils. The shy loner found a rebellious voice and became a ring leader. He once tried to hit a teacher who was attempting to punish him. Then came the coup-de-grace. The curtains were set alight one morning in assembly and Jimmy got the blame. He claims he was playing with a magnifying glass and things just got out of hand. The school decided they had had enough and expelled him. He was fifteen and yet to sit his exams. They had a good case and were deaf to the pleas of his family. Within three years of Shelagh's death it had all gone wrong and the school authorities were unable to make the connection between the two. A promising boy had gone badly off the rails and seemed beyond redemption.

Jimmy was now unrecognisable from the shy, sensitive boy of just a few years earlier. Only the sullenness remained. Laura must have gone through agonies watching this unfold, but was powerless to prevent it. She had lost one daughter and her only son was ignoring her advice to have big dreams, was wasting the talents she knew he possessed. These were dark days for Laura Bradford and her wayward and wilful son would ensure things got much worse before they got better.

3
LAGER LAGER LAGER

Although he was only sixteen when he began his working life as an apprentice welder at the giant Parsons turbine manufacturers, Jimmy Bradford could hardly be called a boy. He had already grown to most of his current 6ft 4ins and, according to one workmate, possessed 'the biggest pair of hands and feet I've ever seen'. Add to that a shock of curly hair and it's easy to see why his colleagues immediately nicknamed him 'The Yeti'.

It was 12 October 1970, just a few months after his expulsion from school. His father, by now a foreman painter at Parsons, was able to pull a few strings to get his son an apprenticeship. After his disastrous time at school, this would be a new start for the boy, he reasoned. He would also be able to keep a discreet eye on his progress.

If Jimmy senior thought the disciplines of a welding apprenticeship would exorcise the demons that beset his son he was mistaken. The dreaded prediction of the careers adviser had come true. Jimmy had been horrified at being typecast by the establishment, yet that rebellious anger had helped fulfil the prophecy. The words of the careers adviser must have rung in his ears as he clocked in as number 14050 at the massive plant. He disguised his anger and frustration, driving them deep within himself.

This was the adult world and he was a small cog in its complex assembly of wheels. He was no longer the dominant force he had been amongst his classmates at school. So he reverted to his old defence mechanism, and withdrew into himself. He worked hard enough at first, tried to apply himself to learning his trade, but secretly hated the rut he felt he had fallen into. One workmate recalls the large, sullen teenager. 'He was a loner,' he said. 'He used to go out drinking and battling with his own mates at weekends. Many's the Monday morning he just didn't turn up to work because he'd been put in the cells for fighting.'

Drinking and fighting. Two pastimes which were to dominate Jimmy's teens and twenties. He had been in plenty of scrapes at school, but now he began to move into the big league. Years later Nail was to describe it as the onset of a dark time in his life.

'Looking back it is like looking at some kind of animal study,' he told Melvyn Bragg during his South Bank Show interview. Yet he could not resist some showmanship to leaven his account. Asked by Bragg what dominated his existence at that time, he cupped his hand around an imaginary pint glass and tossed the 'contents' down his throat. Then he smacked his right fist hard into his large left palm. The cavernous warehouse in which the interview was held reverberated with the noise. Nail could not quite keep the smirk off his face.

He has never been able to resist glorifying the violence of his youth. 'I've lost many a tooth in general misbehaviour,' was one of the boasts of his *Auf Wiedersehen Pet* years. Ten years later he admitted his method. 'I've been told I can terrorise people, and although that side of me is a myth, it is a myth that can work in your favour.'

Just as he was later to use his colourful past as a 'fantastic' reservoir of raw material for his writing, he also used people's preconceptions and prejudices about it to further his own ends. It is an easy myth to sell and there was no shortage of eager buyers in the form of Fleet Street profile writers. Numerous interviewers over the years are found 'cowering' before the brooding presence before them, 'terrified' to ask any difficult questions and if they try brought into line with a glare that could 'cut through the fog on the Tyne'. Nothing wrong with all this, of course. Nail is entitled to use the publicity machine as expertly as he can and the journalists are entitled to produce the most readable copy. But the overall effect has been to gloss over his past.

There is no doubt that his youth and young adulthood was violent. The real question is, what form did it take? That was determined by two things. The size of the boy in the fight, which was considerable. And the size of the fight in the boy, which is more difficult to determine.

There is no question that there was plenty of aggression in him. There was also a cussedness about him, a bloody-minded determination always to have the last word and hang the consequences. Often this led him into violent situations and once there he faced up to what came. But was he a real hard man? Was he someone who enjoyed the violence for its own sake, someone who cold-bloodedly sought it out? There is no evidence of that, at this stage of his life at least.

Drinking and fighting became inextricably linked. They formed an alternative apprenticeship – and one he entered with much more enthusiasm than his legitimate one at Parsons. These Geordie life skills were learned around the pubs and clubs of Newcastle by night and the football grounds of England on Saturdays. Drinking was a way of life to Jimmy and his compatriots. It was important to learn how to drink, to hold your ale. Also, drinking was a wonderful catalyst. With a few pints inside you an ordinary night out could turn into an adventure.

He had grown up watching his father drink his fill after work and stagger home content. That wasn't for him. He wanted to drink in a different way, he wanted drinking to be fun. So Jimmy and his compatriots would hit the town, especially on Friday and Saturday nights.

By this time he had acquired a large circle of drinking friends, who were attracted by his charismatic presence in the pubs and clubs of Newcastle. He was fun to be with, a good laugh. You could always be sure of an eventful night out if Jimmy Bradford was there.

A few 'starters' in their locals in Longbenton or Heaton – perhaps The Sun, The Rocket or The Pineapple – and then it was on the bus to the city centre just a couple of miles away. Perhaps they would go to a nightclub or, if they were lucky, they might to get to hear about a party. If they were feeling less energetic it would be a curry or Chinese to round off the evening. More often than not these nights out would be punctuated by shambolic violence and brushes with the law. And Jimmy was usually at the centre of it.

One favourite haunt on a Friday night was the Mayfair, a popular venue for local bands, and ironically, the place where Jimmy's dreams of stardom had been awakened a little earlier. It was not enough to go there and simply enjoy the entertainment. He had to have a little more spice than that. A game of cat and mouse with the bouncers developed. An accomplice would be instructed to go into the Mayfair and everyone taking part would chip in the entrance fee. He would then go into the gents' toilets where there was a set of emergency exit doors leading to a back yard bounded by a high fence. The rest of the gang waited behind the fence for their co-conspirator to kick open the doors and give the signal for them to come in.

Sometimes it worked. The gang got a cut-price night out and enjoyed the euphoria of their scam. Sometimes it didn't, and they received a few bruises courtesy of the bouncers. Either way it was a story to dine out on.

Another popular late-night game took place at the various Indian and Chinese restaurants Jimmy and his friends visited for an end-of-evening meal. They enjoyed 'doing a runner', that is trying to leave without paying for their food. To be successful at this, a little preparation was helpful. It was a good idea to know the rough layout of the place before going in and finding that the only table big enough to accommodate a large group was a tortuous obstacle course away from the safety of the front door. Signals were also important, but the only signal they seem to have devised was one of the group indicating he was going to the toilet. The potential for disaster here was unlimited as there was no sense of loyalty. People might genuinely have wanted to go to the toilet. Given the amount of beer they had drunk before arrival it was probably a medical necessity. Any of them, on return from the conveniences, might find that all his so-called friends had vanished, leaving him the bill. Mischievous souls like Jimmy would enjoy the odd 'dummy run', which did nothing for the digestion.

One fellow-diner remembers those nights with mixed feelings. 'They used to go to different Indians or Chineses every week and nine times out of ten they would try to run out without paying.

'I always seemed to be the last one out and sometimes they would catch me and make me pay the bill.'

This pattern continued unabated through Jimmy's late teens and early twenties. In the early years he was still living at home, but becoming an increasing handful. His mother was by now despairing of her son. He invariably landed himself in trouble with the police at weekends, either for being drunk and disorderly or for petty thuggery. Most of the time a few hours in the cells to cool off was sufficient but occasionally it was more serious. Sometimes the police would come round to the house in an attempt to scare him into conformity, but nothing worked for long.

He may have had a wide network of acquaintances, but very few got close to Jimmy Bradford. One who did was a boy who had grown up with him on the Longbenton estate, Tom McCulloch. Although ten months older than Jimmy, they had got on well since childhood. Tom, a postman's son, lived in a flat just round the corner from Jimmy's house. They were always calling on each other. The friendship remained strong through their teens and now Tom was Jimmy's closest pal. He too was something of a loner at heart and the two seemed to understand each other.

One of the many brushes with the law came shortly after Jimmy bought his first car, a joint venture with Tom. They had both been mad on cars since they were small boys and, on starting work, had decided to save together for one. Tom was training to be a mechanic so he could sort out any problems which might occur. They just needed to be old enough to drive. Jimmy made sure they wasted no time. Soon after his seventeenth birthday they had enough money, and the hunt for their first set of wheels began.

A friend, David Laidlaw, with whom he was later to share a house, was the son of a car dealer on the Shields Road in Heaton. Jimmy saw an old red Ford Corsair on the forecourt and decided he had to have it. No one can remember if he had passed his test or whether he had sorted out the necessary insurance before he drove it away gleefully with Tom in the passenger seat. What is beyond dispute is how far they got: a lamppost a mile or so up the Benton Road, outside that scene of many a past misdemeanour, Manor Park School. This was 1971, before the days of compulsory seatbelts, when most drivers and passengers did not bother to belt up. The car hit the lamppost hard and both boys hit the windscreen hard. Luckily they were not badly hurt – just cuts and bruises – and were able to make a quick getaway before the police arrived.

David Laidlaw, who now owns the garage himself, remembers the police calling to see his father as the car was still registered in his name. 'They wrapped it round a lamppost. I heard that they went through the windscreen. They were very, very lucky that they were just bruised,' he said.

Another old drinking buddy called Michael remembers the Jimmy of that time with particular affection, not least because he was a passport to a drop or two of illicit alcohol. Michael was two years younger and as such could not accompany the gang out on the town. Jimmy took pity on the sixteen year old.

'I remember when I first left school, he used to pull me in the Butchers Arms and buy me a pint in the snug. I was only sixteen at the time and he'd say, 'I know you can't come with us but I'll get you a few before you go.' I always got on well with him. He was OK, was Jimmy. He was a guy you couldn't dislike.'

Not everyone agreed, however. Least of all the police and others who were required to sort out the mess that followed a typical night out. Things came to a head at home after an episode which could have come straight out of the script of a third rate horror film. Jimmy can remember nothing about it prior to waking up in hospital with a large hole in his head.

'Somebody had stuck an axe in my head – a small axe – I was nineteen. I woke up in hospital and they were darning my head. I said, "What are you doing? Are you cutting my hair?" They said, "We're going to have to cut it. You've got a huge gash. You're bleeding. Your brains are falling out." I went home. I was so drunk, when I woke up I'd forgotten about it. But I couldn't get the pillow off my head. "Mother, mother, get this pillow off my head." She came in screaming. The pillow was claret red. I'd been bleeding all night. I've got a ridge of a scar all down my head. Hairdressers are always puzzled by it.'

Even allowing for the self-indulgently macabre tone of Nail's account of this episode to Chrissy Iley of the *Sunday Times*, it is a gruesome tale.

It was not just his drinking and fighting that was causing problems.

The apprenticeship at Parsons was going badly wrong as well. His heart was not in it and it showed. His employment record contained a number of warnings for 'atrocious timekeeping and attendance' through 1972 and 1973.

Letters were sent to his parents warning that he was putting his place at the factory in jeopardy. It was all to no avail. Jimmy seemed beyond the reach of his employers or his family. He received a final warning in April 1973 and shortly after it was agreed that he should leave without completing his course. His behaviour at Parsons was particularly puzzling and disappointing to his father. The old man could understand a bit of drinking and boisterous behaviour in the evenings, but he had always believed in doing a proper day's work. He felt his son's record of not showing up for work or clocking in late was a reflection on him. When he raised the subject the two men inevitably rowed. Things were becoming too difficult at home and Jimmy decided it was time for him to leave and take up an offer to share a house with a group of his friends. Like many nineteen year olds, he felt restricted at home and needed to spread his wings.

Watching a child leave home for the first time is no easy thing for any parent. It is bad enough if they are going to college or to pursue a promising career, but when a son is fleeing the nest for the kind of life Jimmy was living, it is distressing. Especially for Laura. She could not console herself that he had turned out well. He obviously had not. Worse, she knew he could have done so much better. She knew how bright he was. And how tortured.

He was the last of her children to leave her. Shelagh was dead and Val long married. When the loud, aggressive, wilful and stubborn Jimmy left, the little house on Penfold Close became a sad, silent place.

4
CHIMPY

Laura may have been able to appreciate how clever and under-achieving her son was, but his friends could not. The role he had begun to perform in the last years of secondary school was now being perfected. Jimmy Bradford, the drunken, loud, daredevil. Jimmy Bradford the dangerous clown.

Jimmy Bradford, mad, bad, exciting to know.

Jimmy lived the part. He also found he enjoyed the performance. Enjoyed the power his role gave him. And yet he was also its victim. It carried him to places and situations no one would want to go to.

His friends from this time remember him as a remarkable 'character'. A one-off. Inevitably he acquired a nickname. It is almost a rite of passage amongst young men in Newcastle. Often they did not spare the feelings of the recipient. Even so, Jimmy's was particularly cruel.

'We called him Chimpy,' said Michael, who after serving his drinking apprenticeship in the snug of the Butchers Arms, went on to be a fully-fledged member of the crew. 'Why? Because he looked like one and acted like a big ape. Also he was as thick as pig shite.'

Yet occasionally the guard would slip. One drinking companion who, like Jimmy, subsequently left Newcastle and went on to pursue a successful career in London, offers this assessment.

'There was a dangerous allure, an aura about him in those days. He was loud and aggressive but those weren't the characteristics that singled him out. It was his discontent. If you watched him in a quiet moment you could sometimes sense an intense anger bubbling inside him, he has this very expressive face and you could more or less see his mind working in it. More often than not those were the times to be careful, because you knew trouble wasn't far away.'

Jimmy moved in with a bunch of friends who were sharing a small terraced house on Hotspur Street, in the Heaton district of the city, a mile south of Longbenton. Hotspur Street is a relic of a bygone age. It is one of a small cluster of Victorian back-to-back terraces which survived the upheavals of the sixties' planning revolution. In Newcastle, generally speaking, the closer houses are to the river, the older they are. Workers' houses needed to be close to the workplace and in Newcastle the workplace was stretched along the banks of the Tyne. As the city expanded it became necessary to build further and further from the river. But 150 years ago there was room for lines of small, functional, red-brick homes well within walking distance of the great shipyards and engineering works that formed the lifeblood of the region.

By the time Jimmy Bradford moved in, Hotspur Street offered a quite different set of advantages. Granted, the house and the area had seen better days. Part of a small enclave between Heaton to the north and Byker to the east, it was an impoverished part of the inner city. The houses were showing their age and could not compete with the newer estates which had sprung up in the suburbs. There were no gardens, front doors opened directly on to the street and at the back there was only a small, cobbled yard which led to a narrow path separating it from the adjacent terrace. But for Jimmy and his pals, it was a perfect spot. It was close to the Shields Road with its cluster of welcoming pubs like the Butchers Arms and the Raby Hotel, was a short bus ride from the city centre and just a couple of miles from his old stamping ground of Longbenton.

Material comforts were not high on their list of priorities. In the words of one friend of the group, 'a mattress on the bedroom floor and a tin of baked beans in the kitchen' were all that were required. He might have added a steady supply of drink and women because this is what the staple diet of the housemates seemed to consist of.

Jimmy shared with David Laidlaw, Davey Toole, both from

Heaton, Eddie Black and his brother Ray, who was to become one of his closest friends and his business partner.

The group were all about the same age and had similar interests. They worked all day and liked to play at night and weekends. Not surprisingly the house was something of a bombsite, but that was part of its charm. It was really no more than a place to congregate after work and to sleep when eventually the night's revelry was over. David Laidlaw remembers that time fondly.

'We were all around nineteen or twenty and it was our first time away from home. We lived together for about three years. I'll tell you exactly how Jimmy was. Did you ever watch *Auf Wiedersehen Pet*? That was Jimmy. He didn't have to act, he was just being himself. And he wore the same clobber on the television as he did around the streets of Newcastle. He went round the town just like that.

'He was the same as Oz in *Auf Wiedersehen* when he was out on a Friday night. There were lots of good nights. They were all good nights with him. It was the way he put things over to people really. People used to turn round and say, "Oh, he's a fucking idiot, him." He never used to go looking for trouble, he would go into a pub and would just sit there and after he'd had a few bevvies he would wind people up. I've seen bars clear in minutes, glasses all over the place... But in other places, they loved him. He liked to be the centre of attention though.'

Other accounts confirm that although Jimmy was never regarded as nasty or deliberately violent, trouble used to follow him around, normally because he was unable to keep his mouth shut when in drink. Michael, who remembers the shy schoolboy, goes further. He claims his bark was considerably worse than his bite.

'I remember the aggression that used to come out of him, but if you said "Boo" to Jimmy he'd run a bloody mile. Any spot of bother and Jimmy used to be the first one away. Jimmy's not a fighter, he always came second. He would start it but he wouldn't be there to see the finish of it. The trouble with Jimmy was that if you were sitting having a drink and his mouth was going, he wouldn't let it go, he had to make himself heard. He was always loud, was Jimmy. He was a good laugh, as daft as a brush. Jimmy would swill you with a pint or do something stupid like stick an egg down your shirt. But that is as far as he would go.'

Also, Michael claimed, by the rarefied standards of the Newcastle male, Jimmy's drinking prowess was not that special.

'He was never a really big drinker. He'd have five pints and the slavering would start, whereas a few of us would get through sixteen pints of snakebite in a night.'

One has to treat these assessments with caution, coming as they do from a man who described Jimmy as 'thick as pig shite' after knowing him most of his life. Yet they are not malicious. Michael maintains he always liked Jimmy, that he was very popular generally.

'He wasn't nasty. Anything for a laugh, that was Jimmy. I don't think anyone who knew him then has a bad word to say about him.'

One episode in particular illustrates Jimmy's talent for getting himself into trouble. Michael takes up the story.

'One night we got talking to some girls in a pub. The next thing Jimmy turned round and said we had all been invited to a party. We thought it could be good so we went along. When we got there there was no bloody booze, nothing to drink at all. We were all standing around wondering what to do when one lad walked in with a crate of milk. I said to him, "Jimmy, you fucking bastard, trust you to bring us to a party where the only drink is milk."'

The party limped along for a while thanks largely to its novelty value, but soon it was time to leave. Jimmy, frustrated by the lack of drink, and maybe by the jibes of his friends, was restless, looking for some excitement, possibly looking to re-establish his credibility. It was a mood his friends knew only too well. The fun seekers gathered on the street outside. The only trouble was no one could see where the fun was going to come from.

Amongst them was an acquaintance who had got married earlier that day and, for some reason, had ended up at the milk party. He and his new bride had found themselves the targets of Jimmy's 'humour' throughout the evening which took the form of none-too-subtle remarks about the girl's 'reputation', which was apparently well known to him and his friends. Her husband bit his lip with increasing difficulty all night. Outside on the street Jimmy delivered the coup-de-grâce.

'He just wouldn't leave them alone,' recalls Michael. 'The girl had a bit of a reputation and Jimmy said to her husband, "Brian, she's a canny lass, alright, but she does like sucking my cock." Now Brian was only small but he was a bit of a boxer. When he heard that he hit Jimmy so hard it lifted him out of the clogs he was wearing and halfway across Westgate Road.'

His dignity restored, Brian strode off, his proud new bride on his arm. Jimmy, for once, was speechless.

'At least it shut him up,' said Michael, 'but only for a couple of hours, mind. That memory still comes back. I was sitting at home the other night with a glass of wine and I burst out laughing when I remembered about the milk party.'

The reference to clogs is interesting too. It begs the question of what self-respecting Geordie boy would wear clogs when out on the town with his friends. For although his appearance was grotesquely scruffy, Jimmy was never apathetic about the way he looked. He once admitted to a journalist, 'I have a thing about good shoes, having had to wear such cheap ones as a child.'

There is no indication that his family was too poor to buy him decent shoes. Possibly he was attempting to attach some social gravitas to one of his whims – a liking for fancy footwear.

A few years after the clog incident he is remembered as always wearing either winklepickers or knee-length boots. Combined with his choice of clothing, his appearance was sufficiently bizarre to stick in people's minds.

One friend remembers him as always wearing a black mohair jumper and faded blue jeans. 'If I ever think of him it is with that jumper on. He looked a fucking state the whole time.'

Another claims he didn't comb his hair for five years and loved nothing better than to boast about it. It was as if he was making a point at being as outrageous as possible within the bounds of bad taste. It kept people talking about him, made them remember him.

Jimmy Bradford at that time could not by any stretch of the imagination be regarded as a ladies' man. He was loud, uncouth, dishevelled, with an unforgettable face. Yet, as his friends insist, there was no shortage of girls willing to accompany him back to Hotspur Street after the night's carousing was done. Although rough, Jimmy was not without charm. He had the gift of the gab and liked to display his verbal dexterity. He was also always at the centre of things, demanding centre stage regardless of the consequences – and often the consequences were savage. As such he did have an aura about him, he was unpredictable and therefore dangerous. Women liked to try him out.

No one remembers any serious relationships. It appears that either it did not interest him or appeal to any girl who made his acquaintance. He relationships were short, sweet and uncomplicated. And based on sex.

'He was always having women back at the house,' said David Laidlaw. 'I don't think he was really serious with anybody. He didn't have any long-term relationships, but there were always a lot of women.'

His promiscuity also landed him with another nickname to go with Chimpy, at least among the inhabitants of Hotspur Street. Late one night one of the gang returned home, and going into the kitchen for a drink, was surprised to discover Jimmy and a young lady making love against the cooker. In the throes of passion they appeared not to notice him. As the flatmate watched in a rictus of horrified amazement he realised the couple were experiencing some difficulties. Without hesitation Jimmy solved them by lubricating himself with a handful of oil from the chip pan perched precariously on the stove. From that day onwards the inhabitants of Hotspur Street knew him as White Cap, in honour of the famous manufacturers of lard.

'We called him White Cap after something one of the lads saw – I'm not mentioning who,' said David Laidlaw. 'He was humping one of the birds over the sink. He had his bloody hand in the chip pan and he put it all over his Charlie. It was dripping with fat.'

It is hard to believe that Jimmy was genuinely oblivious to the spectator. Perhaps he performed this act for his friend's benefit. It would have been difficult not to notice someone walking into a small kitchen who did not know what he was walking into. If it was a performance, then it offers an insight into two characteristics. Firstly the lengths he was prepared to go to to preserve his image. He was equal to performing even in this most intimate of moments. Secondly it shows the speed of his mind. To be aware of the intruder, to affect ignorance of his presence, then to make use of the chip oil all in a few seconds, would require masterly composure and dexterity of thought.

If he really was unaware he had an audience it simply shows his no-nonsense attitude to most experiences life had to offer at that time. He had a problem, he found a quick solution and he used it. Sex was sex. It was there to be experienced and enjoyed. A bit like drinking or fighting.

Anyway, communal sex was not that unusual at Hotspur Street. There was one particularly popular local girl who liked to be tied to the bed and have sex with the boys one at a time. Nobody appeared to bat an eyelid. In fact it was regarded as a special treat if they bumped into her out on the town and she was 'in the mood'.

Jimmy was also something of an exhibitionist or, to be more blunt, a flasher. Several old friends remember instances of him exposing himself in bars. He is well endowed and seemed to want the world to know.

'Jimmy has got some weapon on him. He was well hung,' said Laidlaw. 'I remember we went to some hippy bar one night and he just flashed his gagsy. He likes to be the centre of attention.'

An old workmate revealed one of Jimmy's favourite party pieces, one out of his repertoire for livening up flagging evenings. 'He'd go into a pub and say, "This place needs livening up", then put his penis on the counter. He had a penis like a donkey. Then the manager would send for the police and they would come and lock him up.'

What makes a grown man in his early twenties want to do this? In his defence, it seems certain there was no sexual motive. It was far more likely another example of his exhibitionist streak; his desire to be considered a dangerous daredevil, to do things his friends wouldn't dare to copy. Of course it helped that he was well-endowed. A man is hardly likely to place his penis on a bar counter unless he is big enough firstly to be noticed and secondly envied.

If someone had asked him why at the time he would have probably replied, 'For a laugh.' It certainly had the desired effect. It was also a wonderfully effective way of getting attention, and that is what he loved most of all.

By now a quartet of close friends was beginning to emerge. A bunch of real-life likely lads. Tom McCulloch, Davey Toole, Ray Black and Jimmy.

Although they acquired a reputation as a hard-drinking, lively foursome and frequented the pubs and clubs of Newcastle with plenty of gregarious souls, they were, at heart, all loners, all much the same kind of person.

Jimmy's best friend, Tom, is repeatedly described as his own man. Someone who kept his business to himself, who mixed readily but gave little of substance away. He was the only one of the quartet who didn't live at Hotspur Street.

'Tommy used to go his separate way. Tommy was a funny lad. If he got something into his head he would take it his own way, he wouldn't involve anybody else. When I used to go to the town for a drink with Jimmy, Tommy was never with us, he used to go his own way,' said David Laidlaw.

It was with Tom that Jimmy first indulged his developing interest in music. The two would join together with Jimmy on guitar and his friend on drums. Nothing came of it at this stage; it was more hero-worship than anything else. Wishbone Ash were Jimmy's idols, although he also loved blues and soul.

Ray 'Ginger' Black is another mysterious character and remains so to this day. He proved a good, loyal friend to Jimmy but he was something of a mystery to those around him. A man of few words, he now works as an independent glazier in Newcastle, occasionally calling unannounced on his old buddies when the fancy takes him.

'Ray's a great guy,' said Michael. 'When Ray wants you he just appears and you have a drink, then he just disappears. Ray never makes arrangements, he just comes and goes.

'Ray's a funny lad, he doesn't say too much,' is David Laidlaw's assessment.

Davey Toole is another lone wolf. A man of few words, he is still to be found hanging around the Shields Road, the scene of his youthful exploits with Jimmy and the gang. Davey went to school with Jimmy and is the one said by David Laidlaw to have owned the Hotspur Street house.

The four are characterised by the semi-detached nature of their relationship with the world about them. All joined in, but all of them kept something back, some essential part of their being. The other three were obviously reticent by nature, but with Jimmy it was different.

Jimmy disguised his reserve with showmanship, but the public persona was no sham. He later recognised the two facets of his personality and tried to deal with it in *Spender*, the highly successful drama of a Geordie undercover detective that he co-wrote with Ian La Frenais. He told Melvyn Bragg that he wanted to explore the duality in two separate characters in the series. There was the Stick role, described by Nail as the typical Geordie boy-about-town, ducking and diving, living on his wits; a person who can extract humour from almost any situation and who normally emerges from the many crises he gets himself into with a smile on his face. Then there was the detective – solitary, morose, a man with an unhappy past – a man who escaped from his Newcastle roots and was then forced back; a detective who lived cheek-by-jowl with the criminals he was trying to ensnare and who often found himself respecting the criminal underclass more than the 'respectable' masters he was serving.

There is no doubt that Nail feels that his defining characteristics are to be found in Freddie Spender, someone who likes his own space, likes to keep a low profile, a loner. Yet at this time of his life, the Geordie boy had the upper hand and the morose loner was rarely seen. Jimmy was not so much playing a role as allowing the flip side of his character to lie uppermost and bask in the sunshine.

In Michael's words: 'Jimmy's all mouth, but really he's a shy guy.'

5
THE BEAUTIFUL GAME

The gang was well-organised. The leaders would meet on a Friday evening in a river-front pub east of the city centre called the Portland Arms. There they would plan the next day's 'excursion'. Nothing was left to chance. This was the inner circle of the Benders Squad, one of Newcastle's best-known football supporters gangs of the late seventies.

It was a rowdy scene. The pub was always packed with people gathering for a night on the town, yet there was always a quiet corner reserved for the Benders. Nobody wanted to cross them. They sat hunched over a small, circular table crammed with pint glasses and agreed on routes, meeting points and likely targets. After an hour or so they were finished and it was back to the other business of the night – drinking. Indeed, they acquired their name because of their fondness for big drinking sessions. One former member describes the scene in the Portland Arms.

'On a Friday night there was a group of anything between twenty and a hundred people who would meet in there. They would all be going their separate ways – clubbing it or what have you – but everybody would always meet there first. It was a good spot as it was the first pub you came to as you came over to the city from Byker. So you would get there early doors – about seven o'clock – to talk about where to go tomorrow or if it was an away game, what was going to happen the following day on the piss. It was a real spit and sawdust

35

pub. It had a table football machine, a jukebox and a barmaid with big tits – I wish I could remember her name – who was a real character. Everyone wanted to give her one. As you can imagine the manager of that bar could handle himself.'

In the middle of the maelstrom were the top men of the Benders Squad. Eddie Huggans, Dave Smith, Kenny Webster, Terry Mann. Often they were joined by another, a big man who always seemed to wear a black mohair jumper. Jimmy Bradford was not of the inner sanctum but was respected by them and was one of the few who was allowed to get close to them. When the plans were agreed, the peripheral members – who had all made sure they were in the pub – were informed. The gang was rigidly hierarchical. The leaders remained aloof and remote and merely tolerated the more junior elements.

Newcastle is a city steeped in football. The club has a central role in the life of the city that few others enjoy. Its ground symbolises this, being in the very heart of the city centre. In Newcastle just about everybody is a football fan. Jimmy Bradford was no exception. He was immersed in the game. There is a popular misconception that football gangs are not really football fans at all. Any violent incident is normally followed by commentators mouthing the tired cliché about these thugs not being true supporters. The implication is that they are following some other agenda apart from football, that they are professional troublemakers who simply use football as a means to an end. A minority operate like this, but, certainly in the seventies, the vast majority of soccer troublemakers loved the team they followed. This was certainly true of the Benders Squad. They were devoted Newcastle fans first and foremost. They loved the team and made no bones about it. They love the team still. Most still live in Newcastle and are now middle-aged football fanatics who take their children to games. Those that have left the city still go to as many matches as they can.

'My life has changed a lot but football has been the one constant thing,' said one former squad member. 'The fact that you might have got involved in bundling seems pathetic when you look back, but the love for the club was the most important thing. You never thought it was detrimental to the club at all.'

A member's status in the Squad largely depended on his performance on Saturdays. Once you had agreed to go on a trip there was enormous pressure to 'perform' in battle. A kind of chivalrous code in reverse. It was a way of keeping discipline, of ensuring the Benders' reputation flourished. Anyone who fell short of the standards demanded could expect little sympathy. The awe in which the leaders were held ensured that most people did what was required of them.

'If you bottled it you had the leaders to answer to,' said the former gang member. 'You used to see them every fucking weekend so even if you didn't want to be somewhere you would go. Sometimes it was better to take a smacking than run away or avoid the trouble. If you bottled it your name would be shit around Newcastle and you could never wander around the town without the prospect of someone lamping you one.'

Yet Jimmy Bradford appeared to be something of an exception to this rule. The ex-member remembers him being close to the leadership, and present on many outings to opposing club grounds. Yet he does not recall him being involved in any violence. One is reminded of other friends who remember Jimmy as someone who did not go out of his way to seek trouble.

Every major football club had its equivalent of the Benders back in the seventies, an era when football hooliganism was at its most severe. Gangs like them were the scourge of police forces around the country because they were so difficult to spot. They never travelled wearing the team's colours and shunned the places the majority of travelling supporters would congregate. They tried to infiltrate opposing fans' pubs and the 'home' end of the ground itself. They prided themselves on remaining one step ahead of the authorities.

Jimmy once told a journalist, 'There are two kinds of violence. The kind that erupts and the kind that's planned. I was involved in both. In my younger days I used to be involved in the other violence, the premeditated. It's not to do with temper, it's to do with evil. It's a dangerous area for me even to go back and talk about. It was part of the life I lived. I'm not proud of it, and I'm glad I've managed to leave it behind.'

The young Jimmy served his apprenticeship. He went to matches with his compatriots, sang the songs of hate. But slowly his involvement grew. He was a big lad, an intimidating sight. He was loud and aggressive and didn't seem to care about what happened to him. He was perfect raw material. He was also intelligent and soon got bored with the limited off-field entertainment on offer at home matches. As he grew older and could better afford it he started to travel to Newcastle's away games. He fell in with a group of supporters who hailed from his territory: Longbenton, Heaton, Walker and Byker. They were a hard-nosed bunch who shared the same aim: to fly their version of the Newcastle flag around the towns and cities of England. They were all working so had a bit of money in their pockets, and they were all smart and capable.

The former gang member said, 'There was a central group of about twenty but you could probably have got about fifty guys together. These guys were fierce. They could all handle themselves. We had probably the roughest, nastiest mob in the whole country. We had a reputation around the country and we had a massive reputation in Newcastle. Nobody would touch us, people would steer well clear. When I talk about violence or bundling, it was never, say, "Let's go to Cambridge and bash in some shop windows." They went because they wanted to fight with the top boys from another town. When people went to games nobody ever wore any colours. You would try to find the opposition's bars where you could go in incognito and then try to get into the home supporters' end of the ground.

'There was a mob around four years younger than the leaders,' said the former member. 'We would go to games with them. We were their apprentice mob. We would travel with them to away games and get stuck in. Nobody would touch the leaders, they would steer well clear of them. But because we came from the same part of town and some had brothers in the Squad and because we got stuck in at games we were tolerated by them.

'They would talk to us but Bradford always remained aloof. You didn't want to talk to him that much because he did have a reputation as a hard man with loads of bottle. You would never really strike up a conversation with him, although he might talk to you.'

Jimmy was once described as 'intuitively very clever' by a colleague who worked with him closely over several years; someone who instinctively knows what is required of him in any given situation. It is not wholly calculating but it is not wholly artless either. It is a highly sophisticated form of role playing, and Jimmy was an experienced role player – he had been at it since he was thirteen years old.

Among Squad members he was a respected figure, he had power and prestige. He also was able to stand aloof, which suited him very well. People were afraid of him which meant they tended to keep their distance. There was no doubt he enjoyed this image.

'He did have an aura about him. When he walked in people were wary of him. He had something about him', said the ex-member.

That is not to say he had lost his sense of humour. He was still a 'good laugh', although it was always on his terms. No one had the nerve to make him the butt of their jokes. But when the mood took him he liked nothing better than to put on a show for his mates. One evening, returning from an away game the Benders Squad found themselves at a railway station waiting for their connection. There was nothing going on, no sign of any opposition supporters to spice things up, so Jimmy decided to have a bit of fun. He had spotted a group of people at the far end of the platform whom he decided were 'anoraks', boring people whose lives needed livening up. Whether they were boring or not is irrelevant. Jimmy had judged them. He strode towards them, fell to the ground at their feet and, lying on his back, he waved his arms and legs in the air, writhed his body and pulled hideous faces. It was grotesque and frightening and so popular with his compatriots they christened it Jimmy's 'trainspotter dance'.

He used it to entertain his colleagues and terrify the wits out of innocent bystanders. It was so successful it became a trademark, something to pull out of his locker on a quiet afternoon.

The gang spent a lot of time at railway stations. Normally this involved much boredom. It was also a time they were under closer scrutiny from the law than they would have liked.

'I remember coming back from a game at Sheffield Wednesday,' said the ex-Bender. 'I remember it partly because it was the first time I ever heard the chant "Get your tits out for the lads". There were major bundles all the way through the game. When we got to the station there were Sheffield Wednesday, Newcastle and Manchester United fans there – they were on their way home from somewhere else.

'The copper in charge had a loud hailer and he said, "I don't want any abuse when the train pulls away. If there is any foul language I'll stop the train and you're not going anywhere until we've found the culprit."

'My group was in the same compartment as Bradford and as he went past the copper he opened the window and shouted, "Abuse, abuse, foul language, lots of abuse."'

Not very clever or witty, but it illustrates Jimmy's loathing of authority – particularly bumptious men in uniforms. If he could be boorish he could also be brilliant. A memorable Bradford performance came one weekend at the Portland Arms. It was a Friday night and the pub was heaving as usual. Jimmy walked in. His old colleague takes up the story.

'You could never get served at the Portland on a Friday night. He came in and was trying to catch the barmaid's eye but couldn't. So he vaulted over the bar and served himself a pint. The barman said, "Right, you're barred."

'The next evening after the match it was quiet in the pub. In walked this bloke who could only possibly be Jimmy Bradford. You knew straight away, you saw his clothes and you saw the size of him. He had a red plastic bucket on his head and he had cut two eye slits and he just walked in, went to the bar and asked for a pint. The landlord said, "I told you, you're barred." And Jimmy said, "Ah, so you've seen through my cunning disguise." The place was in uproar, it was one of his funniest stunts. It was things like that that made him famous in Newcastle, it was like the *Viz* comics come to life.'

The apex of command of the Benders was a fearsome duo who even now can strike terror into old associates. These are remembered as dangerous individuals it was advisable not to mess with.

The former Bender, who now lives away from Newcastle, said, 'I saw one in a pub in Newcastle a little while ago. I said Hello, how are you? that kind of thing. He gave me a look that I remember from years ago. He said he was doing alright and we left it at that. You don't take liberties with these guys.'

Jimmy was close to them and remains friendly with them to this day. But he was very different. He was the court jester of the group. Valued for his eccentricity, his sense of humour and his outrageous behaviour more than for hard-nosed leadership and organisation.

An idea of the brutality of the Benders comes from one notorious incident in a Nottingham pub. A few weeks prior to this a couple of Newcastle supporters had been beaten up by a known group of Manchester United thugs. The Benders had vowed to have their revenge. They got their chance after travelling to a Newcastle away fixture in the Midlands. The Manchester United gang were also on the road and word reached the Benders that they would be in a particular Nottingham pub in the early evening.

They planned an ambush. They walked in, locked the doors and set about their opponents with a ferocity that shocked everyone who witnessed the scene.

'They shut the door, didn't let anybody out and kicked fuck out of them,' said the ex-Bender. 'I remember there was a big report in the *Daily Mirror* about it. The barmaid at the pub had worked in Northern Ireland and she said it was worse than facing the IRA.

'I don't know if Jimmy Bradford was there, but a few of the Benders were hit hard by it. Some were given very big fines and a couple of the main men went down.'

The Squad really lived for away games every other Saturday. Distance was no object, they would travel as far as was necessary to follow their beloved team. One side effect on the young Jimmy Bradford was that his football excursions gave him a chance to see a bit of Britain. Travel certainly broadened his horizons. It's true that many of these were culturally limited, involving as they did the narrow path of train to pub to stadium to pub to train. But they did help to open up Britain to the young man. They also introduced him to London, which was to prove a powerful allure in the years to come.

The Benders would normally make the London trip several times in a season, especially during the years Newcastle were in the old First Division. Glamour fixtures against the likes of Arsenal, Tottenham and Chelsea were among the highlights of the year. The gang enjoyed journeys to the capital because it was a chance to mix it in the bright lights; a chance to live a little in the smoke, and – of course – to tell the stories of their adventures when they got back home.

As such they always travelled overnight to get the most out of their weekend away. Normally they would arrive in King's Cross station at 6 a.m., grab some breakfast and wander the deserted streets heading south-west towards Soho and its mix of peep shows, sex shops and prostitutes. There they would seek out the various attractions which were on offer even first thing on a Saturday morning. They could wander anonymously in the cosmopolitan atmosphere. Nobody knew or cared who they were or where they came from. It was the kind of thing that would be impossible to do in the close-knit atmosphere of Newcastle.

This sense of anonymity made a big impression on the young Jimmy. These trips were his first experience of London and they opened his eyes. London was no longer a mysterious place hundreds of miles down the A1. It was a real city. Jimmy found he enjoyed his trips to the capital, and not just for the football and the aggro. The life there suited him, he decided. He locked this impression of the capital away and used it years later when he began to look for a life beyond the confines of Newcastle.

6
A SHORT, SHARP SHOCK

There was a strange schism between Jimmy's 'football' life and other areas of it. Friends from Hotspur Street, like David Laidlaw, know little about what he got up to on Saturdays. Although all his closest friends were keen football fans themselves, Jimmy never went to games with them.

'I used to go to matches, but not with Jimmy,' said David Laidlaw. 'We used to be partners on a Friday night but what happened on Saturday was different. He had another set of friends he went around with.'

It is not easy to compartmentalise your life like this, especially in Newcastle which operates like a big village, particularly concerning football, the abiding and unifying passion of just about everyone in the city. Nevertheless Jimmy liked to do it and seemed to be successful at it. It suited his deep desire for privacy. Almost no one was allowed to know him too well. People knew pieces of him, that way no one got too close to the real Jimmy. Only his closest buddies – Tom McCulloch and Ray Black – were granted that privilege.

Most people who knew Jimmy as he entered his twenties had no real idea what he got up to while watching football. There were his stories of course – he was a great story-teller – but most of these were vague and fantastical. They were typical of Jimmy. People enjoyed listening to them because Jimmy was a good raconteur, but no one examined them too closely. Stories of mayhem at matches, of sampling the delights that London's infamous Soho had to offer, were great fun to hear in the same way that Arthurian adventures were great fun to hear. The trick was to suspend disbelief and enjoy yourself – to worry about how close they were to reality was to miss the point.

So it came as an almighty shock when reality took a big pin and punctured the grand romance that Jimmy Bradford had constructed around his life; when the police stepped on to the field of his chivalrous battles for the greater glory of Newcastle United Football Club and frogmarched him off.

He was, of course, no stranger to Her Majesty's Constabulary. They had been frequent visitors at his home during his teenage years and Jimmy had often stayed overnight at their place, particularly on a Friday or Saturday. But this was more serious. This was something that could not be punished with a night in the cells and a ticking off the next morning. This was assault occasioning grievous bodily harm, or GBH.

The occasion was typical. The Benders were returning home from a match against Derby County and decided to stop off for some entertainment in Sheffield. What happened next is unclear. Not surprisingly with Jimmy, several different versions have passed into folklore.

One friend said, 'What happened, apparently, he ran on the pitch and the policeman came to get him off. He said, "I was popped up and this little copper come up to me, he must have been about 5ft 10ins, and I said 'Away.' Then the cop got hold of me so I just kicked him in the face."

His old friend Michael claims Jimmy told him he was innocent, arguing he was the victim of mistaken identity, although how he could be confused with anyone else is hard to see.

'We couldn't believe it when the police came for him. We were just laughing and thinking, "No, man, not Jimmy." He was nowhere near that game – someone on the TV camera must have been a ringer for him. There was fighting in the ground but Jimmy's not a fighter, any bother and he would have been the first away.

'He denied it. He was definitely fitted up. He had got no history of violence on a police record. Once or twice drunk and disorderly –

pissing against the wall or something like that – but never violence, it wasn't his nature. But he just got nailed, nobody could believe it. He just didn't have an alibi. He was innocent, he was definitely innocent.'

Michael recounts this episode with some passion. He is still angry at what he sees as a miscarriage of justice. He has no doubt that Jimmy was telling him the truth.

Jimmy himself has claimed more than once he was innocent. He told the *Mirror* in July 1992 and the *Daily Star* the following January that he was the victim of mistaken identity. Yet in the South Bank Show interview he makes no mention of this, admitting he was sent to prison for GBH, describing it as 'another schmuck thing to do'.

One is reminded of sister Val's remark: 'His stories change.'

His father has made his own contribution to the 'mistaken identity' version of events. He said, 'He was in a crowd of people after a match in Sheffield and the police were looking for a bloke wearing a sheepskin jacket who'd been causing trouble. Jimmy never wore a coat, but that afternoon was so cold he had borrowed his friend's sheepskin jacket.'

John Watson, who was to become a close friend and workmate gives his version of events. 'He was a very keen Newcastle supporter and he got himself into trouble. He assaulted a policeman, I believe. They had stopped in Sheffield on their way home from a match at Derby County. They liked to stop off halfway home to have a gargle. Then they had high jinks, I suppose. He set about a policeman. He would have had to to get what he did.

'He never had any convictions apart from being a bit of a lad. He wasn't a criminal – he didn't go round with housebreaking implements or anything like that, you know. The only trouble he was in was for skylarking about, fighting and that, no real criminal offences.'

This schism in Jimmy's personality is evident again. Jimmy the mischievous knockabout, a bit of a rough diamond but not a bad lad versus Jimmy the frightening football hooligan.

He was charged with GBH and summoned to appear before the Crown Court in Sheffield. This was serious, but Jimmy and his family were optimistic he would be dealt with leniently. It was, after all, just a bit of high jinks that maybe got out of hand. The judge would surely understand that? But after the evidence was heard, Jimmy – who had been around a bit – had a feeling all was not well. This was confirmed as the judge began his address prior to passing sentence by saying nice things about him.

He told Melvyn Bragg, 'The Judge said to me, "It is indeed a terrible shame to see someone of your background and obvious educational abilities ... however..."'

'As soon as they start with the good bits you know you are sunk. If they start with the bad crap they go on to say how you have made an effort and so on. If they start with the good bits you know you are on your way down.'

This was all assembled in hindsight. He had little time in the dock to prepare himself as the judge came to the point quickly.

'However,' the judge continued. 'We cannot have people like you running around the streets of Sheffield like Attila the Hun attacking innocent people. You will go to prison.'

He was sentenced to six months. By the time the shock had registered he was being marched out of the dock to the cells. It was a harsher sentence than he had feared even in his blackest moments.

'I thought, Hang on a minute, but by that time I was being marched down the stairs. All I could think about was the embarrassment of my parents sitting in the gallery.'

It was to get worse. As he sat in his cell, waiting to be transferred to prison, his father came down to see him. He had always had an awkward relationship with his father. In many ways they were too similar; tough, independent, difficult, forceful characters. They had never been particularly close, both macho Geordies who found intimacy with other men difficult.

All this made what was to follow all the more terrible for Jimmy. He was brought to the visiting area and directed to a seat close to a glass partition. His father appeared and sat down on the other side. Then his father began to cry. Big tears rolled down his cheeks. Jimmy had never seen anything like this before from his father. And worse, he was the cause. Worse still there was nothing he could do, he couldn't even put an arm around his shoulder because of the partition separating them.

'The sight of watching my father crying through the glass was something I just decided I did not want to repeat,' he said. 'I did not want to get into any situation that caused him to do that because I felt so bad about it, because he was a big, strong, hard guy and to see him sitting the other side of a glass partition with tears rolling down his face was one of the worst moments of my life.

'So I decided at that point never to put myself in a position where I was going to get into any more scenarios where I would potentially end up in prison.'

This was reality kicking its way into his life with a vengeance; breaking through the outer shell of his career as a soccer hard man and advancing on to the profound illusion of his relationship with his father. For years they had kept a manly distance. Maintained their kinship through a series of clichés. Now, for the first time in years James Bradford senior was able to show what he felt for his son, was able to express his love without embarrassment. And it took a prison sentence to do it.

The effect on his mother was of a different nature. Where his father had broken down in a surprising rush of emotion, Laura was more composed, but only on the surface. For her this was the nadir of her son's life. A downward path traceable from the awful night his sister died. It was also something that did not surprise her as much. More than anyone she knew the inner torment her son had suffered through his teenage years. She was perhaps the only person who intuited what it cost him to live the kind of life he had lived. She was the one who had faith in his artistic abilities. Now she felt it was all ruined. Her only son was incarcerated. All that potential had come to nothing, worse than nothing. He was now a common criminal, locked away so that society could be protected from him.

He was taken at first to Armley prison in Leeds and soon transferred to Strangeways, a grim Victorian fortress in the Moss Side district of Manchester. Prison life is all routine, rules, discipline – things which were particularly foreign to a man who had spent most of his life rebelling against them. Being locked up twenty-three hours a day in a small cell takes its toll on every first-timer but it was particularly hard on Jimmy.

Although he is fond of mentioning his prison sentence, he is less keen to talk about what life was like inside. When tempted to discuss the subject in interviews he has confined himself to the lessons he learned from being deprived of his liberty. What he has never revealed is the horrifying mental and physical effects prison inflicted on him.

He may have appeared tough and ready to tackle anything, the kind who needed a short, sharp shock, but appearances are often deceptive. Mentally he was badly-equipped to deal with prison life. It was only by a Herculean effort of will that he managed to cling on during those desperate months.

The root of his problem went back to his schooldays. To the times he was locked in the stock cupboard as a punishment for his waywardness. The boy who was dragged out of that dark, fetid hole was often more aggressive than the one who was shoved screaming into it. He was not barking his defiance as was supposed but expressing his terror. The humiliation of those brutal punishments never left him. Neither did his claustrophobia. Being locked in a small cell was as close to that dreaded cupboard as it was possible to get.

According to his sister Jimmy suffered terribly with claustrophobia while in prison.

She said, 'Being in prison, I think, had a quite horrific effect on him. Because of the claustrophobia and because of the prison food, the whole experience was a nightmare to him. He lost about three stone. He looked like a skeleton when he came out.'

Val is convinced that the only thing that got her brother through the ordeal was her baby daughter Sarah, who was eighteen months old when Jimmy was convicted. He doted on the little girl, his first niece and the first addition to the family since Shelagh's death. It was typical of his obsessive nature that he began to look upon her as a symbol of hope and innocence amid the squalor and corruption of the life he had made for himself.

All this came out in the regular letters he wrote to Val. Difficult, painful letters. Letters which, at first, he found almost impossible to write. Then they became easier. He found they were having a cathartic effect. It was the first time – in his adult life at least – that he had explored his emotions in this way. This self-analysis was a product of his extreme emotional torment, it allowed him a mental escape valve, a way of freeing himself from the confines of his cell. Little Sarah was the focus of this desperation.

Val adds, 'He wrote to me all the time when he was in prison and I still have the letters. They were almost all devoted to talking about my daughter. She kept him going. All of his letters say, "Sarah is keeping me alive, thinking about Sarah, I want to see her when I get out." She was his motivation, I think, to survive that terrible prison ordeal.'

'Sarah is keeping me alive.' Most probably a figure of speech. But there is a lurid tone to Val's account of this time which is not typical of her. She is normally down-to-earth, practical, undramatic. There is no doubt she was desperately worried about Jimmy's physical and mental health at this time. She had already lost Shelagh and it must have crossed her mind that she might lose Jimmy as well. She knew all about his mental scars dating back to his adolescence. She knew how his claustrophobia would torment him and she heard the desperate, obsessive tone of those letters.

No one was more relieved to see Jimmy emerge from prison. He may have been emaciated, he may have suffered terribly, but at least he was still alive.

His suffering forced him to think. Apart from anything else it passed the time. Now he had plenty of time on his own, something he had always needed but often found impossible to achieve. He used it.

He told the *News of the World's Sunday* magazine, 'Being inside was very strange. I staggered through, it was like walking in the middle of a fog for the first few weeks. I couldn't accept that I was locked up and then one day I said to myself, "Hang on, you're in prison here. This is real porridge that you're eating." I thought, "This is the wrong way."'

In his 1992 interview with Chrissy Iley of the *Sunday Times* he said, 'Prison worked for me for all the wrong reasons. I went in there and for the first few weeks I staggered around in a kind of daze. One day I looked up from my landing and I saw all those other landings, and it hit me: This isn't some kind of stupid tough-guy behaviour. It's being locked up and having your liberty taken away. You have no control over your life. You have no control over anything.'

He realised quickly what a fool he'd been. He was too intelligent to see it any other way. The glamour surrounding the Benders and their ethos was stripped away. He was no longer Jimmy Bradford the alluring and dangerous gang member, he was just one of hundreds of convicts who had been stupid and were paying for it.

It was payback time, payback for all those years of balancing along the edge of what society will tolerate. Prison is never a pleasant experience, but some personalities are more suited to the environment than others. Jimmy Bradford very much belonged to the latter. His hatred of petty authority, his truculence and his inability to keep a diplomatic silence when he disapproved of things were the worst set of characteristics to bring to a prison environment. He was bright enough to learn to bite his tongue, to keep his own counsel, because he knew that was the only way to minimise his punishment. But his time there left him with a permanent loathing for men in uniforms whom he saw as following the rules for the sake of following the rules. This phobia would erupt periodically throughout his life.

This is well illustrated by once incident Jimmy mentioned to Melvyn Bragg. It was breakfast time in Strangeways.

'The food was so bad. The rules stipulated we could not have the same meal twice in a row. I went to breakfast and I stuck my tray out and was dished this pile of slop. I said, "What's this?" and the con who was serving it up said, "It's breakfast." And I said, "Yes, I know, but what is it?", and he said, "It's spaghetti." I said, "We had spaghetti last night for dinner." And he said, "It wasn't pink." They had poured a load of pink dye into what was left from the dinner and we got pink spaghetti. That was one of the lighter moments.'

This large, energetic, impatient, vital man was cooped up in a tiny prison cell. He was forced to live in a regime riddled with petty rules. It was the first hiatus of his hitherto restless life. From this period of enforced reflection he learned, among other things, the value of time.

'That was another thing I got from prison,' he told Melvyn Bragg, 'a real appreciation of how short time is and how valuable time is and how it shouldn't be wasted, and I had wasted enough. I'd lain in enough gutters by the time I came to my senses and decided to try and change things.'

More subtle realisations came to him during those long weeks, triggered by the guilt he felt over the anguish of his parents and more particularly by his father's tears on the day he was sent down. Slowly, he re-assessed his father and the macho image he embodied that had, until now, been so vividly imprinted on his mind and which he so desired to emulate. The first shock he had to come to terms with was his father's apparent lack of self-consciousness as he wept in front of his son.

In reality, of course, people are hard and soft, tough and gentle. It is only when role playing, living up to expectations, that personalities become simplified. His father was not a self-analytical man. He would see no contradiction in his behaviour as his son did. Also this display of emotion did not leave his father diminished in any way. It hadn't diluted his masculinity. Quite the reverse, he appeared more manly for not being afraid to express his emotions, not being afraid to reveal himself for what he was.

As well as writing to his sister, Jimmy had also begun to write letters home to his mum and dad. It was the first time he had expressed himself on paper since his anti-Vietnam poems ten years earlier. He did not find it easy, but he persevered, mainly for the sake of his parents. The letters were nothing exceptional, being largely simple accounts of the minutiae of his life in jail. But he knew they helped his parents and that was important. They also helped him to order his thoughts and give his feelings some kind of outlet.

One thing that is absent from all Nail's musing on his time in prison, however, is true remorse. He says he is sorry for having inflicted the shame on his parents. He says he felt stupid for allowing such a 'schmuck' thing to happen to him and he says he is 'not proud' of the violence which put him there and is glad to have escaped it. But he never says he is really sorry for what he has done. He never says he accepts that what he did was wrong.

To do that he would have to admit that the system was right and that his rebellious ways were wrong. Regret is one thing, humility quite another. And with Jimmy's large ego there was no room for humility. There was no, 'I must mend my ways because what I did was wrong', rather it was, 'I must change my ways because what I did landed me in prison.' The difference is profound and explains the path his life took once he was released.

For once in his life he used the intelligence he had been given. He bit his tongue, curbed his aggressive instincts, learned not to complain, kept his head down and was rewarded with two months off for good behaviour. He had served four months when he was released.

7
STRAIGHTER AND NARROWER

The man who emerged from prison was very different in outlook from the one who went in, but it would be a mistake to assume he was a reformed character. Like everyone who tastes incarceration for the first time, he had made some resolutions. Unlike most, he was capable of carrying them out.

He felt very strongly that he had wasted his life up until that point and that he had to take control of it and push it the way he wanted it to go. But prison did not bring about any profound transformation. As Jimmy himself put it, 'Prison worked for me for all the wrong reasons.'

He still did not believe he had done anything wrong, simply that he had been foolish, so, in his mind, fundamental change was not necessary. He just needed to curb his excesses.

Coming out of prison is not easy, even for a man of Jimmy's strength of mind and self-confidence. He had no job, no money, he looked terrible. For the first time in his life he needed help. His sister Val remembers how hard he found it to bounce back. 'He had a very difficult time because nobody will employ an ex-criminal,' she said.

Help eventually came in the shape of his old friend Ray 'Ginger' Black. The two had always got on well. Ginger, like Jimmy, was bright, something of a loner and very definitely his own man. Along with Tom McCulloch he was the only friend Jimmy didn't feel the need to put on an act for.

Over a drink one night Ginger told Jimmy that he could put a word in for him at a small glass factory where he was sub-contracted as a glazier. He spoke highly of the place and in particular of Joe Watson, the man who ran it. Watson founded his firm in 1952 on a small industrial estate in Byker. A shrewd businessman and a good judge of character, Joe had done well for himself and after twenty-five years' hard work had a thriving concern on his hands which employed around a dozen people.

Jimmy had no experience as a glazier but had nothing to lose. Ginger recommended him to Joe and the three met for a drink one evening. Ginger had been frank with Joe about Jimmy's time in prison but had convinced him that his friend was worth considering for a job. Even so, the recently-released Jimmy was a shocking sight to Joe. 'He looked a real desperate character. He was really down and out, he was unshaven. He was really, really desperate,' he recalls.

Although taken aback by his appearance and demeanour Joe was not a man to be put off by first impressions. He had been around a bit, served in the navy during the War and employed a fair number of men during his years in business. Nearing fifty years old, he was over twenty-five years older than the men before him. As the three talked Joe discerned qualities in Jimmy that were not immediately apparent.

'He seemed a big strong-looking lad so I said he could come down the shop and do a bit of sweeping up. He just looked that rough type that would get stuck into anything.'

Going on instinct, Joe took a chance on him and Jimmy was glad to take up the offer. It is a measure of how far he had fallen that the prospect of a job as a general dogsbody in a small factory was acceptable. He was willing to take anything.

Jimmy found he liked it at Joe Watson's. The boss was a fair man and a man who inspired loyalty and affection amongst his workers. Although his firm was doing very well, Joe was not afraid to get his hands dirty. He worked long hours and managed to be both 'one of the lads' and preserve a boss's authority.

Stan Young, a joiner who was sub-contracted to Joe Watson, remembers how he gave him his break in the business. 'I told Joe I was thinking of starting up on my own boarding up broken windows. He asked me what was holding me back. I said I needed a van and hadn't got a lot of money. He put his hand in his back pocket and gave us £300 and he didn't know me from Adam. There were twenty pound notes, tenners and fivers in a heap. He said, 'There's a start for you and we can deduct so much a week until the £300 is paid." That was my first van. Later, when I got the chance of a better one, he gave me a proper loan.'

Another anecdote from Stan Young gives an insight into why Joe was so popular with his workers.

'I remember one Saturday when I was in the factory showroom and these people were in to buy some patio doors and they asked if Mr Watson was about. I said, "That's him there." Joe was standing close by in a pair of denim overalls eating a pie and this couple just walked past him until I pointed him out again. But that was Joe, very down to earth.'

Crucially, Joe also liked Jimmy, sensing there was something special about this large rough diamond he had hired. He was also shrewd enough to realise that good workers like him do not grow on trees. Consequently Jimmy was made to feel one of the family and his waywardness was tolerated.

'It is a small firm so everybody had to muck in,' he said. 'Within a couple of days he was cutting glass and in six or seven months he was running the shop. He knew how to handle building-type people. You get some funny builders who used to come in and he would tell them to eff off.

'I had a hell of a time with him, of course,' he added with a chuckle. 'He used to go out and get himself in some terrible states. But he proved himself to be a good worker so we just had to put up with it.

'I like Jimmy a lot, we all liked him. He was a character. He didn't go out of his way to be liked but you couldn't help but admire him. He's a loveable character really, in a mad sort of way, but I wouldn't like to get on the wrong side of him, even now.

'When I saw him at this club with Ginger he was down and out, nobody would entertain him. I stood by Jimmy, but having said that I got my money's worth out of him. I wasn't being soft-hearted, he was a handy bloke to have around – any trouble and he would take charge."

It soon became apparent to everyone at Watson's that there was a good deal more to Jimmy than met the eye. His fearsome appearance did nothing to suggest the forceful, intelligent person he showed himself to be in time. Joe Watson, being the shrewd man he is, had recognised his qualities immediately. He would willingly put up with a few eccentricities, apart from his singing, that is.

It seemed that Jimmy liked nothing better than to sing while he worked. Often he would leap up from his bench – even in the middle of cutting a piece of glass – and give an impromptu performance.

Joe winces as he remembers the sound. 'I said to him once, "Jimmy, you'll never be able to sing." He was a terrible singer. I used to tell him to shut up. He used to be cutting glass and he'd get carried away, he'd be getting himself up and singing. He'd stop in the middle of a sheet of glass and sing and shout and wave his hands about. It drove the customers away. I'd say, "For Christ's sake, Jimmy, stop bloody singing. Get on with your bloody work, you'll never be a singer." We all have a laugh about that now.'

Joe grew genuinely fond of his errant employee and their relationship went beyond the professional. Joe became something of a benevolent uncle figure. Jimmy's rough edges were all too apparent and Joe's reaction to them is interesting. Often Jimmy could be unnecessarily aggressive towards visitors to the factory he took a dislike to. Joe says he was not annoyed but 'upset' by this thuggish behaviour.

'It upset me the way he used to talk to everyone else. The only language Jimmy used to come out with was effing and blinding. These commercial chaps used to come and they had to go past Jimmy to our office. And Jimmy used to look at them with that doleful look of his and if they were not put off he would just tell them to eff off. When I found this out I used to say, "Hey, Jimmy, man, these blokes are only doing their job. They are there to sell you stuff."

'I remember one bloke, a Mike Derby from Scunthorpe, came in one day to sell glass. He was full of confidence, you could see he was on the way up. He came in and said, "Where's Joe?" "What do you want him for?" said Jimmy. "I just want to see Joe," he replied. Jimmy turned round at him and said, "Look, you're not getting past this bloody bench", and virtually manhandled him out of the place. The bloke is a millionaire now. But that was Jimmy. Everybody was the same to him.'

Jimmy struck up an even closer friendship with Joe Watson's brother John who also worked at the factory. John was very different from his brother. He was not the type who relished the responsibility of running the factory. He was happiest working as the senior glass cutter. John although considerably older than Jimmy, remained young at heart.

'He never married and was known as the oldest swinger in town,' said Stan Young. 'He lived in his mother's old house for many years. He and Jimmy went home one night and Jimmy asked to be put up for the night. John said, Sleep in my mother's old room, the sheets haven't been changed since she died. That was John. His nickname was Slavers, he was always spitting when he was talking. He and Jimmy were rough and ready, but a good laugh.'

The pair regularly went drinking at weekends, and even spent two weeks in Majorca together one summer. They must have made an arresting sight, the trim older man and his outrageously scruffy young companion. It was a holiday which got off to a painful start for Jimmy, who on arrival changed into his shorts and began sampling local brew and the sunshine with equal gusto. The result was severe sunburn and several painful days made bearable only by the anaesthetic effect of large quantities of Spanish beer. One night the burns were so irritating Jimmy found he couldn't sleep, so he took his quilt on to his balcony and, using it as a mattress, slept on top stark naked so that the cool night air might soothe his torment. It couldn't have been a pretty sight for any passing late-night revellers, but Jimmy would be the last to care.

If Jimmy was popular with the boss and the boss's brother, he did not always get on with his fellow workers. He found his feet at Joseph Watson's very quickly. He had always been a quick learner and soon mastered the techniques of glass-cutting. It wasn't long before he had set up his own glass cutting table, which – in the eyes of some employees at least – challenged the predominance of John Watson. It was a self-confidence which didn't go down well with everybody.

Stan Young remembered the protocol. 'John Watson was the cutter in the place and if anybody wanted to buy glass they went to John and he cut it. He had a special bench. Then suddenly Jimmy set himself up a bench and he was doing it. He was taking over.

'I once had a bit of a row with Jimmy because I boarded up a shop next door to a gentleman's tailors called Fenwicks. It was an old fashioned shop front and it was all bronze. I couldn't fix nothing to this bronze covering so I had to stick patches on. Jimmy went with Joe Watson to sort out the glazing and when he came back he said it was like a patchwork quilt. I thought, You cheeky sod. I always thought he was a little bit arrogant. He was arrogant then and he's arrogant now. He liked to be the centre of attention, that's why he got his own bench and started cutting himself. I thought, Aye, aye, he's going to fill his pockets.'

Paul Clark started his working life at Joe Watson's. The shy teenager was fresh out of school and found himself working on the next bench to Jimmy, who was ten years older and an established figure in the factory. It was not a place for the faint-hearted.

'He was a glass cutter, I was a glazier. I got to know the lad quite well. He was a wild character,' said Paul. 'He was always a very loud, obnoxious sort of bloke. If he didn't like something he let you know about it.

'Most of the time he was alright and you could have a laugh with him but sometimes he could be obnoxious and over-the-top about things. I found that a little bit irritating.

'He was an exceptional character, a one-off. I know a few characters, but I have never met anyone like him.

'He had a lot of energy. He used to sing and whistle all day while he worked. I thought he had a good voice. You could always have an intelligent conversation with him, he was bright to a certain extent. But I think he used to change character of a night time when he went out and got drunk. He was a heavy drinker at that time.'

Paul remembers how Jimmy liked nothing better than to regale his fellow workers with lurid tales of his nocturnal exploits.

It was nothing unusual to see Jimmy lurch into work sporting a black eye or cuts and bruises looking like death warmed up and wearing outrageous clothes. At first workmates would ask if he was alright, what had happened, and that would be the cue for one of his stories. Soon they stopped bothering. Soon enough there would be a

'You'll never guess what happened to me last night…' and everyone knew they were in for another tall tale.

'He liked to be at the centre of things,' added Paul. 'He liked to exaggerate a bit about what he'd been up to the night before, how many women he'd slept with, things like that. According to him he'd had women come to him and run their fingers through his hair. It was all a load of bullshit, nobody really believed it. But that was a part of him, the way he was and you just accepted it. There was one instance of a night time when he had gone out in a nighty or something, drunk as a lord, playing the saxophone on the streets of Gosforth. When he came to work the next day he was that high on the drink. I remember he wore these seal skin boots – size fourteen seal skin boots – they looked like masses of fur. There was all this fur on the outside of them and they came up to the middle of his shins.'

Joe Watson also remembers the states that Jimmy used to turn up for work in. He said, 'He was a tearaway. He would come to my place with black eyes and whatnot. He liked going out and getting popped up every night.

'The things he used to do, you couldn't write them in a book. He'd go into a pub and say, "This place needs livening up", and he'd pull his penis out and put it on the counter.

'He was once in a nightclub and it had these swinging doors and the door wouldn't swing so he kicked the bloody door. The manager said, "You either pay for the door or I'll send for the police." He said, "Well, I've got no money so you'll have to call the police." So he did.'

The resentment of some at the glass factory may merely be envy on the part of less charismatic members of the Watson workforce. There is certainly no vestige of bad feeling on the part of the Watson brothers over the way Jimmy conducted himself as an employee. They were shrewd enough to give him his head because they did not want to lose him.

One of the reasons Jimmy was content to remain at Joseph Watson's so long was that he had other interests to occupy his mind. When he came out of prison he had promised himself to instil some direction in his life and he was true to his word.

As well as getting him the job at Watson's, 'Ginger' Black became his business partner. The duo set up a business renovating old property and either renting or selling it on. The origins of this enterprise are unclear. Accounts from Joe and John Watson imply that the impetus for the scheme came from Ginger and that Jimmy was invited to join him.

Joe Watson said, 'He used to do jobs for Ginger on the side. Ginger was a regular builder and Jimmy used to help him at weekends.'

John concurred. 'He and Ginger used to renovate houses. Ginger had the know-how for that.'

Jimmy tells a different story, suggesting the property company was his idea and that Ginger became his partner. Whatever the genesis, it was necessary for him to put his hands on a considerable sum of money to finance the enterprise. And he needed it quickly.

Jimmy finds it impossible to keep a smug tone out of his voice when he offers a terse account to Melvyn Bragg.

'When I got locked up I decided I never wanted to get locked up again. So when I got out I decided to get some money together quickly – overnight, really – and just went into property.'

'And that's it?' replied Bragg somewhat disdainfully.

'That is. It's as much as you are going to get.'

Jimmy's enjoyment at suggesting to the eminent interviewer that there are more things in heaven and earth than can be dreamt of in Hampstead is palpable. But it also puts an unpleasant gloss on exactly how he got his money.

It is fair to assume that the finance did not come from the high street banks. Jimmy Bradford was hardly a customer with a good credit rating. It is obvious from the suppressed glee of his tone that the source of the money cannot be revealed. But what strings were attached?. How dirty did he have to get his hands to finance his attempt at rehabilitation? Was the money given in the form of a loan or did he cut in some hidden partner into his new business?

Jimmy was not a reformed character. As he himself said, prison worked for the wrong reasons. As the Thatcher era dawned, Jimmy Bradford, proud working-class boy, was infused with the entrepreneurial spirit of the age and became a property developer, possibly with the help of financiers who would not be found advertising their services in Yellow Pages.

Jimmy saw this enterprise as a bulwark against the gutter, a chance to channel his energies into something more positive than they had been hitherto expended. But it was more than that. It allowed him to operate outside of a system which he despised and which he perceived as having dished him out a raw deal. Working for themselves, he and Ginger were free to be as unorthodox as they liked. It also allowed Jimmy to be the entrepreneur. To wheel and deal, to duck and dive to set up and clinch deals, to drive hard bargains, to work hard and make good profits. He found he loved it, loved the chance to make a profit out of his wits, courage and hard work. He could not have chosen a better time to explore this side of his character. He was the perfect Thatcher disciple.

It was hard work, of course, especially when combined with days at the glass factory. But Jimmy did not mind that, he had never been afraid of work. He was simply glad to have found a purposeful direction for his energies. However they managed to set things up, wherever they got the money from to finance it, Jimmy and Ginger managed to make a go of things. Their modus operandi was to search for run-down houses, of which there was no shortage in Newcastle at the time, renovate them and sell them on at a profit.

At first it was incredibly tough because the pair had to do almost everything themselves. Scour property auctions and re-possession lists for something suitable, then gut the house and renovate it before selling it on. They made their money on the sale and then had to use most of it to buy another house. Although they did the heavy work themselves, neither had formal training in any of the crafts and they occasionally had to hire specialist help, which cost money.

Margins were tight at first but they persisted and the business began to run more smoothly and profitably. As the finances improved there was less pressure to get an immediate injection of cash from sales. The boys began looking at the rental business. Newcastle was home to two universities and a big teaching hospital. As such there was a huge demand for flats or houses where several students could share. It was a scene just made for Jimmy and Ginger. Freed from the necessity of securing an immediate sale, they found it profitable to rent houses out to students. A decent-sized house could accommodate five of six tenants and provided a lucrative income which always came in handy in case of cash flow problems. They became landlords.

It was not all grab, grab, grab, however. Jimmy used his know-how in the property market to help his friend John Watson. John was living alone in his late mother's old council house in Byker. It was a rough area and John, who was by now in his early fifties, did not feel safe there.

Joe Watson remembers Jimmy's reaction. 'The house John is living in now is the house Jimmy got for him. My brother lived in a council house and we would say to him, "You want to get yourself away from there because it is a real rough area." But he refused to go. When Jimmy came he said, "You will have to get yourself away from here because there is all sorts of trouble going on. I'm going to get you a house, I'll keep a look-out." He was seeing all the properties because he was doing this thing with Ginger.

'He said, "Where would you like to be?" My brother said he wanted the same area – Byker. So Jimmy got the house for next to nothing, he did everything up, arranged the mortgage, arranged everything. He said to John, "You'd better bloody move or I'll break your effing neck." John was terrified so he moved into this house and he's been there ever since. That was Jimmy.'

During his many hours of reflection in prison, one evening from his boyhood kept coming back to him. He remembered his youthful self-confidence after watching Michael Caine in action on the shoot of Get Carter outside the Mayfair. He remembered how Caine had been the focus of attention apparently without trying. He remembered how everyone's eyes had been drawn to the star. 'I can do that,' he had told himself then. In the darkest period of his life, alone in a prison cell day after day, that memory kept returning. It was not so much the acting that fascinated him, rather it was Caine's ability to captivate an audience.

The easiest way he could see for himself to try something like this was through music. He began to cherish the idea of being a rock and roll star. When he came out of prison, armed with his new determination, he resolved to do something about it.

Jimmy decided to form a band. He persuaded Tom McCulloch to join as the drummer then recruited local musicians Robbie Lockhart and Micky Hutton, a shipyard worker who went on to become an actor, stand-up comic and television presenter. The King Crabs were born.

If the Crabs set out to be a serious musical outfit, something went badly wrong along the way. Their music is largely forgotten but the group itself is seared on the memory of anyone who ever went to see it play in the pubs and clubs of the Tyneside region. In particular they remember the frightening and outrageous lead singer.

The Crabs were a product of the punk rock era. They emerged just as the iconoclastic genre became infectiously popular. But the Stranglers they were not. More a poor man's Sex Pistols. They played mainly cover versions of punk and traditional rock songs peppered with the occasional offering of their own. Jimmy has since admitted that their music was hopeless. 'We just made a lot of noise. I always felt I had to take a bit of the heat off the band because if the audience concentrated too much on the band they would twig to the fact that we were not very good. It was my job to keep them pre-occupied.'

His performance on stage more than made up for their artistic shortcomings. He found he loved it on stage, loved the chance to perform. Soon it was his performance which dominated everything else. One of his favourite attires was a skimpy dress – worn without underwear – and a pair of pit boots. Once after breaking his toe on stage he appeared with a trainer on one and the boot on the other. The sight of this 6ft 4ins broken nosed, gap-toothed man squeezing his sixteen stone frame into a woollen dress was a sight to behold. Often the dress did not stay on too long. Jimmy whipped himself into a frenzy of bad singing and foul language which culminated in him stripping his clothes off and cavorting on stage stark naked.

The Crabs quickly acquired cult status in and around Newcastle. There was no act to touch them for outrageous stage behaviour. They were particularly popular amongst students and also had a large female following, who enjoyed goading Jimmy to strip so they could judge for themselves if the rumours about his ample size were true.

Jimmy needed little encouragement. Once up in the spotlight he appeared to have little self-control. He would regularly drink pint after pint of beer on stage, think nothing of exchanging four letter language with his audience and once even dived into the crowd intent on attacking one heckler who had particularly annoyed him. One of his favourite stunts was to swing from the light fittings above the crowd, shouting and screaming at them.

Buried somewhere beneath all this mayhem was the music. Nobody remembers much about it. The popular joke was that the Crabs were a rhythm and booze band. Nobody went to see the King Crabs for the music, they went to witness the outrageous lead singer.

Dave Taggart, whose band Dance Class often shared the bill with the Crabs, remembers their Sunday lunchtime gigs. He told *Today* newspaper, 'We played a place called the Geordie Lad. We used to tell the punters to bring eggs and tomatoes and throw them around. Then it got on to bags of flour but stopped after we had to pay the cleaners £40 because they would not touch the place.'

Dave also remembers Jimmy as the man who handled the financial side of things, who negotiated the band's fee and who made sure everyone always got paid. 'He was very loyal to his friends. He was the guy who always sorted out the money and paid the lads.'

David Laidlaw remembers the day he walked in on a rehearsal and Jimmy cajoled him to join in. 'He said, "Have a go." I said I couldn't sing. He says, "Go on, do your bit, man."

'The band were good fun, a good laugh. They were very popular with the lads up here, but their music was a load of shite really, to be honest about it.'

Even Joe Watson remembers the King Crabs. 'Jimmy used to go round with this group and do some terrible things. He used to strip bollock naked on the stage and the women used to say he had a penis like a donkey. I'm not exaggerating here. He used to borrow my van and they used to go out to these country places. You can just imagine them going off and stripping off at these really dignified places. The managers would chase them out. That's the way they were.'

John Watson, more circumspect, less articulate than his brother, saw the Crabs play at a large pub called the Chillingham Arms in Heaton.

'It was certainly pretty outrageous. But that was Jimmy, larger than life. Jimmy was boisterous.'

One of the 'dignified' venues to which Joe Watson referred was at the ancient Saxon village of Warkworth, thirty-five miles north of Newcastle overlooking Alnmouth Bay on the Northumberland coast. The village is famous for its magnificent Norman castle, the Hermitage, spectacularly hewn into rocks above the river Coquet and its medieval bridge. Between these landmarks the village itself snakes and weaves along narrow lanes, the design of which has remained unchanged since the Middle Ages. Modern Warkworth is a peaceful mix of solid pubs, hotels and souvenir shops. Its many attractions regularly pull in thousands of tourists every year and the village relies heavily on this trade. Visitors tend to be middle aged, middle class and in search of a peaceful interlude.

One bunch of visitors which were none of the above were the King Crabs. Locals still talk about the night Jimmy Bradford and his group descended upon their community. They joke that Warkworth had seen nothing like it since the notorious Duncan, Earl of Fife stormed the place and butchered 300 inhabitants in 1174.

The local folk club, run in the late seventies by Mark Dixon and Tony McKay, had heard of the Crabs from friends in Newcastle and decided to try and book them. Although the club was based at the Black Bull, the room they used was too small so it was arranged for the concert to be held at the bigger Hermitage Hotel, named after the famous religious retreat in the cliffs above the village.

Nobody in the village was prepared for what ensued once the Crabs got into their stride. Jimmy was up to his usual tricks – skimpy dress, foul language, the lot. His pièce de resistance was a Tarzan-like swing on a chandelier hanging invitingly over the edge of the stage which took him flying above his audience. This was too much for the landlord, who promptly called time on the concert, paid the band and kicked them out of town. They have never returned.

A rumour circulated around Newcastle that the locals banned the band from the village but John Morton, landlord of the Black Bull, says this never happened.

'It was the talk of the village at the time and the landlord of the Hermitage was furious. No one had ever seen anything like it around here. I think the folk club had a bit of explaining to do afterwards. But as for a ban from the village, that was a rumour that got a bit out of hand. I don't know if he's ever been back since, mind you. If he has he must have passed through incognito.'

With Jimmy at the helm the priority was entertainment, raising the band's – and his own – profile. He understood early on the need to be noticed, and he went about trying to make it happen. If no one paid much notice to a song he had laboured long and hard to compose then he would give them something they could not ignore. And he was ideally equipped for that role.

He is not nor never was a man completely dedicated to his 'art'. He is an entertainer, someone whose ego is satisfied by being in the spotlight, by the applause of an appreciative audience. It is simply that music happens to be his favourite form of entertainment. It is not something he is prepared to dedicate his life to, it is something he happens to prefer.

The pattern was set in those early years. He entered the eighties as a man with his fingers in many and varied pies. He was a glass cutter, a property developer and a singer. Three seemingly incompatible occupations which were seamlessly synchronised by the force of his personality. And underpinning that, of course, was his relentless ambition.

8
MIRIAM

Jimmy drove himself on and on. The property business was, by now, beginning to blossom thanks to the hard work he and Ginger put in and to his abilities as a businessman. His energy, always impressive, was a formidable ally now he had learned to channel it in the direction he wanted it to lead him.

Val McLane is convinced Jimmy would have become a property millionaire if he hadn't made it in showbusiness, such was the intensity of his energy and ambition. He may have got there, but his first priority remained music. He wanted, above everything, to be a successful singer. Yet he was still a long way from his dream. He might have been the owner of a few houses, he might have had some money in his back pocket and he might have found some minor celebrity on the Newcastle pub circuit, but Jimmy Bradford remained essentially a product of his upbringing.

He looked like he had just lumbered off a building site with his broken nose, missing tooth and unkempt hair. He was larger than life in every sense – physically huge and possessed of a personality that veered erratically from the manic to the malignly sullen. Then there was the drink. He liked to drink, he liked to get drunk. It was woven into the fabric of his life. And when he was drunk he was even more difficult to handle; more boisterous one minute and more sullen the next.

There was also another element to his personality, one which had remained largely hidden since he was a small boy. The part of him which snuggled close to his mother on the school bus while the other children played happily together, the part of him which he had submerged since the death of his sister. Many years later it was still there and it had no small influence on his behaviour.

He was a man who had never had much trouble attracting women. His extraordinary personality ensured there were always plenty of females who were keen to try him out. Going back to his days at Hotspur Street and the girls who used to accompany him home after a night out on the town through to the mornings after the nights before at Joe Watson's when he liked to brag about his conquests the previous evening.

What characterised all these liaisons was their brevity. For Jimmy it was almost always a case of 'wham bam thank you, mam'. As for the girls, once they had experienced this exciting creature, they were generally content to leave it at that.

Nevertheless it is unusual that apparently none of these flings developed into something that could be described as a relationship. There was no regular girlfriend throughout Jimmy's teens and early twenties. It was partly because of the circumstances under which he met women. – pubs, club or gigs. But also it seems the loner within was unable to make any connection with the women his alter-ego ended up with.

One associate who worked closely with Jimmy for several years noticed that he often behaved in a curiously old-fashioned, sometimes chivalrous way with women and eventually concluded that he was never particularly at ease with the opposite sex.

Certainly his autobiographical small screen creation, Jed Shepherd, hero of *Crocodile Shoes*, is chivalrous with women to the point of abstinence. And in his own life, amid all the casual, drunken sex and macho bragging about his sexual antics, he managed to preserve a rather quaint romanticism somewhere deep inside him. He didn't let it show – his public persona wouldn't allow that – but it was there and it survived the mayhem of his early life more or less intact.

Hand in hand with that secret idolisation of romantic love, was chauvinism, a product of his upbringing in a society where men's and women's roles were clearly delineated. Most working-class women in sixties and seventies Newcastle (Val McLane is one obvious exception) stayed at home kept the family together, often with little money and coped with the drunken excesses of their husbands. Jimmy admits as much. 'The women up north suffer most,' he once confessed. Yet ask the typical Newcastle man of the time about his attitude to women and he would declare them wondrous creatures to be revered for their ability to cope in adversity. He would be respectful towards them, he would even be chivalrous. It is this very combination of chauvinism and chivalry which characterised Jimmy's view of women when he finally met the girl of his dreams.

Miriam Jones stepped into his life from a different world. She was the daughter of a BBC radio producer who was brought up in the liberal-intellectual traditions of rural north-west Wales. Her elfin features belied her strength of mind, independence of spirit and penetrating intuitive skills. She came to Newcastle after winning a place at the city's university. Although Miriam's upbringing was middle class through and through she had none of the pre-conceptions about Geordie life she may have carried with her if she had come from the Home Counties. Her strength, assurance and open-mindedness were useful attributes as she adjusted to a way of life totally different from that she was used to. They were also pretty handy in dealing with Jimmy Bradford.

They met in 1980 when she moved into one of his student flats in south Gosforth. He was her landlord. She had already heard of Jimmy Bradford as he had quite a reputation amongst students for his performances with the King Crabs. He lived close by at the time and they shared the same local pub, the Brandling Villa.

Ironically it was Jimmy who felt the difference in their social positions more keenly than Miriam. It was simply not the done things for a self-respecting Geordie lad like him to fraternise with a student. Students were normally treated with a mixture of envy and contempt by the locals. Yet despite this Jimmy loved her straight off, he admits. He couldn't reveal this kind of thing to his friends and he was careful not to betray his feelings to Miriam at first. But it would not be denied. For the first time in more than ten years the serious side of Jimmy's personality demanded to be heard and what's more demanded he act in a way which threatened his reputation. He listened and took a big risk. It was to be the most important decision of his life. Typically he went after what he wanted with relentless determination. He pursued her.

Carol Johnson came as close to Miriam as anybody during her friendship with Jimmy. She told Carol a few years later that Jimmy seemed to always to be around. 'She said he was everywhere she went, he was in every pub she went to,' said Carol.

He may have been brutish and ugly and most definitely not the sort of man Miriam was used to but he had redeeming qualities. Carol sums up his appeal. 'He's always had some sort of attraction for women. There is something about him. It's that raw, animal thing. He's unusual in his looks – you couldn't say he was handsome – but he's handsome in an ugly way. He's so strange looking he's attractive. He's definitely got charisma, everybody says that. Women were intrigued by him, he was a challenge. This big brute of a man was a challenge. And he grows on you.'

There was no doubting his charm. One old colleague said, 'He has enormous charm. He can be very charming, certainly when he wants to be and sometimes when he doesn't particularly want to be.'

This charm had the effect of persuading people to look again at Jimmy. Miriam may not have been impressed with what she saw at first, but then the thought struck her she may have misjudged him. He intrigued her. They began dating. The huge, loud, rough-looking working-class man and the petite student made an unlikely-looking couple. How would she handle such a monster? At first there were some culture clashes. Their first drink, then their first meal could be scenes from a seventies sit-com.

'I loved her immediately, and I took a risk,' he said. 'To go out with a student was anathema, just not done. I remember when we went for our first drink she said she wanted a pint of Bass, and I said, "Are you a lesbian? You can't drink that, I'm not buying it for you."'

He remembers the first time Miriam cooked for him with a mixture of nostalgia and shame. She prepared ratatouille, a dish

Jimmy hadn't encountered before in his culinary world which had hitherto consisted of traditional home cooking and various cheap take-aways.

'I was worse than Sid the Sexist,' he said. 'I sat down, looked at this food, and poked it with a fork, lifted bits of aubergine and said, "What's this? Where's the meat?"'

Miriam was wise enough to see these outbursts as a mixture of genuine astonishment and Jimmy playing the role of outraged plebeian. She was also acute enough not to try to 'change' him, to convert him to middle-class gentility. Anyway, she liked him as he was, did not want to mould him into something he was not and was strong enough to deal with any disapproval of their relationship from friends or family.

The sexual encounters of his earlier life had left unusually few emotional marks. At twenty-six, he was relatively inexperienced in matters of the heart. It must have seemed strange to Miriam that this big, confident, worldly wise man four years her senior was an emotional adolescent. And having listened to his alter ego in the first place he allowed himself free reign to fall in love with all the intensity of his secret nature.

Miriam intuited that there was a good deal more to this man than met the eye. From the first she was able to pierce his armour and communicate with the person inside. She offered the emotional nourishment that he had not known for so long and he did not waste the opportunity.

Miriam was completely different from any other woman he had met. Think back to the Jimmy Bradford who stumbled into Joe Watson's factory in the mornings bragging about how lots of women loved to run their fingers through his hair. Even allowing for the standard male posturing, the women in his life appeared to fulfil one purpose – that of satisfying his macho urges. They were there to re-inforce the identity he had created for himself.

Because she saw something in him that most other people missed and because she was able to communicate with that inner self, Miriam was not fooled by Jimmy's image. As such Jimmy did not feel the need to pretend with her. Gradually he opened up to her. He talked to her about things he had never been able to say to anyone else in his adult life. He talked about his ambitions. She listened, careful not to pressurise him into change. But simply by being around, being able to listen, understand and offer discreet advice, Miriam helped to open doors in Jimmy's mind he had hardly dared go near since his sister's death.

She was also able to give foundation to his ambitions to be a showbusiness performer. Her father had worked for the BBC, she had an insight into this world which Jimmy certainly did not. Simply telling her about his dreams and to hear her explore the possibility with him, not laugh them back into his face was encouragement enough.

There was no outward sign of the subtle changes in Jimmy wrought by Miriam. To the outside world he was the same Jimmy Bradford. The only difference was that he was now going out with this rather well-to-do student.

Within a short time Jimmy and Miriam were oblivious to the various jibes -'God knows what she sees in him. Maybe she likes a bit of rough' – and soon after the comments stopped. This relationship which everyone thought so unlikely became established and people accepted it.

By the time she finished university, their relationship was solid enough for them to decide to live together. This was a big step for both of them. Miriam was committing herself to Jimmy and to Newcastle. Jimmy was following his heart and was not ashamed who knew it. It was an important step in his regeneration.

By the time Carol Johnson got to know them, Jimmy and Miriam had been together just over a year. Already the depth of their bond was apparent.

Carol says, 'I think she is strong. She is not given credit. People dismiss her as the little woman, Miriam in the background but I think that is far from the truth. On big issues in their life she actually has a big influence on Jimmy. I think she has anchored him. His life could have been completely different had there not been a Miriam in it. I think he may not have been where he is today, he would have been off the rails. It was obvious he respected her and took notice of her. People only saw the public side when he dismissed her – 'I'm going partying and you bugger off home' – but she is the mainstay of his life, he has needed a Miriam Jones in his life.'

Jimmy has described Miriam as 'the luckiest thing that ever happened to me. She is the first and only woman I have ever loved.'

His life now had a centre, a heart. He had a person he could confide in and a place where the real Jimmy Bradford could re-establish himself.

9
THE ENTERTAINER

As Jimmy entered his late twenties there were signs that he was trying to drag himself away from the world he had grown up in. There was no dramatic upheaval, no obvious casting off of his old friends and lifestyle; rather there was a gradual broadening of his horizons, prompted by his ambition, his inquisitive mind and a handful of people around him.

For although he looked and acted for all the world like the Geordie lad whose misspent existence was confined to the pubs and clubs of Newcastle and who knew little of life beyond its boundaries, this was not strictly true. His sister Val was now an established actress with a reputation not just in the north-east, but nationwide. His girlfriend wasn't a local working-class girl but a middle-class graduate.

He had already decided that if he was to satisfy the demands of his ambition, London was the place to do it. It offered him the chance to develop his career as a musician. He may have been well known in Newcastle but he had found that his reputation and that of the Crabs was not conducive to being taken seriously there. Also he realised that the potential for making serious money in the property business was far, far greater in London. And he badly wanted to succeed at something.

Jimmy himself had become increasingly fascinated with London and by now had spent a good deal of time in the capital, especially in the months following his release from prison. Ever since his weekends away with the Benders Squad, London had represented something of a promised land for Jimmy. Even as a teenager intent on violence he had gleaned the wealth, power and energy of the city and felt the opportunities it offered compared with Newcastle. He never lost this sense of London and his sights remained fixed on the place from then on. With money in his pocket and with Miriam's encouragement, he visited there more than ever and began to acquire a circle of London friends.

This easing towards London was made possible in the main by the music business of which he was a fringe member. His activities with the King Crabs had given him a certain notoriety, a profile, if not for musical excellence then at least as a performer that people took notice of. He made no secret about his ambition to be a singer and would cultivate friendships with people he thought might be able to help him along. The Crabs offered him a chance meeting with a woman who would become his closest friend and give him invaluable access to the glamorous rock and roll world he aspired to.

Carol Johnson decided to go to the Honeysuckle pub in Gateshead one night in the autumn of 1981 to see a local band she had heard stories about. She was late. By the time she arrived with some friends, the group was already well into its routine. The pub was packed and she had to walk across the front of the audience – close to the stage – to reach some seats she had spotted in the opposite corner of the room. She looked up and saw the lead singer – clad only in a ballet dress and pit boots – making a beeline for her.

'He jumped off the stage and threw this little ballet tutu over my head. he wore nothing underneath so I was slapped in the face with his tackle, I got a good old whack in the face from his tackle. That was my first encounter with Jimmy. He had already been on stage a while by then so it was not a pleasant experience. I sat down – he was crazy to watch – he was jumping out to the audience, stamping about, screaming and shouting.

'I can't remember any of the songs, but it was nothing like his singing now – chalk and cheese. It was the look of him, this bloody massive bloke in a ballet dress and pit boots and an old nylon mac, leaping out at people throwing his tackle into their faces. In the break he came over and laughed and said he hoped he hadn't offended me.

I was laughing and I got chatting to him. I think there was a lock-in that night so we stayed back and had a few drinks and he told me they were playing a few nights later at a club called Top Cats – it doesn't exist now – in Longbenton and said why don't you come along. When I got home and Brian arrived I told him about this guy. I said you have got to see him to believe him. I have never seen anything like this. I went to Top Cats and afterwards was drinking with Jimmy and he came back to the house and had a few drinks – Southern Comfort was his tipple at that time.'

Carol's home was enough to make Jimmy's eyes pop out of his head. She and Brian lived in a huge Victorian house called Danemede in the upmarket Jesmond district of Newcastle. It came complete with swimming pool, games room and a bar – known as the Pig and Whistle to the steady flow of musicians and celebrities who came visiting. This was the big time and Jimmy was being afforded a peep at it. It was an opportunity not to be missed. Jimmy had always been good at grasping opportunities when they came along.

'He became a permanent fixture around Danemede,' said Carol. 'He just hung around a lot which did not bother me because there was something about him. A lot of people took an instant dislike to him, he had a reputation for being a bit of a wild lad when he had a drink – very unpredictable, you never knew which way he was going to swing so people tended to keep out of his way when he'd had a few drinks. But there was definitely something about him that attracted me to him. Charisma. I liked him, but I didn't fancy him, although lots of women did.'

Carol and Brian owned a video shop – called Roxy Video – on the Shields Road in Heaton and asked Jimmy to do some glazing work there. Then Carol hired him to carry out some major improvements she wanted doing to the swimming pool. Brian was not happy with the arrangement. According to Carol, he disliked Jimmy at once and was suspicious of his motives for hanging around his home and his wife.

'Brian was very wary of Jimmy from first meeting him,' said Carol. 'He was never altogether at ease, he always felt a bit intimidated by him. He thought he was unpredictable, he thought he was a lunatic. He wasn't happy about me knocking about with him.'

But Carol enjoyed knocking about with Jimmy. The two hit it off. Also Brian's lifestyle took him away from home so much that she had plenty of time to give to her new friend. Many people assumed that Carol and Jimmy were having an affair because they spent so much time together. The truth is that although they got close on one or two occasions, it never actually happened.

She said, 'I didn't initially fancy him but he grew on me and I loved being in his company. He liked my company as well. We had a kiss now and then, a daft thing. It wouldn't have taken much doing, I don't suppose, if I'd wanted to, but I didn't. Once we were going through town [Newcastle] to the bars and we stopped in the middle of the road and he put his arm around me because there was a car coming and said, "I've got this overwhelming urge to kiss you." He often used to say things like that. I'm sure lots of people believed we were having an affair, I'm sure lots of people thought there was more to me and Jimmy Nail than a platonic friendship. We were touchy people, he would walk along and put his arm around me and we were very close.

'Once or twice he would try it on and I would just dismiss it. In drink – I don't think he would have done it sober. He always thought Brian didn't appreciate me. "I'd look after you better than him," he'd say. But I always knew it was done in a jokey way. I knew he would never leave Miriam. I would never take him up on it. If I'd decided I was going to have a fling, that's all it would have been. There were loads of times when we had the opportunity, we were together, we were drunk, but we never did.

'The closest we got was a kiss and not even a long, lingering kiss. I think we both felt a bit funny about it. Once we had got that out of the way it was much easier and a friendship came out of it, whereas if we had slept together that would have blotted it. I could never have looked Miriam in the face.'

Gradually the friendship between Jimmy and Carol involved their respective families. Miriam was invited along to gatherings at Danemede. If Brian was openly antagonistic towards Jimmy, Miriam never was to Carol. If she did worry about her partner's relationship with this effervescent woman, she never showed it. In fact she and Carol became close friends, even though the latter still regards her as an enigma.

She said, 'Sometimes I used to think, God, she shows no emotion at all, surely she must get annoyed at the way he goes on because sometimes it was so obvious the way he pursued me. I got on with her very well. She wasn't a friend that would pour her heart out, she would keep her own counsel. She is a very private person, that's her nature, nothing will change it.'

If the sight of Jimmy was an extraordinary one to Carol's rock music friends, then the sight of this huge man alongside his petite, well-mannered, quietly spoken, reserved girlfriend was even more dumbfounding.

'Miriam is so delicate and refined and polite and pretty, standing next to him it was like Beauty and the Beast,' said Carol. 'I used to think, God, they are the most unlikely couple ever. But she never used to be fazed by it. She was very tolerant, very patient. God knows what went on behind closed doors. Nobody ever knew because she never told anybody.'

It became apparent that Miriam had developed a highly effective way of dealing with Jimmy's outrageous public behaviour. She simply retreated. She went home and left him to it.

'When things got too heavy, too hot for her to handle, she would just go home,' said Carol. 'I could tell sometimes she was upset or hurt or angry but she kept it down, she suppressed it.'

Jimmy made no attempt to hide his envy of Brian Johnson's position as a major international rock star. It was what he wanted for himself more than anything else. Despite Brian's dislike of Jimmy he too recognised a certain quality in him which led him to believe he would make it one day.

'There was definitely something about him which made me think, and made Brian think that he would make it,' said Carol. 'Brian said, "There is something about him I don't like but there's something about him that tells me he'll go after what he wants and I probably will see his name in lights." He always said he would. he wasn't going to give up and he really believed it. It wasn't just "Maybe I could do that", it was "I'll do that, I'll be famous, I'll be on his [Brian's] level one of these days." I think he set that as his target. After meeting Brian he thought, "If he can do it, I can bloody well do it."

'But he thought it would be as a singer. His dream was to do stadiums and arenas not poky pubs and social clubs. He used to say to Brian, "It must be magic when you play these massive arenas in America and you peep out the curtains and see thousands and thousands of people all come to see you, and you step out on that stage and they light their lighters…" You could see his eyes light up.'

He may have longed to be a rock star but Jimmy displayed a sizeable chip on his shoulder when it came to the acting profession. It wasn't as if he had had no contact with actors. His sister was a well-known performer with a network of thespian friends and acquaintances who must have bumped into her 'difficult little brother' over the years. Now, with Carol, he was displaying the old prejudices against the many actors who visited Danemede. Things came to a head at a major fancy dress party at the house towards the end of 1981. It marked a turning point in his relationship with Carol. The party was a grand one, even by the standards of Danemede. There were dozens of showbusiness luminaries there – actors, singers, musicians, some friends of Brian's had even travelled from New York for the occasion. Then there was Jimmy, jobbing builder and part-time club singer.

She said, 'I invited Jimmy because he was working on the house. He had done some work at the video shop and I told him there was a lot of work to do at Danemede, there was a swimming pool unfinished, there was masses to do. He was glad of the work and I was glad to be able to get somebody to do it. I was organising this fancy dress party and he said, "They will all be bloody posers and that shower, not normal people. I'll not get an invite to that." I said he could come and why not bring Miriam along. "Are you serious?" Yes. "Oh, right. great, great." He got really excited.

'He turned up as a convict. Miriam had made him the suit and painted the arrows on it and he got the ball and chain and welded it to his ankle. She was dressed as a domino with bin liners with big white spots on. But he frightened everybody at the party and got so out of control Brian asked him to leave. He had the actor Christian Rodska up against the wall menacing him and saying, "Why are you poofs, all actors are just poofs." He had probably had a bottle of Southern Comfort by then. Christian said to me, "Bloody hell, who's he? What's his problem?" And I said, "Oh he's the builder and he's got this daft band going, and he runs round with his dick hanging out and this frothy ballet frock."

'People were bemused by him at first and then very wary of him and then half a dozen were frightened of him by the end of the night. The final straw for Brian was when Jimmy picked up the chain with the ball on the end and bashed it on the pool table. How it didn't shatter I don't know. Then he picked up his ball and chain, jumped on the pool table and started dancing around. Brian went berserk, saying, "This guy is abusing our home. He is in our bar intimidating people and jumping on the pool table. I've always wanted a pool table and he is wrecking it." That's how he was when he was drinking. He was not pleasant, he could turn very nasty and woe betide anyone who got in his way when he turned nasty because he is a big feller – he was well-built then – nobody wanted to have a run-in with him.'

Miriam having long gone – no doubt anticipating trouble – Jimmy was left to find his way home alone still wearing the convict's outfit complete with ball and chain. Not surprisingly, he was stopped by the police. Instead of explaining what he was doing, he got angry at their interference and only narrowly escaped being arrested.

Worse was to follow. Brian had long been jealous of Jimmy's friendship with his wife and only kept his feelings under control with difficulty. One Sunday evening, he and Carol had just returned from a christening in Birmingham, when there was a familiar knock at the door.

Carol said, 'We'd only been back five minutes when Jimmy landed on the doorstep and Brian just lost it. He said to me, "What does he want, why is he always here? I'm getting pissed off with this Jimmy Bradford feller here all the time." Jimmy then made some comments to Brian about how he didn't look after me properly and how he was always gadding about. Brian said, "Mind your own business, and what the hell are you doing here anyway? What exactly are you hanging round 'wor lass' for?" They were in the kitchen and I was trying to fill the dishwasher and they had a scuffle. Brian pushed him and Jimmy came back with his fists up as if he was going to hit him.'

Carol intervened, telling the two men to calm down. Brian wasn't the only one getting heartily tired of the turbulent Jimmy Bradford. Possibly as a result of one of his newfound circle of showbusiness acquaintances putting a word in for him, Jimmy was offered the chance to be a roadie to a group on tour in Germany. He jumped at the chance, taking time off from Watson's. Jimmy was certainly ideal material for such a job. Big enough to handle all the heavy lifting work and capable of dealing with any trouble that might come their way. Unfortunately but unsurprisingly it all went wrong within a few days. Whatever happened, the band decided pretty quickly that they needed to dispense with Jimmy's services and abandoned him, penniless, in Germany.

Little is known of the episode apart from what remains in the memory of Stan Young, the joiner who was sub-contracted to Joe Watson at the time. Stan remembers Jimmy regaling workmates at Joe Watson's with the tale, claiming that he was so hungry as he hitched his way home that he ate a can of dogmeat. As with all Jimmy's stories it is rich in the macabre. Then again, as his listeners were aware, with Jimmy anything was possible.

'He actually ate a can of dogmeat, he was that hungry. This is what he told the lads, of course,' said Stan, adding as a postscript to the anecdote, 'There's nothing wrong with dogmeat. It doesn't kill dogs.'

If Jimmy was changing, it was only slowly. Miriam took great care not to interfere in the way he ran his life, intuiting, no doubt, that trying to change him would be useless.

'She accepted him for what he was,' said Carol Johnson. 'I don't think she ever gave him an ultimatum – stop drinking, do this or do that. He did his own thing. Nobody stopped him. He did what he wanted to do and she cared enough about him to go along with that.'

Neither had Miriam's influence curtailed his activities with the King Crabs. In fact, her presence had added a whole new dimension to Jimmy's performance. He discovered that despite the difference in their respective sizes, some of Miriam's clothes were useful for wearing on stage. One woollen dress was a particular favourite, because although Miriam was a size ten, the material stretched sufficiently for Jimmy to squeeze his bulk inside. He must have looked a memorable sight. Given his height the dress would barely have covered his hips and with the wool stretched to the limit, it would have been just about transparent. Once he wore one pit boot and one trainer. Legend has it he explained this with the comment: 'One to kick you with and one to run away in.'

The anecdote has become part of the stock Jimmy Nail material for journalists remembering his colourful past. Maybe this is why it now jars with him so much. He later told the *Sun*: 'The one thing that drives me insane is this story that "Jimmy always used to wear one Doc Marten and one trainer – one to kick them with and the other to run away with." Do people really think I'd come up with something that corny? The real story was, there was a ruck in a bar. I went to kick this geezer, missed him and kicked a cast iron table and broke my big toe.'

It wasn't a stage gimmick, it was a necessity brought on by a bar room brawl. He is happy to recall the fights in public. What galls him is the idea that he might be accused of coming up with a 'corny' idea and that journalists are perpetuating the 'myth'. It is acceptable to have a dark past, but not very cool to pull a cheap publicity stunt.

By 1981 Jimmy had, by sheer force of personality and effort of will, propelled himself to the fringes of the showbusiness world through his relationship with Carol Johnson and her husband. He had established himself as a 'personality', a 'character', a rough-hewn Geordie boy who was good entertainment as long as he didn't get too much drink inside him. But that was it. He may have been known in Newcastle and he may have had a few influential and capable people batting for him. But it wasn't really getting him anywhere apart from a few prestigious parties where he played the local drunk. He was still Jimmy Bradford, the glazier who dabbled in property, acted the fool on stage and drank a lot. He may have been an impressive figure in the pub or at Joe Watson's factory with his tales of London and drinking and womanising but it was a small stage to perform on.

He needed a break. And, of course, he got one.

10
THE BIG BREAK

In 1980 Newcastle-born film director Franc Roddam returned to his home city and discovered that a large number of his old pals and associates were absent. Starved of work, they had abandoned Thatcher's Britain for the building sites of Germany where there was good money to be earned far from the clutches of the tax man or, as the joke went, their wives.

He did a little research and discovered that his old buddies were the tip of an enormous iceberg. A huge and well-organised black economy had developed which supplied around 30,000 British building workers to satisfy German demand for their skills. It gave him an idea.

Roddam began to develop an outline for a drama based on a group of Geordie builders in Germany. He was convinced it would work and took it to the BBC where it apparently rested untouched for the best part of a year. Eventually, losing patience with the Corporation, Roddam reclaimed it and approached his friends Dick Clement and Ian La Frenais. Clement and La Frenais were already highly-esteemed comedy-drama writers with hits such as *The Likely Lads* and *Porridge* to their names. Roddam knew if he could get them on board people would take notice.

The trio met in Los Angeles and discussed the idea. Clement and La Frenais, both Newcastle boys, were very enthusiastic. Roddam said, 'Ian la Frenais was so excited, he said "I want to go away and write it now, I feel so good about this programme."'

They decided to collaborate and eventually produced a ninety-minute feature-length script. They took this to the programme controller at the former independent television company ATV and asked him to commission the film. He came back to them with some bad news and some good news. He didn't want to make a film out of the idea. Instead he felt it would suit a series of thirteen hour-long episodes and wanted it as quickly as possible. It was a dream commission.

The project was unusual in that it was produced by an independent production company. The practice is common now, but was virtually unheard of in the early eighties. Witzend Productions was co-owned by Clement, La Frenais and Allan McKeown. Clement and La Frenais produced a pilot script for the first episode and documentary producer Martin McKeand was approached to join the team. He liked what he saw and decided to take the plunge into drama. True to his documentarist roots, he made a crucial decision to cast the three central Geordies (Oz, Neville and Dennis), who were the heart of the show, not from established north-east 'names' like James Bolam or Alan Price, but from young unknowns. McKeand reasoned that if the series was to work the main characters had to be realistic, they had to have grit and the best way to get that was to cast people whose real lives were not so far removed from the roles they were to play.

By now the producers had hired Roger Bamford as director and he, McKeand and ATV's casting director Barry Ford called Dave Holly, the local Equity organiser in Newcastle and asked to see every member – male and female – in the region.

Newcastle is a hotbed of acting talent these days but it was not the case then. The industry on Tyneside was moribund. The last major film to be shot on location was *Get Carter*, starring Michael Caine more then ten years earlier, the film that fired Jimmy's showbusiness dreams. Holly, an engaging Geordie, knew opportunities like this didn't come round very often and went to work rounding up all the local talent he could muster.

The secretary of the Equity branch in Newcastle was one Val McLane, a well-respected and talented actress who dovetailed a burgeoning West End stage career with family life in Newcastle. It also just happened that she had insisted her younger brother Jimmy join Equity as a singer, well aware of his desire to make it in showbusiness.

Although he had been told to round everybody up, Dave Holly had also been given a brief on what the producers were looking for in their lead roles.

'Barry Ford rang me to say they were looking to cast some people for this new project about Geordie brickies who were working in Germany. I didn't have a massive brief on what they were looking for but I was told that Oz was big, loud and gormless. There's one in every squad,' he said.

'I had known about Jimmy a little while because as a TV rep for Equity I had a general register of people in the north-east who were Equity members and were available for work. In the main they were extras or walk-ons but some had done small roles. It was to keep them away from local variety agents who would charge them God knows what in commission.'

Jimmy was just another name on Dave Holly's list. But there were two things in his favour. One was his sister. Holly had mentioned the approach from Ford and asked Val if he should put Jimmy's name forward.

Val said, 'I was the secretary of Equity for some years and worked very closely with Dave Holly. At the time that they auditioned for *Auf Wiedersehen Pet* I was doing *Andy Capp*, playing Florrie opposite Tom Courtenay. At the time they were doing these auditions I happened to be at home for a month in between the transfer of the show from Manchester to the West End and that was when I got the phone call from Dave Holly saying should I include your brother because he has got no acting experience. And I said, yes, get him in there. He said, "Will you guarantee that he can act?" And I said, "He's a natural. Get him up there, get him an interview." I was desperate to help him, I would do anything to help him – he was having such a difficult time.'

Dave Holly remembered what Barry Ford told him. Someone, big, loud and gormless. He hadn't met Jimmy but they had spoken on the phone. 'His sister told me Jimmy may be interested in doing some work. I rang Jimmy and arranged for him to go round for the audition.'

As asked, Jimmy had sent in a photograph of himself with a note containing a few basic biographical details.

'The letter I got from him had a little photograph taken at the booth at the Central Station. He had a green T-shirt on and the brown leather jacket that he used in *Auf Wiedersehen Pet*. At the end of his note it said, "If Oliver can't do it, give us a bell. Jimmy." He meant Olivier, at least I assume he did. But he spelt it Oliver.'

The letter amused Holly and the photograph stuck in his mind. He made a mental note to recommend Jimmy as one of the possibles for the Oz role as long as he lived up to the stories he had heard from Val.

Jimmy had two very influential people batting for him. But they could only do so much. When it came to the crunch, he was on his own.

The crunch very nearly didn't happen at all. On the day the producers were due to meet him for the first time, Jimmy was in the middle of some renovation work at his home and was not inclined to abandon it. This was a very curious reaction considering how obviously ambitious he was. It can be explained by the nature of his ambition. He regarded himself as a musician. He had never acted and had no particular desire to become an actor. The audition had been arranged by his sister and he was being pressurised to go. Jimmy was not a man who reacted well to people telling him what to do – it awakened his stubborn, awkward streak. He was a musician, not an actor, hundreds of people were going and nothing would come of it. At this point Miriam stepped in.

She reminded him that people had gone to a lot of trouble to set this up and he shouldn't let them down. He had nothing to lose, he might as well give it a try. Eventually she won him over, he downed tools, put on an old raincoat and went along.

Dave Holly offers the version that has passed down to him. 'From what I can gather, Jimmy was doing some sort of renovation at the house – which in his book probably means devastation or destruction – but he was doing something at home and Miriam said, "You've got to go for this." And he said, "No, it's a waste of time", and she said, "Well, the lad's got you an audition, get yourself along." Otherwise he wouldn't have come, he'd have just carried on with what he was doing. He came under duress because he did not expect to get anything. Jimmy never had this burning desire to be an actor, it just happened for him.'

Jimmy wasn't in a good mood. He felt ill at ease, although he wasn't going to let it show. His mood wasn't improved when he saw the people running the audition. They seemed irredeemable 'theatre types', the darling and cravat brigade he had met and terrorised at Carol's party. The thought of performing for them was anathema. But he also remembered what Dave Holly had said about them looking for a loud, obnoxious, aggressive Geordie bricklayer. If that's what they wanted that is what he was damn-well going to give them. He was perfectly qualified to do that, at least.

It was the middle of a hard week for Messrs McKeand, Ford and Bamford, the trio who were painstakingly seeing everyone who had responded to their audition invitations. Most were terrified, nervously answering the questions put to them and being obsequiously polite.

Then Jimmy arrived.

One member of the casting team recalls the scene. 'We went up there for about a week and we saw well over a hundred people. We cast quite a few characters out of that. And one of the people who came into the casting session was Jimmy. I don't remember the exact words he used but he was pretty obnoxious. My job was to ask the questions and get these people talking. With Jimmy it wasn't a question of asking him anything, he just talked. He came in and said words to the effect of, "Make your minds up quickly, I'm not going to hang around." He looked pretty ill at ease to be there.

'He was dressed in a terrible, baggy mac and looked, literally, as if he had just come off a building site. Barry Ford was completely gobsmacked. I was slightly surprised. He was certainly very different from most of the actors in most casting meetings I have been in.'

Dave Holly was hovering and witnessed this extraordinary meeting. He said, 'He was big and stocky, he was exactly what they were looking for and he went in and he saw these guys sitting with their cravats on. Now Jimmy's idea of theatre and television people was that they were all poofs. He didn't know anything about them, he had never met them before, he had never stood in front of a camera before, he had never auditioned before and he took a bit of umbrage that they were standing there – ponces, as he thought – questioning him. And he thought, "Ah, I canny be bothered with this." So he was a bit aggressive, which he apparently was like all the time then.'

Legend has it that Jimmy walked into the session, informed his interviewers he didn't really want to be there, that his car was parked on a double yellow line, he had better things to do so could they just effing get on with it.

Ford, McKeand and Bamford emerged from the session in a state of shellshock. None could believe what they had just heard. Not only because of the astonishing rudeness of the man but also because he was just perfect for Oz. He fitted the role to a tee. If Clement and La Frenais had designed the ideal person to play their creation they could not have done any better than this terrifying man who had just walked in off the street with no previous experience.

The trio looked at each other and Roger Bamford simply said, 'We'll have him.' There were lots of other people to convince, notably Clement and La Frenais, who had created Oz, but the three men knew they had made an extraordinary find.

Dave Holly added, 'When they came out of the casting session, they said to me, "What do you think?" I said obviously Oz would have to be Jimmy and I thought Dennis would have to be Tim Healy. They said, "Dead right." Later Barry Ford sat with me and said, "Don't let anybody tell you that anybody but you discovered this guy." Because nobody would have found Jimmy in a million years.'

Ford, McKeand and Bamford knew there and then that they had found Oz. Even though this was only a casting session – the first hurdle – they knew they could not let him slip away. They still had no idea if this man could act, they had only been chatting with him. He hadn't done a screen test or read from the *Auf Wiedersehen Pet* scripts. Nevertheless they knew he was the one.

'It was not quite as simple as that, because they had a lot of people to convince. Having cast all the main parts, at least in their own minds, they had to involve Dick and Ian as soon as they had a fairly short short list,' said one source close to the decision-making team. Nobody told Jimmy, of course. As far as he was concerned it was a question of 'Thanks very much we'll let you know in due course.'

Time was tight and the producers quickly arrived at a short list.

Joe Watson remembers Jimmy turning up for work after being told he had made the second casting session in London and being very unsure about what to do.

'He said to me, "What do you think I should do?"' said Joe. 'Well, he liked London, he used to get down to London and stop down there. I said, "You'll see your London friends, they'll put you up in a hotel, you'll have a good night on the piss. He says, "Argh, nothing will come of it."

'He said he was undecided, saying, "I don't want to go really." It was the girl he was living with, Miriam, that made him.'

The casting team source takes up the story.

'We had this short list casting session, seeing two or three people for each part, which involved getting thirty or forty actors down to one of those rehearsal rooms in London. Jimmy turned up and apparently he was amazed to see how uptight everybody was. He came in and just looked around and there was a man being sick in the corner, somebody else shaking with fear. Jimmy couldn't understand this at all, as far as he was concerned it was just something he was doing.'

The opinions of Clement and La Frenais would be crucial. Jimmy's future may have hung on the few minutes he spent reading lines from one of the *Auf Wiedersehen Pet* scripts, but no one appears to have told him that. He was as cool as a cucumber and as contemptuous of these 'arty farty' people around him as at the first session in Newcastle.

Nail told Melvyn Bragg his memories of that crucial session.

'I remember we were in a large room and there were two guys sitting in the dark and they were chuckling. At one point I shouted over, "Oi, you in the dark", and a little squeaky voice said, "Yes?" "Do you mind not chuckling, because I am trying to read this and it does not help when you are chuckling. Alright?" And this voice said, "Right-ho."'

The two men in the dark were none other than Clement and La Frenais themselves. This inspired complaint did more than any number of lines of script to advance Jimmy's cause. What he also didn't know was that the two writers were already on his side, having had him discreetly pointed out to them.

La Frenais said, 'As soon as we saw him we said, Oh God, let him be able to act, because he was just so perfect.'

When the auditions got underway everyone was surprised how well Jimmy acquitted himself. Everyone assumed, and were not disabused of the notion by Jimmy, that he really was a wide-eyed innocent in his early twenties, fresh off the back streets of Newcastle. What they didn't realise was that there was more to Jimmy than met the eye. His age for one thing (he was nearly twenty eight). They didn't know that his sister was at that time starring in a West End musical and they didn't know that he lived with the daughter of a BBC producer who was able to give him valuable advice.

Val had, in fact coached Jimmy prior to the second casting session when he was required to read from the *Auf Wiedersehen Pet* script.

'He brought the script back to me after the interview and said, "What do I do with it? I don't know what to do with it." So I coached him into reading it very naturalistically and when he went back he got the part.'

When Jimmy took a script and began reading Oz's lines with passion and panache, McKeand, Clement, La Frenais et al were so delighted that this find could act as well they almost forgot to be surprised.

'There was never any question he could act. I don't think I would have cast him in an Oscar Wilde comedy but he was certainly very convincing as Oz, and that was what we wanted him to be. He had enormous physical presence. At that time he was very much larger – or broader – than he is now, he looked a real bruiser,' said the source.

There was one more hurdle to overcome. The paymasters had to approve. McKeand organised another screen test for all the main characters in London and the plan was to film each member of the provisional cast performing in character. Jimmy received a letter informing him of this along with some scripts so he could learn his lines. His reaction shows how inexperienced he was despite the calm assurance he brought to the auditions.

'When the scripts arrived I saw these documents that to me looked like the Holy Bible. I went into a terrible panic. I said to Miriam, "How am I going to memorise all of this? This is a nightmare. Look, hundreds of pages of gibberish." She said, "Keep calm. You don't do

The Bradford's council house on Penfold Close, Longbenton, Newcastle, where Jimmy grew up.

Jimmy Bradford senior.

Joseph Watson's, the glazing firm on the Walker Industrial Estate, Newcastle, where Jimmy worked from 1977–82.

The King Crabs *circa* 1979. Jimmy is second left and his best friend Tom McCulloch is far right.

Top left: With Tim Healy and Carol, enjoying a boozy lunch, 1983.

Above: Jimmy in boisterous mood at Carol and Brian Johnson's fancy dress party at their home, Danemede, in 1981.

Left and below: Jimmy and Carol, Danemede, 1983.

Jimmy and partner
Miriam in London,
1984–5.

Jimmy gets down to
his friend's level,
Danemede, 1984–5.

Jimmy tries out his
musical skills,
Danemede, 1984–5.

Above left: Jimmy with Kevin Whately (*left*) and Timothy Spall (*centre*) on location in Germany for *Auf Wiedersehen Pet*.

Jimmy in full *Morons from Outer Space* costume, 1984.

Above right: Jimmy on the set of *Morons from Outer Space*, the film he made with Mel Smith and Griff Rhys Jones, 1984.

Jimmy meets his match on the Quayside, Newcastle, *circa* 1985.

Jimmy with co-stars in a publicity shot for the TV film
Shoot for the Sun, 1987.

Below left: Jimmy with Miriam and their two sons.

Below right: Jimmy and Miriam at the *Evita* premiere, 1996.

Jimmy with Madonna and Antonio Banderas, *Evita* premiere, 1996.

it all at once, you do it in little bits. I will read it with you." So that is how we did it.'

Slowly, Jimmy got the hang of it. With Miriam's patient help he found it a good deal easier than he first supposed. By the time of the screen tests he was word perfect. He joined the other main characters which included Tim Healy, Kevin Whately and Tim Spall for the tests. All the major players, although unknown, were experienced actors. Jimmy and wrestler Pat Roach were the only ones without any acting experience. Whereas Roach was one of the six central characters, his role as Bomber was considerably less demanding than Jimmy's.

It is probably as well that Jimmy at this stage did not fully realise the size of the part he had taken on. He was still blissfully ignorant of what was to be demanded of him. He gave his usual confident, abrasive performance at the screen test and managed not to look out of place amongst his vastly more experienced colleagues. The tapes were sent to Margaret Matheson, Head of Drama at the newly-formed Central Television. She approved of the casting and the project went into production.

Having belligerently browbeaten the entire team responsible for *Auf Wiedersehen Pet* and treated them in a way none had ever been treated before by a would-be actor at a casting session, this audacious upstart had won a leading role in a flagship television drama. It is every young actor's dream, but for someone with no acting experience or ambition it was a truly astonishing achievement.

In the general euphoria at having discovered Oz incarnate no one really stopped to consider how Jimmy Bradford had carried this off. There wasn't time for such reflection. They had thirteen hours of television to produce and little more than a year to do it in. Anyway, why look a gift horse in the mouth? At the time everybody assumed he was simply being himself and by a happy coincidence that fitted the requirements for Oz exactly. It was only much later – after years working closely with Jimmy – that one colleague wondered whether things were quite as straightforward as they appeared at the time.

Referring to Jimmy's first dramatic appearance at the casting session he said, 'It was either intuitively very clever or worked out in advance. In retrospect, I realised it was a very clever act. Everything in his life has been a very clever act.'

Jimmy had the confidence and composure to manipulate these astute professional judges. Acting the Geordie thug was second nature to him by now. If he could fool the much more knowledgeable observers to be found on the streets of Newcastle, he could fool this group of middle-class television people. Yet this thesis is only partly correct. If it was all a carefully calculated performance, Jimmy would have had to prepare in advance what was required of him and there is no evidence that he did this. Quite the reverse. He was not even planning to go. It was only Miriam's last minute intervention that got him to the audition at all. The truth can be found in Jimmy's attitude to the casting session. He did not take it seriously. Dave Holly remarked that he had never yearned to be an actor, he always wanted to be a professional singer. Therefore he did not arrive for the audition believing the fulfilment of his dreams was a short performance away. Quite the reverse. He was convinced that nothing would come of it and was not overly bothered either way. This gave him his confidence and his contempt for those who had gathered to judge his qualities. He turned on his 'Geordie boy' act for them but it was no calculated thing, more a spontaneous assumption of a familiar role.

The biggest surprise for Jimmy was getting beyond the first hurdle. He had never expected it, especially after insulting most of the people making the decision. His apprehension can be gleaned from his reaction – shock and alarm – to receiving a script in readiness for a reading test at the next casting session. Behind the arrogant, aggressive man who appeared at each audition there was a person exhibiting all the uncertainties of a novice entering a strange new world. With the benefit of good advice from his sister, and from Miriam, he was able to hide his nerves better than most.

Even when he was finally offered the part of Oz, Jimmy did not regard it as a dream come true or the watershed in his life that it turned out to be. He looked on it as a lucky break, something that sounded interesting and worth pursuing for a while. He had little to lose.

When he arrived at Joe Watson's factory one morning and gathered his workmates round to tell them that he had won a starring role in a new television series, most thought his imagination had been working overtime even more than usual. They were used to Jimmy's tall tales but even he had never come up with anything like this before.

'When he first came up with the story, "I've landed a star part, etc., etc…" nobody actually believed him because he used to come up with some cock and bull stories,' said Paul Clark. 'It wasn't until they saw his face on TV that some people were convinced. People did not believe it until they saw it, because he would say this and say that. I believed him. You cannot really say something like that unless it is true because people will find out anyway. There were a few people round Joe Watson's who said to me, "How's that knacker got on the telly?"'

Bragging in the workplace aside, Jimmy knew he had to have a serious talk with Joe Watson. He had been at the glass factory for five years. It had given him with a steady income while he and Ginger worked to establish their property business. It had also provided him with a couple of good friends in Joe and John Watson. Jimmy liked it there and felt a debt of loyalty to the man who had given him a chance when everyone else could not see beyond a jail sentence for GBH. Joe gave him his blessing, saying he had to give it a try. 'He just had to go. It was certainly better money than I was paying him to cut glass,' he said, ever the practical businessman.

Jimmy decided to leave Watson's and give acting a try. A couple of days after he made his decision he started talking to his workmates about what professional name he should give himself. If he was going to have a go at acting, he was going to do it properly.

Joe takes up the story. 'He said to me, "I've got to have a professional name. What do you think?" The previous day he had to open a crate of glass in the factory. He had to get on top of it to pull the nails out with a crowbar. He pulled one nail off and it fell on the ground. Then he jumped off and onto that nail. It went right through his foot. You can imagine the language. His pal Ginger said, "Why not call yourself Jimmy Nail?" and that was it.'

The name was perfect. It exuded menace, which was exactly the image Jimmy was looking for. There was no more discussion. The cap fitted and Jimmy wore it from then on.

He had one other thing to sort out before he leapt from the relative security of his old life into the great unknown of this new opportunity. He had to settle with Ginger.

Apart from Tom McCulloch, Ginger was his oldest friend. He owed him a lot, for it was Ginger who dragged him up by the boot straps when he was struggling to find his feet after coming out of prison. He got him the job at Watson's and he had been a loyal business partner.

Jimmy had harboured hopes that he could somehow keep the business partnership going alongside his work on *Auf Wiedersehen Pet* in the same way he had managed to combine it with working at Watson's. Then the first three scripts arrived and he realised for the first time the size of the role he was committed to. Oz – along with Neville and Dennis – dominates the early episodes of *Pet*. It was an incredible challenge for a non-actor. As the reality of his task hit home Jimmy knew he would have to dissolve his partnership with Ginger and that it was not going to be easy. He didn't want to dissolve the friendship as well.

Jimmy gave his side of the story to Melvyn Bragg.

'I had a property business at the time. I had a partner. I said to my partner I will take a year off, I will do this and we will resume afterwards. But we never got to resume afterwards, things went a different way.'

The impression Jimmy gives is of an amicable parting of the ways. People who were around the two men at the time remember it differently. The problems began when Jimmy, not content with walking out and leaving the business to Ginger, also asked to be bought out.

'Jimmy reckoned he was owed a bit of money when he was set to go,' said Joe Watson. 'Ginger got some advice from a trader that he should not give him anything as he was the one paying tax and everything. So they fell out.'

Michael gives his version. 'I know Ray owed him money and still does. They fell out over that. I was surprised because Ray is not like that, he would give you his last penny. I don't know the ins and outs of it, they kept it very quiet between the two of them.'

Ray might be the sort of man who would give you his last penny, but this dispute was not just about money. Ray and Jimmy were very much alike. Both were loyal to their friends, both were essentially private men, who went their own way and had their own standards. Ray felt that Jimmy, going as he was to pursue a potentially lucrative career as an actor and leaving him in the lurch to carry on their business as best he could, was trying to take advantage of him by asking for money. Jimmy – always a tough negotiator and good businessman – simply felt it was his due and that he had a right to ask for the cash. Ray dug his heels in and Jimmy never got his money. The two old friends parted with bad blood between them. Jimmy, sceptical as he was about his new career, may well have fully expected to return to his partnership with Ginger after a year and sort things out then. Of course, it never happened. A year on and the amount of money involved – a few hundred pounds – was a piffling sum for Jimmy. But that was not the point. Ginger was not one to court Jimmy's favour once he was famous and Jimmy was as stubborn as ever if he believed he was in the right. There was a barrier between them and neither was inclined to make the first move towards tearing it down. It was a feud that was to keep them apart for years.

This was the only blot on Jimmy's landscape. He might not have appreciated the full potential of what was being offered him but there was no doubt it was a good deal better than the life he was leaving behind. His family – particularly Val, Laura and Miriam – was delighted. The three most important women in his life had all, at different times, spotted potential in him. Persuading him to realise it had, until now, proved beyond their capabilities. Now he was on the brink of achieving something, on the brink of putting his gifts to their proper use.

Although it was Val and Miriam between them who were responsible for pushing him, it was Laura who took the deepest satisfaction. Her son was going to star in a television series. The boy who she knew had a way with words was going to use his skills at last. Maybe the words she repeated to him during his formative years had done some good after all. The boy she had despaired of during the torments of his teens and twenties was finally showing her he had listened to her advice.

'Have big dreams, son, because there is nothing you can't achieve.'

11
AUF WIEDERSEHEN JIMMY BRADFORD

In the late spring of 1982 Britain was a country pre-occupied with events on the other side of the world. The Falklands War exerted a powerful hold on the nation. Normally level-headed citizens became vociferous patriots. There was little middle ground; opinions were polarised. Arguments about the wisdom of sending a task force halfway round the world to liberate a tiny group of islands were often shouted down by those who wanted to give the Argentineans 'what for'. After all, they were clearly wrong to invade the islands and could not be allowed to get away with such unprincipled aggression.

Armchair generals sprouted up everywhere, notably in pubs up and down the country. Here the tone was often of noisy patriotism or worse. Dissenters were regarded with suspicion.

One such establishment was the Brandling Villa in Gosforth, Newcastle. It entertained its fair share of supporters of Margaret Thatcher's unequivocal foreign policy who were similarly not afraid of nailing their colours to the mast. One of the most energetic participants in the vigorous discussions which took place as events unfolded was a large, scruffy man who came in every night with a bundle of papers and took his place in the same corner.

For long periods he would keep his own company, poring over the sheets and sheets of paper he carried with him, occasionally muttering to himself and at other times bursting into loud tirades against Britain's older enemy, the Germans. But there were times during each evening when he couldn't resist joining in. When he did he was always the loudest, most stubborn participant. Eventually, after a particularly vociferous outburst, the landlord decided he had had enough. However, being a discreet man, he also decided to delegate the task of barring Jimmy Bradford to his barmaid, Tina Brown.

She was loath to tell him as she had grown very fond of this strangely engaging character. He was rough around the edges, but she could see there was no harm in him. He had told her all about the major new television series he had landed a starring role in and about how much he had to learn in only a few short weeks. She even helped him rehearse by standing in for characters he was playing opposite.

'He used to come in nearly every night. He was quite a character. There were no airs and graces about him, he was like Oz in real life. He didn't put it on. He was just like Oz. I used to read his scripts out of *Auf Wiedersehen Pet*. He used to stand at the bar shouting out his lines and waving his scripts. I used to listen. He once said, "Tina you'd make a good German barmaid." I used to laugh about that.

'He used to stand at the bar swearing and the manager didn't like it, but that was just Jimmy. That was just him and everyone who knew him loved him.

'This particular day the manager went mad with me for serving him because he was barred. I said I didn't know. He said, "Well go back and tell him that he's got to go out", which I did do, and, Oh, he went mad. He crashed his drink on the table and said "This isn't the only pub I can drink in, you know. There are other pubs."

A parting shot worthy of Oz.

Once he realised the size of the task before him Jimmy got down to work. He wasn't sure what all this would lead to – and he retained a healthy cynicism about its long term prospects – but he had decided to do it and was determined to give it his best shot. It was the kind of challenge he had been secretly yearning for and he was set on doing himself justice.

An obsessive man like Jimmy cannot do anything by halves and so it was with his preparation for *Auf Wiedersehen Pet*. He immersed himself in the character of Oz, which may seem a contradiction given the observation of so many people that he was so like the character that acting was unnecessary. His sister Val is the first to point out that playing yourself is not as easy as it sounds.

'People come up to me and say, "Oh well, he was only playing himself", but little do they know how difficult it is to actually play yourself in front of a camera.'

The character was someone who spoke lines written by someone else, who interacted with other characters and did things which were determined by the writer and director.

But Jimmy decided the best way to do himself justice was to become Oz. He has since rationalised this by admitting he is not the world's greatest actor, that he cannot pretend, that he cannot do a role justice unless it feels real. Oz – a marvellous creation – certainly felt real to him and he invested all his powers in the role. He was not an actor at this stage. He had no experience of preparing himself for a part. He was not the seasoned professional who could step in and out of character at will. He was a novice who was determined to use the power of his personality and his formidable obsessive determination to make up for what he lacked in experience and craft.

It was this huge effort – largely unseen except by those closest to him – which was the reason for his astounding success in the role. It also accounted for the severe personality problems that were to plague him as his star rose to undreamed of heights.

These huge preparatory efforts were well disguised when the cast and crew met up to begin filming *Auf Wiedersehen Pet*. The main actors were as unlikely-looking a bunch of thespians as you could imagine. The most established was RADA-trained Tim Spall who was playing Barry, the biker from Wolverhampton. Kevin Whately and Tim Healy – Neville and Dennis – were both aspiring local actors. Chris Fairbanks was a little-known actor/writer and Gary Holton was a rock star turned actor. Then there was professional wrestler Pat Roach, all 6ft 5ins and nineteen stone of him, whose small screen career to date had been confined to Saturday afternoons on Grandstand, alongside such luminaries as Mick McManus and Jackie Pallo. The final member of this motley crew was, of course, Jimmy Bradford, or Jimmy Nail as he had then begun to be known. All of them except Jimmy were acquainted with the televisual medium and its peculiar demands. Yet this big, strange-looking man, although quiet at first, soon did not seem overawed in the slightest. In fact it wasn't long before he established himself as the dominant force in the group.

The series was shot mainly at Elstree studios in Hertfordshire and was the last major drama to be made there. Francesco Reidy, the floor manager, vividly remembers the extraordinary cast of characters that was assembled. It was his job to work closely with the actors to ensure they had everything they needed to prepare for shooting.

'From the beginning, Jimmy stood out from the rest,' he said. 'I don't mean in terms of talent, as he was quite a nervous performer at first, but he stood out as a dangerous character. He was suspicious and unpredictable and he didn't really understand the process that made it all work.

'He was suspicious of almost everyone at first and took time to accept them. He seemed convinced that most of us were secretly homosexual and waiting for a chance to pounce on him.'

The stand-off did not last. Jimmy soon discovered that these so-called poofs regularly put in long, exhausting days and still had enough energy left to carouse into the night. One evening, exhausted after a hard day's shooting, he was invited into Reidy's dressing room.

'At the end of the shooting days he was exhausted,' said Reidy. 'David MacDonald (my senior on the floor) and I were still fresh and had a tradition of starting and ending the day with a glass of bucks fizz. We called Jimmy in, he collapsed in a chair and we handed him a glass. He drank and looked up, too tired to speak. I looked at him and said, "Well, Jimmy, do you still think we're a load of poofs?" There was a moment's silence, then he laughed. We all laughed.'

Encounters like this helped to break the ice. Soon the actors and crew began to forge friendships during long evenings in the ATV bar at Elstree. The actors were all given nicknames as part of the bonhomie. Tim Healy was 'Chairman Tim' in keeping with his air of authority; Tim Spall was 'Barry the Radish', after the character he played; Kevin Whately was 'The Altar Boy' as he was generally well behaved. Jimmy was known as 'Dangerous'.

Reidy and Jimmy became friends. Although just twenty-one, the floor manager had been in the business for five years and was steeped in anecdotes which he liked to share over a few beers in the evening. Jimmy, of course, had plenty of stories of his own.

Once, prompted by Gary Holton limping into a pub which he explained as an old injury sustained falling off the stage years ago in the musical *Hair*, everyone was charged with telling a tale. 'To be truthful, we were all being a bit "lovey dovey showbiz"', said Reidy. 'It came to Jimmy's turn. Taking my hand and placing it on his head, he smiled and said, "Can you feel that crease in my skull?" I could and recoiled at the touch of it. "What happened?" I asked. He explained, in a very matter of fact way, how he had been attacked in Newcastle and his assailant had tried to place a short axe in the centre of his head. We sat there in shock. I remember thinking, this is a guy who is frightened of nothing.

'When we were out drinking he was more unpredictable than ever. Most of the time he was a really good laugh and loved to tell stories of his previous life in Newcastle. One such night in a bar in Muswell Hill [north London] he suddenly stopped, mid-sentence, and walked to the opposite side of the bar, stood facing a man who had apparently briefly made eye contact with him a few seconds earlier and said, "What's your problem, pal?" I could see the whole place erupting into a Western brawl. In the end the man apologised, not really knowing what his transgression had been in the first place. Jimmy came back and stood next to me and carried on the conversation as if nothing had happened.'

The shoot took place at a particularly difficult time. The old ATV company was being wound down to make way for Central Television and consequently there were many technicians who were about to lose their jobs and knew this was their last project. They were disillusioned and apathetic and consequently industrial relations were seriously strained.

'Labour relations at the studio were absolutely appalling,' said one member of the production team. 'There were a lot of people who knew they were going to be sacked, a lot of people who knew they were moving and we had not a tremendously helpful workforce. Also industrial relations in the industry were very bad – there had been a major strike a couple of years before. It really was a struggle to get the thing made at all.'

The sense of unreality was heightened by the nature of the drama they were making. It has been described, with the benefit of hindsight, as ground-breaking television and it certainly was. But at the time it was viewed by the establishment within ATV/Central as something of an oddity, certainly the cast was unlike anything that had been seen in the studio before.

'It was very much us against them, we were very much on our own,' said one production source. 'We were not helped by the system of the management there at all. This was partly because it was an independent production, partly because of the kind of people we were – they really did not know how to handle us. They were used to doing historical dramas – *Disraeli*, *Edward and Mrs Simpson*, that kind of thing – and then there was this gang of noisy Geordies let loose on them.

'We would rehearse or tinker around for three or four days then do a couple of days filming. It is a bad way of working but it is the way that programmes got made at the time. What tended to happen on the rehearsal days particularly was that we would rehearse all morning, break for lunch and most of the cast would stay in the bar until the middle of the afternoon, then roll home. Six or seven pints at lunchtime would be the norm. People in other shows tended to keep well clear.

'Jimmy at that time was totally in character. He was drinking with the best of them, possibly even more than the best of them. On the second week into rehearsal he didn't turn up and Francesco Reidy had the idea of phoning round all the police stations in Newcastle to find out if he was at any of them. He eventually turned up halfway through the day.'

The ATV bar became a notorious place, a place other actors and especially executives avoided like the plague. The *Pet* cast and entourage completely took it over and no one was arguing with them. It did not help that the bar was part of an open plan room that included the canteen and, in a discreet corner, the executive dining area. Here there were white table cloths and sober-suited managers sipping half bottles of wine. Some would be entertaining guests, others would be trying to enjoy a quiet break in their hectic schedules. Unfortunately peace and quiet were luxuries they got used to forsaking when the *Pet* cast was around. Just a few yards from this haven of respectability the scene was more in keeping with a Wild West saloon. Shouting, swearing, raucous laughter and all sorts of wild antics were the norm. It all helped to foster the feeling that the *Pet* team was a nuisance to be endured.

The source remembers one incident typical of the time. 'There was one guy, he was famous in light entertainment at the time although I now forget his name, who Jimmy took a dislike to for some reason and he took a very cordial dislike to Jimmy. On one occasion Jimmy decided to spend the whole of lunchtime falling around barking at this man. Again not the way to endear yourself to management.

'Kevin Whately and Tim Spall were the two sanest of the lot,' said McKeand. 'Pat Roach kept himself to himself. Pat doesn't drink, as far as I remember. The rest were not stand-offish, they certainly entered into the spirit of things but never got out of hand. Jimmy and Gary Holton acted in character, their behaviour was very similar to their characters in the show.

'Gary was equally as wild as Jimmy but in a very different way. To begin with Jimmy and Gary worked as a team, as a couple. They were the two bad boys. I can't remember who cooled on the friendship first, but I think in a comparatively short time they stopped being a couple.'

The pattern was set. Jimmy was the centre of attention again. He was the loudest, the brashest, the most outrageous, the one who always seemed to have a story to tell, normally about his colourful past, his misbehaviour, his time in prison.

If their time at Elstree was eventful, it was nothing compared with the location shoot. Very early in the schedule the team moved to Germany for ten days' intensive filming. The potential for general misbehaviour was enormous and, as it turned out, fully explored.

The forty-two-strong team was ensconced in Dusseldorf's Inter-Continental Hotel. They were a group of British actors and television professionals and were treated like kings. For Jimmy this was like entering a whole new world. But, as usual, he took it all in his long stride.

The schedule was punishing. Working days of between twelve and fourteen hours were followed up by equally tiring nights letting off steam. If their German hosts thought they were entertaining a celebrated group of British thespians, they quickly had cause to re-appraise their guests.

'It was a very long and very trying ten days,' said the production source. 'They were a fairly uncontrollable bunch. There was one notorious occasion when the police were called by staff at the hotel and there was a chase. I believe the police were armed and actually drew their weapons. It started because of some dispute between Jimmy and the night staff and he was chased through the hotel. An actor called Ray Winstone was only in one episode but because of the peculiarities of scheduling he was with us like a permanent member of the cast. The rumour was that in order to escape the police Jimmy spent the night in Ray Winstone's wardrobe. The next morning I was summoned into the manager's office. He said, "It is a great privilege to have you and your film crew here and some of your actors. But those two, Mr Nail and Mr Holton, are not actors, they are animals. In Germany actors are people of distinction and your people are not like this at all. I will have to ask you to take them away."

'I had to do a lot of fast talking then because that would mean moving everyone out and it would be difficult to find forty-two rooms in Dusseldorf. After half a morning's pleading I came out of the manager's office and there was Jimmy in the bar and I went up to him and said, "God, you've just got me in the most dreadful trouble. I've had to do a lot of fast talking." Jimmy said, "Was it about last night? Well, I suppose I was a bit out of order…"'

Part of Jimmy's fascination for the other cast and crew was his unpredictability. One minute he would be the loud-mouthed bar room bore, the next he would come up with some memorable comment or one-liner. He was, as those around him were beginning to realise, a deceptively complex character.

The production source said, 'Based on what I saw of him during those six or seven pint lunches at Elstree, as I did almost every day, listening to him sometimes being very amusing and sometimes fairly boring and pontifical, you wouldn't think he was very astute or clever.'

But a comment Jimmy delivered, with perfect timing, in the bar of the Dusseldorf Inter-Continental caused him to think again. 'It was a great quote of the time. He looked round the very crowded bar and said, "Isn't it amazing, here I am, a simple lad, plucked from obscurity and surrounded by glamorous boilers."'

Jimmy brought the house down with that one and the source still wonders whether it was off-the-cuff – as it was made to appear – or carefully planned. 'It was a very peculiar line just to come out with. It sounded spontaneous. It did actually sum up the life of many of them at that particular point.'

Jimmy was also attracting attention because of his astonishing performance in the role of Oz. There may have been lots of antics after work was over, but when they got down to business Jimmy was highly professional and an incredibly quick learner. All doubts about the gamble the casting team had taken on him were, by now, completely dispelled. As Ian La Frenais said, 'When we went to Germany we realised it wasn't a risk, he was a real find.'

A crew member said, 'It was extraordinary. He learned very quickly. He says he learned by watching, particularly Tim, who was the most established professional. Jimmy was certainly very good at picking things up. He very quickly learned what the camera was doing, he learned what lens was what. Later this became a bit of a problem when he very definitely had an opinion about all kinds of things.'

Jimmy is more self-critical.

'I went into it not knowing anything,' he said. 'At one of the first rehearsals somebody said, "We are going to block this." I thought, "Block it? What is that? Is there going to be a fight?"

'Tim Healy explained what blocking was. Tim Spall looked after me extraordinarily well. I did not deserve the kind of care and attention Tim gave me.

'I remember a scene and I was obviously talking over everybody's lines and he took me to one side and said, "Nothing happens until you have finished." Although it was only a small thing, it was a real revelation. I realised this was not real life, you do not have to fight for space in a conversation. It is structured. Nothing happens. You can wait for your moment and then proceed. But of course I was haring in and butting in and stopping people's dialogue and everything. So little things like that were huge in the amount of help they gave me.'

Jimmy may have been green but he did not have to be told twice. 'I have always been a quick learner. I have always been able to pick things up pretty fast.'

Midway through filming the team was forced to take a four month break because Elstree was committed to completing another drama. It was a chance for Jimmy to reflect on the extraordinary change in his life, time for him to evaluate what had happened to him. Back home with Miriam, his friends and family, he spent hours telling them the stories of his adventure. Miriam told Carol Johnson at this time that Jimmy had taken to his new life 'like a duck to water'. The more he told them, the more Val and Miriam were convinced that Jimmy had done extraordinarily well for a novice performer. They told him this and impressed on him the opportunity that was before him. He respected their opinions, listened and took stock.

Jimmy had very quickly found his feet with the rest of the *Auf Wiedersehen Pet* team socially. When they re-assembled after the break, he set out to establish himself professionally. He astonished people around him by taking in so much so quickly. Once he felt he knew enough to voice his own opinion, he wasted no opportunity to do so. As the series went on he got many an experienced technician's back up with what was seen as his incredible arrogance, presuming that he knew better than people who had been in the business for years.

One colleague said, 'I think he decided to take television quite seriously early on, but possibly he didn't start off doing it. I don't think his career was going anywhere, certainly not as a singer. He was making most of his money, I believe, out of property dealing. I think he thought of television as an alternative, but it wasn't until he'd been doing it for a bit that he realised it could be really quite big.'

Jimmy acknowledges the debt he owes Tim Spall and the two have remained close friends. It was during one of his many conversations with Spall at this time that Jimmy decided he had at last found his niche.

Ian La Frenais takes up the story. 'It was a very confusing time for Jimmy because he had been put into this other world and I think he really didn't know quite how to act, except that he was probably acting up to our expectations of him which was this frightful, frightening super-yob. Tim Spall said to him, "You're home", which was meaning, "You've found a place", and I think Jimmy found that very profound and it was a pivotal point. There was a place for him.'

The *Auf Wiedersehen Pet* project had put more than a few noses out of joint, from stuffy television executives to technicians to German hotel staff. The team felt it was being viewed with disdain by the establishment, and that served to bind them closer together. It fostered a team spirit, at least among the actors, director and production team. There was a 'We'll show 'em' mentality which was a very positive force in one sense, but also allowed novices like Jimmy to speak his mind more easily than he would have been able to in a more conventional production.

By the spring of 1983 the series was finally in the can. No one had any real idea how the show would be received and the producers were convinced that the powers that be at Central did not give much for its chances of success. Their indifference was revealed by a sequence of events involving the *TV Times*. A journalist from the magazine had gone to Germany with them for the ten-day shoot. She was very enthusiastic about the material she had collected and predicted it would make a cover story and four inside pages.

'When the *TV Times* came out we were not on the cover and there was just half a column inside,' said the production source. 'So I phoned this girl in some anger and said, "What the fuck has gone on after all we did for you?" She said she had written it all up and offered to send me her copy, but her editor did not think the programme had legs and didn't want to give it big coverage.

'They didn't like it, they didn't know what to do with it and weren't very keen on it at all.'

If the television executives didn't know what to do with this new show they had been lumbered with, the press certainly did. It had all the ingredients to whet the appetites of tabloid showbusiness editors. A major new series starring, not established actors, but a crew of rough-and-ready characters whose real lives mirrored their screen personae. Plenty of scope for behind-the-scenes stories there. Rumours were already beginning to circulate about rowdy antics on location in Germany. The press sensed *Auf Wiedersehen Pet* would stimulate lots of juicy copy.

One of the earliest stories was published in the *Daily Star* in October 1982 – more than a year before *Auf Wiedersehen Pet* made its debut. It began, 'Watch out! A wild, earthy bunch of likely lads are heading your way.' It went on to describe the seven main characters as 'a battling, boozing, bird-pulling gang of building site workers' who would be 'invading' the nation's television screens the following year.

Referring to Martin McKeand's decision to go for unknown players it continued, 'With Jimmy Nail, who plays a character called Oz, he has undoubtedly struck gold. Nail is as tough as his name, a six-foot battling bruiser of a man who sports a smashed-in nose and has lost many a tooth in real-life brawls.'

Jimmy is then quoted as saying, 'Oz is something like I used to be. I've led a bit of a naughty life up to now. Oz is a hard man, a general ne'er-do-well. He's nothing like me now, unless I think back to last Tuesday...'

By early November the following year – just days before launch – the *Star* was calling the gang 'The Magnificent Seven' and were tipping the show to be as big a cult show as Alan Bleasdale's *Boys From The Blackstuff*. The article makes much of Central's decision to hire a Hamburg brothel 'complete with prostitutes' for a day to film one scene.

McKeand made sure he stoked the fires. He told the paper, 'Who needs stars when you have magnificent characters like these?'

Jimmy was described in the usual hard-man terms and told the reporter, 'I've lost many a tooth in general misbehaviour.'

So far, it's all jolly, knockabout stuff. The show's publicity machine feeding reporters bits of background information to produce headlines and heighten public anticipation. The quotes are pretty standard fare. Jimmy – as he will do throughout his career – likes to make capital out of his misspent early life, he likes to play the Geordie thug, to use it for effect. It wasn't until later that things got nasty.

During filming in Dusseldorf one or two journalists had been invited out to meet the cast and gather material for use around the time of the launch. One reporter was tipped off by a member of the public relations team that Jimmy had had a pretty colourful adolescence and had 'done time' for assault. Picking his moment carefully, the journalist pulled Jimmy aside during a break in filming and asked him about his early years. Jimmy was not only a novice actor in those days, he was a novice at dealing with the media.

The reporter said, 'I had been told that they were an incredible bunch of characters and one of them had been in Strangeways. Someone on the programme had slipped it to me that there was a good story there. I sat on a lawn cross-legged with him and put it to him and he came out with it all quite happily. I prompted him and he talked. He was utterly wild in those days. I was pretty petrified when it all went in the paper. It didn't go down terribly well with him, I don't think. To be frank I was absolutely bloody petrified of him. I remember at the end of the interview he held up this huge fist in front of my face. He was very impressive then, impressively frightening. He was a fearsome sight with a tooth missing and God knows what else. He held it up in front of my face and said, "If you get any of this wrong this is going straight through your face."'

The story was published on the morning after the first episode went out. The newspaper had calculated it would have maximum impact once Jimmy's face had been seen on television. The programme makers were not exactly displeased – it was yet more high-profile publicity.

A major press conference with all the main actors had been arranged a few days after the show's launch. It was a chance for any journalists who hadn't visited the set to glean stories from the cast and was therefore a good way of keeping the show in the headlines. What they hadn't reckoned on was the frenzy of interest the story about Jimmy's criminal past had created. The assembled reporters were only interested in that one thing. As soon as the press conference began, Jimmy was swamped with questions. Things quickly got out of hand.

One reporter said, 'All the hacks got stuck into him. He was shouting and God knows what. Eventually he went to the toilets, pursued by reporters. Then there was this incredible haranguing match between the urinals.'

The overnight success of *Auf Wiedersehen Pet* took everybody by surprise, let alone Jimmy. Although initial viewing figures were not sensational – around the six million mark – the characters made an immediate impression with their audience. Ratings rose steadily over the first six weeks and reached the ten million mark by Christmas – a tremendous performance and a complete justification of the decision to recruit untried actors. Television hadn't seen anything as original and fresh in years. The scripts were spot on and the actors – especially Nail, Healy and Whately – conjured up the right mix of humour and pathos in their respective characters. But, amazingly for a complete novice, it was Jimmy who stole the show. Crucially, he invested enough rough lyricism in the character of Oz to make him truly memorable. It was a tremendous achievement.

After a week's break over Christmas *Auf Wiedersehen Pet* came back even stronger. The first shows of the new year of 1984 attracted audiences of more than twelve million and held them until the series finished at the end of February. Central had a massive hit on its hands. The unknowns who had made up the cast were now household names. All the misgivings about the show were conveniently forgotten.

An indication of the way in which people took the show – and particularly Oz – to their hearts comes from Dick Clement who was at a Liverpool versus Newcastle United football match shortly after *Pet's* release. 'The Newcastle fans were chanting, "Ee ay adio, Oz is better than Yosser",' he said. 'You thought you have somehow tapped into something that is right in the British consciousness.'

Jimmy was under a great deal of stress. He had been transformed from an unknown to a national celebrity literally overnight and he found he was horrified by it. Up until the evening the first show was broadcast he had been totally unprepared for its effect on his everyday life. It had not occurred to him that he would become a face familiar to millions across the country, that he would be pointed at and stared at by total strangers in the street. And it happened so fast.

Jimmy was famous. He was a star.

This acting business which he had got into almost by accident and which he had struggled to take seriously had turned him into a massive and instant success story. He had always enjoyed being the centre of attention but always on his terms, when he chose it. Now he was powerless against the consequences of his fame. His treasured privacy was under threat.

It is very rare for someone to be so famous so fast. It is also extremely disconcerting, especially for a man of Jimmy's temperament. For despite his showmanship he remained essentially a private person who resented this mass intrusion into his personal life.

Carol Johnson remembers the aftermath. 'It was the big time for Jimmy. He was just famous overnight. I thought, "My God, he's done it." He hated it, but he also craved it. He said, "I'm sick of people bothering me wherever I go." I said, "Well, that's what you wanted. This is what you craved."

'Then the change came. He was always a bit arrogant, but he became unbearable. He got very pompous and big-headed, well above his station, he was nasty to people, ill-mannered, thought he could dictate to everybody. It was, "I'm not Oz. I hate people saying I was not acting. I'm not like that." I said, "You are. Everybody says that. That's why you got the part."'

His sister is more sympathetic. 'I went out with Jimmy a lot after *Auf Wiedersehen*. He was never aggressive to the public when they called him Oz, which they did all the time. They came up to us in pubs, trains, wherever we were. They all came up and said, "Hello, Oz, here is a pint of lager", and he very politely said to them, "No, excuse me, Oz is a character. I'm not Oz and I don't really like lager."'

He told Melvyn Bragg, 'It was very, very difficult to deal with. I did not realise how valuable anonymity was. The speed at which it happened. Anonymity on Friday night and complete ape-shit city on the Saturday morning. I went out and people started pointing in the street. It was as if I had landed from Mars. And it never stopped.'

12
MOVING ON

Over the coming weeks the phone hardly stopped ringing. There were offers of all kinds of things; acting roles, television commercials, personal appearances. Wherever he went he encountered the same reaction. "Hey, look, there's Oz from that new series. Looks just like he does on the television."

Life was looking good. Money was being thrown at him from all angles. His talents were in demand. Yet all was not well with Jimmy. He was unable to enjoy his success. This wasn't only due to the consequences of fame. There was something else eating away at him. Something which he had forced on to the back burner for the months he was busy shooting *Auf Wiedersehen Pet*, but which now pushed itself forward to grill his conscience with a vengeance.

One night, in July 1983, his great pal Tom McCulloch had disappeared. He left his parents' home in his red Triumph 2000 car for a night on the town and that was it. No one ever saw him again.

As Jimmy's fortunes had begun to rise, so Tom's had fallen. He had been unemployed for fourteen months and his main diversion and source of income was the King Crabs. But when Jimmy won the Oz role, he no longer had time for music. The Crabs naturally fell apart as Jimmy had been their guiding and driving force as well as their main commercial attraction. None of the other three was close enough to think about continuing as a group. Tom – the drummer – drifted out of the music scene.

On his disappearance, Tom's family called the police and a major search got underway, with other British police forces and Interpol alerted. They even dredged part of the River Tyne. To no avail. No trace of Tom, his car, or any of his belongings was ever found. There was no indication that he had intended to disappear. He had taken nothing with him that night to suggest this. He had said nothing to anyone in his family which gave any clue as to what happened to him.

Jimmy felt a mixture of grief, guilt and determination to do all he could to find out what had happened to his friend. Grief for the simple loss of his closest and oldest pal; guilt that he was so distracted in the immediate aftermath of the disappearance. Guilt also – however irrational – that he had been given a wonderful opportunity while his old sparring partner had come to grief. All this fired his determination to discover his friend's fate.

Since Jimmy landed his television role he and Tom had seen less of each other than usual as Jimmy was so busy learning his lines. Jimmy was by now living in Gosforth, three miles from Tom, who was still in Longbenton. Their paths crossed less and less often.

In the weeks after his friend's disappearance Jimmy began to use his connections in Newcastle to see if the grapevine could provide an answer to the question that began to gnaw at him. All he got back were dark stories about Tom mixing with the wrong company and upsetting dangerous people.

There were no shortage of rumours around Newcastle about what happened to Tom McCulloch. Some said he had been violent to a girlfriend, and her father, who had underworld connections, had vowed to 'sort him out'. Others that he had been sleeping with a married woman and her husband had found out. Others claimed he had been 'mixing with the wrong sort' and had fallen foul of the wrong people. Most are convinced Tom was killed, although when asked to elaborate invariably evoke a street wisdom which suggests it is unwise to delve too deeply into the subject.

Joe Watson said, 'Tom McCulloch just went missing. They reckon he was sleeping with a married woman and they reckon her bloke found out, found them together... Anyway, Tom McCulloch was never seen again. You keep away from those kind of things.

'It upset Jimmy very much, and he didn't get upset easily. He was upset but he kept it to himself, he didn't go screaming about. He was also determined to find out what had happened to him. I wouldn't like to repeat what would happen if he found out. Jimmy wasn't bothered by gangsters, he would take anybody on, you just couldn't tell him.'

John Watson added, 'I heard all sorts of rumours. I wouldn't like to repeat them, but he wasn't seen any more. Interpol were informed and everything, but nothing came of it. He just disappeared off the face of the earth. I knew Tommy a little bit, he was a wild lad. He was on a par with Jimmy when they got a drink or two.'

David Laidlaw recalls similar stories about Tom McCulloch. 'Tom McCulloch was Jimmy's best pal. I think Jimmy's had Interpol on the case and everything, but no one has come forward. He was a naughty lad years ago. I remember he was going out with a girl, a beauty queen. He was knocking her about. Her Dad said to me, "I'm going to pull his effing head off. I'm not having this, him coming round and battering her." I also heard stories that he got involved with the drugs lads.

'Jimmy was very upset. He will not let it loose. It's still there as far as he's concerned. I think that the only time Jimmy will give his mind a rest is when we actually know where he is. I think it will be with him for the rest of his life.'

Jimmy himself has said very little on the subject in public.

He told the *Sunday Times*, 'We were petrol pump attendants together when we were fifteen. Best job I ever had. No commitments, no responsibility. It sounds sexist but it had the wonderful bonus of the legs when the women got out of the cars. It was a dream.

'Tom was in my band with me, the Crabs. He was the drummer. I've only got a few photographs of him from that era. They were bad photographs so his face is fading as time goes by. I have dreams that he's back and he's all right. And I wake up and I know he's not. He went out of the house, picked up some cash, he was on his way to a nightclub, and he never made it. Vanished off the face of the earth.'

Yet another person close to Jimmy who disappeared from his life without warning. Just as Shelagh was partying one minute and dead the next, so Tom was out on the town and never returned.

The eulogising of the summer holiday job at the petrol station and the lurid melodrama of his friend's face fading out of his life on the old photographs indicate he has spent many hours musing on his fate. It shows what Chrissy Iley calls his 'bleak fatalism', an attitude of mind which serves to temper his successes and aggrandise his failures.

The Northumbria police were quoted in the Newcastle-based *Sunday Sun* newspaper, who splashed the story in 1991, as saying, 'There's neither rhyme nor reason to this. Mr McCulloch vanished without trace yet there's no evidence of foul play. We don't have a single clue.'

Whether they acted on a phone call they received from a former girlfriend of Tom's not long after his disappearance is not known. Certainly nothing appears to have come of the information that she and her husband passed on to them.

Julie Hunt met Tom when she was sixteen and he was nineteen and they went out with each other for two years. During that time she got to know Jimmy very well as he and Tom were inseparable.

Although she and Tom remained friends after their split, she is kinder in her assessment of his friend. 'Jimmy was a very loveable rogue, a great guy, a bit of a wayward character when he was younger but would never do anybody any harm. He got into trouble quite often, doing stupid things. Tom could be a bit naughty. Put it this way, if you needed anything Tom would help you. He wasn't such a bad person. We stayed friends after we split up until he disappeared. We would just like to find out who did Tom in.'

Julie Leyland, as she now is, and her husband Gordon are convinced Tom was killed and that it was a professional job. They are sure because of a conversation between Tom and Gordon just a few days before Tom disappeared.

Gordon tells the story. 'I spoke to him shortly before he went missing,' he said. 'The clutch had gone on my car and he came round and he fixed it. A couple of weeks later somebody backed into my car – it damaged a wing and a few other things – and I asked Tom could he fix it, and he came round and said "No problem." He had an old white Rover. He said, "I'm in a bit of trouble." He asked my advice because although I'm not a villain I'm a bit of a Jack the Lad. He showed me a shotgun in the boot of his car. He said, "I have been knocking around with a bird whose husband is dying of cancer." He was well known in the town and he said there was £5,000 on his head.

He asked my advice. I said, "There are only two things you can do, Tom. Either go and sort him out, or disappear." The next thing I know he disappeared. He just disappeared. He went out one night to Maddison's club and he never come back. He was done in, definitely.'

Tom told Gordon the name of a man who he said had been handed his contract. The man was well known in certain Newcastle circles for sorting out such problems. His name was given to the police.

'He is the local villain of Newcastle,' Gordon continued 'The man who had cancer had hired him. That's what happened. He is definitely dead. I don't think it's possible he staged it. We have a friend in the CID in Newcastle and Julie asked him to try and sort it out. The police turned up nothing at all, not a thing. I think it was a professional job. This man is a well-known villain. He would be the man a villain might turn to if he wanted a job done. He was put away.'

'I know Jimmy was devastated,' said Julie. 'I think it is a lost cause now. I just think it is so sad that nobody can do anything about it. I would just like to see justice. Not just that, I would like to know what happened to him. You can't just sit on this.'

It is difficult to reconcile the statement from Northumbria Police that 'there is no evidence of foul play' with the testimony of Gordon and Julie Leyland which they say was passed on to Newcastle CID. It may well be that the police have no idea what happened to Tom McCulloch but they can hardly claim there is no evidence of foul play. The man was carrying a shotgun in the boot of his car because he thought his life was in danger a few days before he disappeared and had the name of a hit-man he believed had been hired to kill him.

All this did not help Jimmy. If Tom had told Gordon Leyland the truth, then his friend could hardly be expected to find the people responsible where the police had so obviously failed. Joe Watson may have claimed Jimmy wasn't bothered by gangsters and would take anybody on, but this was the real world not some imaginary one created by Jimmy's bravado. He was as powerless to help his friend or even find the truth about his disappearance as anyone else.

Tom's disappearance broke his parents' hearts. Thomas, a postman, and Margaret were left shocked and bewildered . Her sister in law Catherine McCulloch said of Margaret, 'She was never the same.' They experienced the peculiar agony of not knowing what happened to their son. They could not grieve because they were not sure he was dead. They were left with a dwindling hope that they would see him again. Jimmy often visited the old couple in their council flat. He could do nothing to comfort them other than let them know he shared their anguish.

Both are dead now. They died none the wiser about their lost son. Tom's sister Lynn and his aunt and uncle Robert and Catherine McCulloch still wonder every day. So does Jimmy.

13
THE BIG SMOKE

Jimmy and Miriam decided to live full time in London. It wasn't the major sea-change in their lives it might have been, more a shift of emphasis. Their time seemed to be divided almost equally between the two cities so it made sense to have homes in both. They kept their terraced house in South Gosforth to use as a base in the north.

It was a time of turmoil in his life. He had the unwelcome demands that his instant celebrity posed and he was still shattered by Tom's disappearance. He found he needed his home city and his old companions. The result was frequent visits to Newcastle. Moving out created a nostalgia for the old place. Moving back was never a possibility, but he needed a regular fix of what he was familiar with. Joe Watson and his workers became used to the phone call out of the blue from their now famous ex-colleague. 'Joe, I'll be down to make the tea,' was the usual refrain. And he would appear for a cup of tea and a chat.

During one of these chats over tea he persuaded Joe that he could use his fame to help the business. He suggested a local newspaper advert. He would arrange it all, Joe just needed to be there and pay. Joe agreed. Jimmy hired a photographer and they turned up at the factory to organise the picture that would be the centrepiece of the advertisement.

'He brought a photographer along and they did a picture in the car park, Jimmy and the lads standing there with one of Joe's window frames and a van in the background,' said Paul Clark. The photo went in the (Newcastle) *Chronicle* with a slogan 'Joe Watson's windows are the best, says Oz. He knows, he used to work there.' Jimmy did that for nothing for Joe, he just had to pay for the photographer. That was very good of him.'

One Newcastle friend who spanned the two worlds Jimmy now inhabited was Carol Johnson. She was based in Newcastle, but was frequently in the capital because of her husband's lifestyle and her own business interests. Now Jimmy was no longer the odd-job man Carol had a soft spot for. He was famous in his own right. He had achieved what he declared to Carol and Brian he would achieve. Now he was an equal. His new status did not affect his relationship with Carol. She was used to inhabiting the celebrity world and was not fazed by a bit of showbiz success. But it did help heal the rift between Jimmy and Brian. The latter began to take someone he had hitherto regarded as an undesirable oik a bit more seriously. He, Carol, Jimmy and Miriam began to spend time together as a foursome.

Even though Jimmy was a celebrity now, he still had stars in his eyes about the world Brian and Carol inhabited, a world where international rock stars dropped in for coffee or champagne, depending on the occasion. He liked nothing better than to mingle in this company and once he had his feet under the table lost no time in telling these top musicians of his plans to release an album. Jimmy gave them the full force of his charm and was convincing enough to persuade some that they should seriously consider giving him a try.

Only one thing tended to get in the way. The drink. More particularly, Jimmy's personality change when drunk. One incident sticks in Carol's mind. AC/DC had played a gig at Wembley Arena which Jimmy attended. After the concert the band and its entourage went back to its hotel, The Capital, just behind Harrods in Knightsbridge.

'We all went back to the hotel,' said Carol. 'Jimmy was starting. He was getting annoyed. What triggered it, I think, was that he stood in the audience and watched them perform and he wished it was him. He came back to the hotel. Miriam came with him but left after an hour, she must have had an idea of what was going to come. Jimmy stayed and he started getting belligerent. We all disappeared to our rooms and he went rampaging through the hotel, screaming abuse, asking where we were. He was chucked out and as he left he jumped on the bonnets of about five cars parked outside. He had to pay for the damage. The next day he was on the phone apologising, saying he was out of order and could he come round to the hotel. I said that Brian was going to do an interview for Alan Freeman so I was hanging around at the hotel with Cliff Williams, the bass player of AC/DC and his wife. A few other people were there and Jimmy came over. As we sat there having a few drinks this messenger arrived with a huge case of champagne for me from Fluff Freeman as a thank you for letting Brian go for the day. Cliff Williams said, "Great, good on Fluff Freeman." I opened the box up, asked for ice and we started drinking. Cliff's closest friend, Laurie Wisefield, the guitarist from Wishbone Ash arrived and Jimmy sat there and said, "God, that's Laurie Wisefield, one of my heroes, I don't believe it." He was awestruck. He said, "I've got to talk to him."

'As the day went on we were all talking and drinking and he did get chatting and he seemed to get on with him OK. But, as usual, the more drinks that we had, Jimmy changed. Mr Hyde came out again. He could be lovely, then he had a few drinks and everybody would start leaving. I drifted off. Brian came back and he took one look and said, "Let's get out of here." We went to our rooms and Laurie knocked on the door and he said, "That lad, that Jimmy guy, he's after me to play on his album and I said yes, he seemed a nice guy and I said he could get my number from you. I've changed my mind. Don't give him my number. I don't think I could work with him."

'He always had a streak of paranoia in him as well, especially when he had a drink. He believed everyone was against him. He said he was misinterpreted, misunderstood. I said, "Jimmy you haven't got a chip on your shoulder, you've got a giant bag of King Edwards. You turn people against you because of the way you behave when you've had a drink. That's the bottom line. They don't change, you change."'

Another introduction Jimmy was keen for Carol to effect was with Peter Mensch, manager of AC/DC and Def Leppard amongst others. A very powerful and influential figure in the world of rock music and a man Jimmy felt it was essential he met. One evening Carol took Jimmy along to a party being thrown by Mensch and his wife Sue at their home in Kensington, west London. There was a small but high-powered gathering and Mensch was in no mood to be accosted by Jimmy.

'Peter was very wary of him,' said Carol. 'He said, "What have you brought him to my house for? I can't do anything with him. He's not in a heavy metal band, he's not a rock and roller."'

Jimmy might have been able to get away with it a few years earlier, but not any more. The drunken antics cut no ice in this new world, a fact which gradually dawned on him as he tried to establish himself. But it was not all drink-sodden embarrassment. Carol remembers his charm, energy and 'can-do' spirit with great affection. Despite his often glum, haunted look, he was a man who was living his dream and occasionally he allowed himself to enjoy it.

'We had great fun together,' she said. 'We could go out drinking together, especially in Newcastle. We would hit the clubs and then go back to my house. He always stayed whether Miriam was with him or not. My Dad was at the house at the time and he thought nothing of it. We'd have a few drinks, he'd go off to the guest room, I'd go to bed and the next day he'd go back to London, or whatever, and that was how it would go on.'

One difficult time for Carol was illuminated brilliantly by Jimmy, providing her with a memory she will always cherish. She was hospitalised with an abscess in her groin. One afternoon she was feeling particularly down when a familiar face popped round the door to the ward. Jimmy came striding towards her bed clutching a bottle of Opium perfume in one hand and one of Jack Daniels whiskey in the other. He silenced the excited hubbub that had risen as the patients began to recognise him by shouting the immortal greeting, 'Hello, Johnson, how's your fanny?' A few seconds of shocked silence was broken by Carol's laughter. Everyone joined in. When the ward sister arrived to see what the commotion was about, Jimmy turned on the charm and managed to persuade her to put him and Carol in a side ward where they were able to drink to their hearts' content. 'We got as drunk as skunks,' said Carol.

The terrifying ex-convict was now a self-assured celebrity, able to bestow kindness on his old friends. He was changing, yet the public's perception of Jimmy was as Oz, the unreconstructed Geordie. This would prove a destructive tension.

14
LIVING ALRIGHT

In the spring of 1984 – after four years together – Miriam became pregnant. The news delighted Jimmy and heightened his sense of the profoundly changing nature of his life. Tommy McCulloch had been missing more than nine months by this time, but Jimmy had been so pre-occupied working on *Auf Wiedersehen Pet* and moving to London that the whole thing was still painfully fresh in his mind. His brooding, fatalistic nature turned in on itself. The unborn baby became for him a symbol of the fresh start he had been allowed which his best friend had not.

The revulsion he felt at being recognised in public and, worse, the way he hated being confused with Oz – however light-hearted the intention – had curtailed his socialising. He found it impossible to walk into a pub now, even though he had spent all his adult life doing just this. He still drank – and drank a lot – but it was now seldom in public.

His increasing isolation and brooding about Tommy also set him thinking about the old band – the King Crabs – and his musical ambitions. The one thing he craved above anything was to make it as a singer. The Crabs, he knew, had been more a novelty act than serious musicians but within the confines of the north-east they had achieved a certain cachet because their charismatic lead singer had been a marketable commodity.

Also, some of the *Pet* actors regretted not recording the show's theme tune, 'That's Living Alright', after seeing Joe Fagin's version reach number three in the charts. Again timing and marketing were the factors behind Fagin's success.

The businessman in Jimmy knew that if he was going to carve out a musical dimension to his showbusiness career now was the time to do it. Yet he was determined not to be yet another actor riding on the back of a spot of commercial success. There was no way he was going to give the public a musical Oz, which would have been the easy thing to do. He wanted to give them the musical Jimmy Nail.

The music industry did not seem so keen on the prospect. After *Auf Wiedersehen Pet* when Jimmy let it be known he was interested in establishing himself as a singer all he got were the knee-jerk reactions he had feared. 'Quick, cheap, cashing-in deals where they would have liked to see me on Top of the Pops in a donkey jacket and carrying a hod,' was how he later summed them up. 'I refused to get involved with that sort of garbage.'

To the average record company executive Jimmy Nail must have appeared insufferably arrogant. Here he was, an ugly, hulking Geordie who got lucky in television presuming to tell them how he wanted his musical career to develop. They knew best, to cast him how the public know and love him and watch the money come in. It was a tried and tested formula and, let's face it, Jimmy Nail was hardly hearthrob material. They tried the suggestions on Jimmy and met with a resounding no. Who on earth did this man think he was? Another stroppy actor taking himself too seriously, no doubt. If he didn't want to play ball there were plenty of others who would. Jimmy Nail's musical career could have died before it began if it was not for his characteristically dogged determination.

He was not backward in coming forward. He was confident of his musical abilities and not afraid of buttonholing whoever he could find to tell them so, as Peter Mensch and Laurie Wisefield could testify. And he did have ability. Francesco Reidy, whose friendship with Jimmy continued after *Auf Wiedersehen Pet*, remembers his surprise at the discovery.

He said, 'He had two genuine musical gifts. The first was his voice which had a great quality and range and the second was a natural ear for musical structure, that is to say harmony, melody and composition. We sat down together at my Fender Rhodes piano to work out an arrangement of the song Gigi. As we looked at the ideal base line he would constantly insist on a particular note being the right one – banging various keys on the keyboard with one finger until he found it – to underpin a given phrase or chord. Very often the choice he made was wrong in my opinion as it broke the accepted rules of music. It was only when we played the end result that I realised how good it sounded. His head was not cluttered with all the various limitations that a formal musical training can create. He was arranging by simply using the natural gifts and instincts that he had.'

With the help of Allan McKeown Jimmy recorded a demo album of his own songs. It was a big step. He was laying himself bare as never before. The intention was twofold: to realise his long-standing musical ambition and to hack down a clearing in the confusing foliage between himself and Oz.

This was not as straightforward as it sounds as, by his own admission, he had put rather too much of himself into his famous small screen alter-ego. The mental process going on at this time takes us right back to the sullen, reserved boy in Newcastle who allowed himself to be submerged under the smothering influence of the loud aggressive, centre-stage-seeking young man. The public were seeing – and adoring – this outrageous figure. They were invading his precious private life. Jimmy didn't know quite what to do about that at this stage. He certainly looked like an Oz – there was nothing much he could do about that – but he didn't have to sound like Oz. This priority is expressed by Allan McKeown in a newspaper report about the demo tape. 'Jimmy is a fantastic prospect with a fantastic voice. He sounds nothing at all like Oz.' The point is hammered home with a quote from an anonymous 'close friend' who says, 'Jimmy has an incredible talent. When the public hear his music they will realise he and Oz are a million miles apart.'

The trouble was that the public never got to hear it. No one offered him the recording contract he had set his heart on. There was acute disappointment, a bruised ego and the desire, after exposing something of his heart to the world and being rejected, to retreat back into his shell. But above all Jimmy was angry. Angry with the music industry for rejecting him. He had failed this time, but he was determined not to give up. He vowed to have the last laugh on all the doubters who could not see further than his broken nose and missing tooth.

He was being pressed into signing up for the second series of *Auf Wiedersehen Pet* and decided to use the opportunity. One of the stipulations he made was that his contract contained a guarantee that he be given the chance to sing in the series. It was the perfect opportunity to put his abilities in the shop window.

As it turned out, he would not need it. In the autumn of 1984 his backers negotiated a deal for him to record a cover version of the Rose Royce classic 'Love Don't Live Here Anymore'. Jimmy remembers its genesis thus, 'Recorded somewhere in north London. Can't remember where, exactly – I was drinking for England back then. Track had its beginnings in the Barge in Little Venice. Late night with Tony Mac [McAnaney]. Listening to it the next day in a café, it sounded OK. Roger Taylor heard it, liked it, co-produced it with Dave Richards and that was the start of this little adventure.'

The Roger Taylor referred to was no less than Queen's drummer and a major player in music production at the time. His presence was a testimony to Jimmy's impressive powers of persuasion. Nevertheless the record had a difficult and protracted birth. They took it round various record companies all of whom turned it down, saying Jimmy should make a comedy record instead. Jimmy was furious. He'd already had enough offers to be the singing Oz to line his living-room walls. He may have been furious, but he did not give up. Eventually his persistence paid off. He approached Virgin, who agreed to release it. A date was fixed in the following spring.

Crucial as his music was to him, it only claimed a part of his time. Jimmy was also busy negotiating to appear in Mel Smith and Griff Rhys Jones' film *Morons From Outer Space*. It was to be directed, coincidentally, by Mike Hodges, director of the inspirational *Get Carter*. Jimmy signed up to play Desmond, one of the morons. It may not have been Michael Caine, but it was a start; his big screen debut. The film was put together during an intensive ten-week shoot in the summer of 1984. Mike Hodges remembers Jimmy as a charismatic performer and polished professional who had an air of confidence which suggested far greater experience in the business than he actually possessed.

'I had only seen him in *Auf Wiedersehen* and I hadn't seen him a lot in that because I had been out of the country while it was being transmitted,' said Hodges. 'I found him a real, natural talent. He has got such an extraordinary face. He just had this great ability to deliver funny lines. I think he is terribly good in it. I was never conscious that he was as inexperienced as he patently was. I was never conscious of him having not learned his trade. Lines were learned, he was there on time, the lot. He was one-take Jimmy as far I was concerned.'

Once again, as in *Auf Wiedersehen Pet*, Jimmy was concentrating all his energies on conquering this new medium. Hodges was obviously greatly impressed, especially as he had not experienced most of the Oz-mania that had swept through Britain in the months prior to filming. Not only was he surprised by his abilities but also that this bright young actor was a long-standing fan of one of his previous works. It was over a cup of tea during a break in filming that Jimmy told the director all about the evening he watched him shooting the scene outside the Mayfair Dance Hall. He said watching the film being made, then seeing the finished article at the cinema, seeing his home city used so evocatively to convey atmosphere, had inspired him. *Get Carter* became something of a cult picture in the north-east when it was released in 1971, everyone in the city wanted to see it. Jimmy and Hodges hit it off. It heightened his sense of achievement to be working with the man who, to the sixteen-year-old boy watching in the crowd all those years ago – must have seemed like a remote god able even to command such stars as Michael Caine.

Although *Morons* was well received in the United States – one critic called it 'Swiftian', according to Hodges – it attracted very mixed reviews in Britain. Hodges himself admits it was a flawed picture. But for Jimmy it was a relatively high-profile debut, even if the role of

Desmond – an outrageously clad alien one brick short of a full load – smacked a little too much of type-casting for his liking.

By this time he was a father. Miriam had given birth to a boy, with her partner present, in February. They had decided to call the child Tommy after Jimmy's missing best friend. Jimmy had done a lot of brooding about the disappearance in the month's leading up to his son's birth and giving him the same name was a kind of exorcism. This way his old buddy would always be with him through his son. Also it gave him a sense of renewal, a sense that life had to continue without his great friend.

He may have been present at his son's birth but he wasn't around much in the months that followed. The great British public, already conditioned to expect Jimmy Nail to be loud, uncouth and obnoxious, were in for a shock when his debut single was released in April 1985. Even allowing for the ultra-smooth, professional production, Jimmy's voice was remarkable, not only for its quality and range but for its ability to convey emotion. It was certainly not the kind of voice you would expect to be emitted from his hulking frame. The public might have been shocked but not unpleasantly so. They liked what they heard and bought the record in sufficient quantities to propel it to the undreamed of heights of number three in the charts. Jimmy was a pop star, and he had done it without gimmicks or building site props. He had done it on his own terms. So determined was he to pare down his appearance, to let his music do his talking, that he made his debut on Top of the Pops in a drab raincoat. He stood centrestage, surrounded by dozens of jigging, bright young things, a dowdy, gap-toothed giant, ponderous amid the lithe dancers all around him, yet delivering a sweet sound that belied his appearance.

His handling of this musical success bears all the hallmarks of a man who believes he has made it. He told one journalist, 'I have been singing for years in rhythm and blues bands, I have been involved with it from a very young age. It's good now to look back at the times I'd work my butt off at gigs. Sometimes it would cost me more money to do the show than I got at the end of the night. Sometimes there were more people in the band than the audience.'

This comment shows Jimmy is keen to hammer home the point that he is a serious musician. To do it, he serves up the old cliché of himself as the struggling artist who has served his time, suffered his apprenticeship at the sharp end and is now reaping the just deserts of his years of toil.

Everything was happening for Jimmy at once and, typically, he was determined to embrace it with as much vigour as he could muster. After all, he had a family to support now. Three months after Tommy's birth Jimmy called him 'the light of my life' and that he loved the peace and quiet of home life. Yet his hectic schedule meant that he saw very little of the boy or his home at that time.

15

AUF WIEDERSEHEN
REVISITED

There had to be another series. Thirteen million viewers for one thing. Talk of it being a landmark in television drama for another. Tremendous characters who had been enfolded to the bosom of the nation for a third. It really was just a question of when.

As far as Central was concerned it couldn't come soon enough. The series had been a big feather in the cap of the fledgling television company. It had gone a long way to establishing it as a major player in the scramble for prestige following the re-organisation of independent television.

Only now the circumstances were entirely different. This time the boot was on the other foot. The producers and stars, far from outcasts, were being entreated to work together again. Witzend were engaged to produce, Clement and La Frenais were to be involved in the scripts. All that was required was for The Magnificent Seven to sign on the dotted line.

They were not hungry unknowns anymore. They were famous, in demand, feted. Some were big stars. Instead of eager novices, desperate for work, there were agents to contend with and newly-inflated egos to assuage. None was resting between roles anymore, all had busy schedules which had to be accommodated.

The months following the first series were lucrative for them all.

Pat Roach was busiest and enjoyed the highest profile, winning roles in the James Bond film, *Never Say Never Again* opposite Sean Connery, and *Indiana Jones and the Temple of Doom* with Harrison Ford. He played Little John in George Segal's *Robin Hood* film and starred as Captain Oates in ITV's account of Captain Scott's assault on the South Pole, *The Last Place On Earth*.

Tim Healy starred as Andy Capp in the Newcastle Playhouse and made several commercials. Gary Holton returned to music, playing in *Pump Boys and Dinettes* at the Piccadilly Theatre in London. Tim Spall played the Dauphin in Shaw's *St Joan* and Ligurio in Machiavelli's *Mandragola*, both at the National Theatre. Kevin Whately did a nationwide theatre tour in the title role of *Billy Liar* and filmed a three part Agatha Christie thriller for the BBC.

Jimmy was no slouch, either. He appeared in a BBC mini-series *Master of the Game* and episodes of *Spyship* and *Minder* as well as *Morons From Outer Space* and launching a singing career.

They were all hot stuff and making the most of it, striking while the iron was hot. Even so, they all knew that a new *Pet* series was not to be sniffed at and it was relatively straightforward to get them to agree to appear. Except for one, that is. The Jimmy Nail who entered into negotiations for the new series was a very different proposition from the one who had appeared in the first. The rave reviews he had received for Oz, the advice of those closest to him and his subsequent successes had convinced him that Tim Spall was right, that he had, at last, found his niche. This was a business to be taken seriously.

He had not been one of the highest paid people on the first series. He had been an unknown – not even an actor – whereas someone like Spall was an established performer. He had accepted this as fair but did not forget it. When contract negotiations opened for series two he was told that Central wanted to pay the seven main actors the same amount. The company reasoned that as all had contributed to the programme's huge success it was the fairest way to do business. Jimmy disagreed. He argued that he was a bigger name than some of his co-stars and, applying the standards of the first series, should be paid a bigger fee.

It is difficult to argue his case. All – with the possible exception of Chris Fairbanks – were enjoying an extended honeymoon with the

British public. Jimmy had probably made the most impact because of his extraordinary performance, but the others were by no means overshadowed. However difficult his case, Jimmy continued to argue it with his customary stubbornness and determination.

At one point he even pulled out of the new show and the story was leaked to the press. On 15 July 1984 the *Sunday People* carried an article claiming Jimmy had quit the series because his television bosses would not pay him a star bonus. It quoted Jimmy as saying, 'Yes, it's true. I'm not doing the new series. I'm very disappointed but that's the way it is.'

This is a wonderful example of talking yourself up. Tell enough people you're worth more and some will begin to believe it. The story also quotes a Central 'insider' as saying, 'The company want to give all the actors the same amount, regardless that some, like Jimmy, have developed into much bigger stars than others.'

The controversy seems to have blown over pretty quickly, however. Central held firm and Jimmy eventually accepted its terms, doubtless realising that it made much more commercial sense to be in the second series than out of it. His stance was a minor irritant at the time but a foretaste of the attitude he would bring with him to filming, which went some way towards souring the genial camaraderie which characterised the shooting of the first series. There would be more minor irritations before shooting began in earnest.

In the early days wardrobe had the task of assembling the clothes to be worn by the seven stars. It was deemed important for reasons of continuity that as many items from the previous series be used again. It was deemed particularly important that the battered leather jacket worn by Oz, and which had become his trademark, be unearthed from the bowels of the Central wardrobe department. The problem was, no one could find it. Several searches had drawn a blank and the bad news was broken to the producers. In the general discussion about what to do that followed Jimmy piped up with the news that he had the jacket. He explained that there had been a sell-off of clothing at the end of the first series and he had snapped it up as a souvenir. The relief that followed was soon replaced by astonishment as Jimmy explained that he was quite happy to hire it out to Central for the duration of the shoot as long as an appropriate fee could be agreed.

He had them over a barrel and he knew it. Eventually they settled, but not before Jimmy had extracted a decent deal worth a few hundred pounds out of them.

The anecdote gives a good illustration of Jimmy's mindset at this time. He came to the second series the wised up professional determined that no one was going to put one over on him. He had the self-confidence and experience by now to speak up if he was unhappy with anything and he was certainly no respecter of reputations.

Work on the second series began early in 1985 against a background of appalling industrial relations at Central's Nottingham studios. One member of the production staff said, 'In the second series Nail was by no means the biggest problem. That was the absolutely appalling management-union relations and the fact that it was almost impossible to get anything done. Management didn't seem terribly interested in making programmes, only breaking the unions and the unions realised it was their last chance of making big money out of a programme. Nobody except us was interested in getting a programme made.'

The other major headache was Gary Holton, who played Wayne. The producers realised to their horror that Holton was deep into the downward, self-destructive spiral of drug addiction and was a nightmare to work with. An insider revealed, 'Gary Holton was a terrible problem. I have never worked with a totally self-destructive drug addict before. He was making life extraordinarily difficult for everybody. I realised that a coke addict – and God knows what else he was on – not only destroys himself but pretty well destroys everything around him. He was totally out of control for the last couple of months. We were trying to keep him and the show going.'

If anything, these problems inflamed Jimmy further. Although they had briefly been buddies during the early weeks of the first series, the friendship between Jimmy and Holton had quickly cooled. Now, Jimmy viewed him as a rival, and a rival who was getting all the attention. Drug addict or not, that just would not do, so Jimmy did what he had seen and heard of other actors doing when they didn't like something. He resigned. A source on the series said, 'Jimmy did resign once, complaining that we were paying too much attention to Gary and not enough to him. We didn't actually take much notice of that and he turned up again the next day. There was a lot of that kind of thing but then there is a lot of that kind of thing in showbusiness. There were other actors working there at the time who did a lot of that and I think he saw them doing it and thought "Maybe I'll do it too."'

No one was safe from the wrath of Jimmy Nail, not even Ian La Frenais himself. In fact it appeared to crew members that Jimmy went out of his way to antagonise the great man. It did not matter a hoot to Jimmy that this was a celebrated writer and that he was a novice actor. If he didn't like something that La Frenais wrote he made no bones about telling him. There was a real friction between the grammar school boy made good from Whitley Bay and the ex-welder from the heart of Newcastle. Fortunately for both it was a constructive friction. Both had the self-confidence and good sense to see the positive aspects of this relationship.

'By the second series Jimmy had become very shrewd,' said La Frenais. 'He was asking all sorts of questions and picking on the script. He was always being nasty to me. But behind it all he was right. A lot of the things he was complaining about, he was right. He was a pain in the arse is what he was, but he was usually right because he was learning a lot and learning about the character and in the same way learning he couldn't stay as Oz. He was horrible to me at times, very unpleasant which probably was based on the fact that we were both from the north east.'

La Frenais tolerated this upstart's impudence because he was convinced he had talent and because he judged his heart to be in the right place, that his complaints were borne out of a desperate desire for the show to be as good as it could be. This reading of the Nail psyche is shared by a senior member of the crew, who could not help like and admire Jimmy despite his tantrums.

'There was an occasion in the second series when he got very involved in a scene he wasn't even in, involving Bill Patterson – who played Ally Fraser – and his girlfriend. Jimmy, for some reason, I don't know why, seemed very concerned that the scene was not written or played properly and he certainly made his feelings known. He had a very strong professional interest in the way things were done and also he cared very much about the show.

'I remember one time when Ian La Frenais was visiting us from LA and Jimmy gave him quite a heavy time about what Jimmy saw as his lack of involvement. Later he and the director were in a restaurant and suddenly Jimmy appeared and said to La Frenais, "I want a word with you." La Frenais groaned and went over and sat with him. He felt, quite unfairly, that La Frenais wasn't caring enough about it. It is important to make the point that he was not just being bloody-minded. I'm sure Jimmy genuinely cared about the show and thought it could be better and made no bones about telling anybody, whether it was another actor or the director. A lot of what he does would be completely unacceptable from somebody who didn't care. That care underpins his actions.'

It is the ability to look into the eye of the storm he creates around him which seems to be necessary when dealing with Jimmy Nail. Only strong, self-confident professionals who are secure enough to take criticism need apply.

These tantrums were punctuated with Jimmy's ability to land himself in trouble, a talent which he had not lost on his way up. This first manifested itself in the Nottingham studios where he fell foul of a race he detested above most others – the security guard. One crew member tells the tale.

'The one thing that used to get Jimmy going was men in uniforms. He used to get paranoid about them, particularly the kind of people who join security companies. On one occasion they tried to throw him off the site. He was needed for a scene and he had to get changed very quickly. But there had been a mix-up in dressing-room keys, so he kicked down the door to his dressing room, for which the security people wanted him arrested. I had to try to explain to one of these thickos that he had gone a bit over the top but if he was arrested and sent away for three days it would be very bad. What was important was to get that man on stage and they didn't understand that. I think he objected to those kind of chaps in office. Presumably he would not make a policeman his hero if he objected to all men in uniform, but he objected to the self-appointed people in uniform, the Group Four mentality.'

The second brush with authority came while the crew were filming on location in Spain. It all began when Jimmy decided he didn't like the bedroom he had been given at the hotel and told the management.

He was given another room but was soon on the phone to them complaining the bed in the new room was not to his liking. When he failed to get what he considered was the proper response he decided to remove the offending bed. Horrified staff were confronted by a furious Jimmy dragging his bed out of the door and down the corridor. The language barrier only inflamed things, so staff decided to communicate in a lingo that might have more impact. Armed police were called and had surrounded him – pistols drawn – by the time the long-suffering production team managed to calm things down and avoid the time-consuming business of extricating him from a Spanish jail.

Another fraught day resulted from the decision to cast Jimmy's sister Val McLane in the role of Tim Healy's sister. It was only a minor role and Val was needed for just one day's shooting, but that was enough for the rest of the cast and crew involved. She did just one scene with Jimmy but the combination provided director Roger Bamford with what he regarded as his worst afternoon of the shoot. One crew member said, 'They certainly have a very complicated relationship. She didn't have a huge amount to do and she was professional and fine. She did one scene with Jimmy. Constant bickering. Older sister. I don't think it was particularly Jimmy's fault, I think it was just as much Val's.'

Jimmy's insistence on singing in the second series – which he'd had written into his contract – baffled the production hierarchy. This was negotiated at a time when he was desperate to parade his talents as a singer. The fact that he had since had a chart-topping single didn't dampen his enthusiasm. Jimmy was absolutely determined in the teeth of a good deal of opposition to the idea.

'He was prepared to take it to the wire. I don't know what would have happened if we had said no,' said one insider.

Eventually he got his way. His big moment came when the gang visited a country and western dance and the compere asked for a guest singer. Oz stood up and obliged. Interestingly he did not attempt to sing in character. He sang it as well as Jimmy Nail could. 'He was obviously putting his singing talents in the shop window,' said the source.

Despite the show's many problems Jimmy remained intensely loyal and dedicated. He desperately wanted it to be as good as it could be and was prepared to put anyone's nose out of joint – figuratively speaking – to achieve that end. Roger Bamford and he always got on and Bamford remains Jimmy's favourite director to this day. But he could not direct all episodes of the second series and a replacement – the respected Tony Garner – came in at relatively short notice to take the helm for four episodes. Over dinner one evening he admitted he had not seen all thirteen programmes in the first series.

'Jimmy was absolutely outraged by this and came out with a "How can you sit there…?" type of speech. They didn't get on at all well. Tony is a very good experienced director but it was quite obvious their relationship was completely gone,' said one member of the dinner party.

The shoot lurched from crisis to confrontation through the autumn of 1985. When they returned from Spain, producer Martin McKeand could see the end in sight and began to think his troubles were over. There were just a few weeks' filming left which should have been completed by Christmas, he calculated.

They were in the middle of filming a snooker match in which all the main characters were taking part, a tremendously tricky operation because of the difficulties of maintaining continuity. They stopped midway through the scene for a few days' break. During that break Gary Holton died. His last weeks had been a sordid and tragic descent, He became a pathetic figure, pursued by reporters seeking to verify the rumours of his drug addiction.

The cast and crew returned from the break in shock. Although Holton had become increasingly out of control and an irritation to everybody, he remained by and large a popular figure who had worked cheek by jowl with most of the cast and crew over two gruelling shoots. The cast were once more the object of close tabloid scrutiny and something of the us-and-them mentality of the first series returned.

Apart from their shock and grief, Garner and McKeand had to resolve the thorny problem of finishing the shoot without Holton and resolve it quickly. The remaining scenes were hastily re-written and the snooker scene completed and cut in such a way as to cover up the inescapable fact that one player started but could not finish.

Holton's death meant that the shoot could not be completed by Christmas as originally planned. This created a major problem for the producers as the actors' contracts expired several days before filming was complete. Whatever the reason – colleague's death or no – this put them in a very strong position. 'I don't know what deals were done but the actors were in an extraordinarily strong position to make all kinds of demands, which I believe they did,' said a source.

They soldiered on until just before Christmas, feeling anything but festive. The last straw came on the final day before the holiday. Chaos erupted by mid-morning when the electricians downed tools and walked out. One crew member recalls the pandemonium that ensued. 'Halfway through the morning the electricians walked out through the studio and down the corridor. In reception there was a carol service being recorded live and they just walked through it. At the same time coachloads of audience were arriving for the afternoon recording of *The Price is Right*. It was a scene of absolute farce and chaos. That was when we decided to go home.'

Everyone followed the electricians' lead and decided to down tools until the New Year. It had been a dreadful few weeks but McKeand was at least hopeful that with the actors' individual deals sorted out he could quickly wrap things up after the holiday.

The return in early January was characterised by a collective desire to finish the project as soon as possible. It had not been a happy shoot and it was now hanging over a month after it should have been done and dusted. There was a spirit of conciliation in the air, old grievances were pushed aside so that things could be concluded and *Auf Wiedersehen Pet 2* consigned to history. Within a few days it was just about in the can and the sense of relief amongst the actors and production team was palpable. The evening before the last day's shooting there was a large and good-humoured gathering for dinner. The mood was convivial as everyone knew they were almost there. Jimmy seemed as happy as the next person. Everyone dispersed relatively early ready for the final day's work.

The general spirit of co-operation was shattered first thing the next morning. Everyone involved appeared on set early to get things going. They were shooting a group scene involving the whole cast. Then Martin McKeand got the message that Jimmy was remaining in his hotel room and refusing to work. The spirit of determination was shattered. Everyone hung around wondering what to do. Eventually McKeand was told there was a phone call for him from Jimmy Nail. A colleague says, 'Jimmy got it into his head that he and Tim Healy were being asked to do a scene from another episode that we wanted played another way and technically if they did that they were entitled to another episode fee, which was several thousand pounds. Jimmy somehow saw this as being asked to do something for nothing which he thought was disgracefully unfair and he went on strike.'

He told McKeand on the phone that Central owed him the episode fee and he wouldn't come out of his hotel room until he was paid the money up front in cash. A furious McKeand organised a hasty meeting with director Roger Bamford and they decided they could shoot the scene without Jimmy which they proceeded to do, leaving him to stew in his room.

The source adds, 'He turned up at lunchtime saying he had thought about it and he was ready to play the part and that we could discuss the other matter later. He was told "No, it's all right, you can go home, we don't need you." It was a very depressing end to a very traumatic shoot. It reached a point with Gary dying and the enormous industrial unrest when some of the actors really thought there was a jinx on the programme. Everyone was very depressed and at the end of the shoot at 5 p.m. everyone just literally walked away. They didn't throw a party or even go for a drink.'

It would be difficult for anyone to argue that Jimmy's last tantrum on the shoot of *Auf Wiedersehen Pet* was because he cared about the show so deeply. It seemed calculated to bring about the maximum disruption at a time when that was the last thing any single member of the cast and crew wanted. It seemed all about ego, about playing the temperamental star to the end. One colleague is of the opinion it is more about a working-class chip on his shoulder and a heightened sense of injustice bordering on the paranoid. 'He was always very distrustful of management because he felt they were trying to take advantage of a simple lad. I think that feeling was always there.'

It was this which sparked his final tantrum, he believes. 'After a jolly evening he had gone away and started brooding,' he adds.

The complex character which is Jimmy Nail was not finished yet.

After the sad dispersal of the afternoon a group of about a dozen people who had been closely involved in both series decided the occasion could not pass unmarked and arranged to go out for dinner at a country pub close to the studio. The mood was sombre but improved later as the wine flowed. At around midnight, just as the party was planning to head back to their hotel for a few late drinks the door opened and in walked Jimmy.

One diner said, 'He came in, sat down and said let bygones be bygones, that type of thing. When we asked for the bill we found it had already been paid by Jimmy. I don't know what the psychology behind that was.'

Possibly it was the Nail way of saying sorry. They returned to their hotel and by now Jimmy was forgiven. They carried on drinking into the small hours. One senior member of the crew found himself deep in conversation with Jimmy. 'He started talking about this idea he had, something he really wanted to do which was a series on a Geordie detective. I wished him good luck with it.'

Even then, at the end of a traumatic series, in the early hours of the morning after an extremely convivial evening, Jimmy would not allow himself to relax. He was always planning his next move. This project he was nurturing would come to fruition as *Spender* but not for several years. Not before Jimmy properly found his feet in this relatively new world he was inhabiting and radically re-invented himself to suit its requirements.

16
RECONSTRUCTING JIMMY

It may have been a nightmare to make, but *Auf Wiedersehen Pet 2* proved just as big a commercial success as its predecessor. Audiences peaked at fifteen million. The pain had been worth it. However, there were never any serious plans to make a third series. A combination of the cracks in relationships and the fact that by now the main stars were such busy people meant it was highly unlikely it would ever be possible to get them all together again. The will was not there. Unlike many a successful series, *Pet* did not limp on one step too far. It retired at its peak and its reputation became all the better for it.

Jimmy had tried but could not properly claim to be the biggest star spawned by the show at the end of the first series. But he had a legitimate claim to that honour now. Whereas the other five (Holton was dead) either remained as actors with varying degrees of success, Jimmy was the one who possessed the formidable drive – some would say ego – to explore as many avenues as he could. Singing, film and television acting, song and script-writing; he was full of ideas, ambition and energy. Not only was he proving a potent creative force, he also enjoyed the wheeling and dealing, the negotiating, the setting up of his various artistic manifestations.

Jimmy, Miriam and Tommy had settled in a surprisingly modest suburban semi in leafy Cricklewood, deep in bank manager country, the unremarkable commuter belt of north-west London. The apparent peace of this existence was deceptive. Like many a set of net curtains in the area, the well-tended façade of the Nail household disguised enormous emotional turbulence. Jimmy was still driven by formidable demons. Those closest to him say they came from deep in his background.

Ian La Frenais, himself a working-class boy made good, offers this assessment. 'There was a determination to succeed and prove himself, married to the fact that he didn't want to go back to what the option was. Michael Caine said he always had the fear that someone was going to tap him on the shoulder and say, "Right, you've had your taste of it, now back to the factory." It's that working-class thing. You know where you've come from and you don't want to go back, except for visits or to shoot a television series.'

His sister Val connects his ambition with the traumas of his early life. 'I think Jimmy would have been a success at anything because whether it was to do with the trauma of losing Shelagh – which of course affected him – or whether it was to do with prison, I don't know, but he became obsessive and ambitious and determined that whatever he did he would succeed. When he went into the property business, if he had stayed in that, he would have become a property millionaire. He's got a marvellous head for business. He's very interested in business, wheeling and dealing is his forte. He has an obsessive personality.'

The one thing he had set his heart on above everything else was to make it as a musician. It remained his first love. He had a vision of playing the big arenas – like he had watched Brian Johnson do – and having thousands of people in his thrall. He was driven towards this goal, yet the ferocity of his ambition was counterproductive. It compelled him to do everything his way, rendered him incapable of accepting help and advice from experienced people in the business.

Things started brightly enough. He was handed an album contract by Virgin on the back of his successful single, and he set to work. He had recorded some songs two years earlier for the demo tape and was also keen to develop new material. But it was a debut album and if he thought he was to be left entirely to his own devices by Virgin he was mistaken. This was exactly what he expected, however, and viewed any attempt by the company to contribute or offer advice as interference not to be tolerated.

A Virgin executive said, 'The problem was Jimmy simply refused to take any advice from us. When it came to producers, even the songs, he insisted on having it his own way. He was very awkward and difficult to work with.'

Jimmy soldiered on, resolutely going his own way. Because of his independence and his commitments to filming *Auf Wiedersehen Pet 2* the album took much longer to complete than Virgin would have liked. As it began to come together other problems emerged. The company's marketing men were convinced that Jimmy should be sold as what is known in the trade as 'MOR' – middle of the road; safe, conventional, easy listening. As such they began to work on getting Jimmy the kind of publicity they thought would suit his image. A spot on the *Des O'Connor Show* was mentioned. Jimmy hit the roof. He had an entirely different view of his place in the musical pantheon.

'They lump me in with all the soap stars who are making records,' he complained. 'They think because I'm an actor, I'm automatically a novelty act. They forget I've sung blues and rock and roll since my early teens.'

'The thing was, he has this idea of himself as a cool, credible artiste', said the Virgin source. 'In fact he was plain MOR. Not that there's anything wrong with that. But Jimmy would not accept it. So, for example, we were steering him towards appearances on the Des O'Connor Show and he just refused. He felt he belonged on The Tube, and of course they wouldn't touch him with a barge pole.'

The album, *Take It Or Leave It*, was eventually released in the spring of 1986 – far later than Virgin had calculated would be the optimum time – and it bombed.

'People left it,' was Jimmy's wry comment years later.

'It took him at least a year to get the album together and, of course, by the time it was released the moment had passed. Commercially it was a failure. In the end we let him go. That's the truth behind Virgin not doing a follow-up album. Clearly Jimmy chooses to see it otherwise.'

The Virgin source is obviously keen to stress that one of the main contributing factors to the album's failure was Jimmy's refusal to heed the advice of the experts. This might be so, but it is difficult to agree that the timing was entirely wrong. Although Virgin say 'the moment had passed', that by the time the album was released Jimmy's hit single was a distant memory, the launch did – intentionally – follow hard on the heels of *Auf Wiedersehen Pet 2*, which was attracting huge audiences. One thing no one could argue with was the public response. Jimmy was determined to do it his way. He played a high risk strategy and lost. If it had sold he could have stuck two fingers at all the 'experts' who had tried to advise him. As it was they did just that to him.

For a man who was beginning to have grave reservations about the public's perception of him and who was also chastened by the failure of his unrefined energy to produce the results he wanted, Jimmy made a surprising choice for his next project. He agreed to appear as a small-time drugs dealer operating on an Edinburgh housing estate in Peter McDougal's play, *Shoot for the Sun*. The character, Geordie, was an axe-wielding thug who supplied addicts on the estate with drugs and then terrorised them into paying their debts. The play was a powerful exposé of the horrifying effects of drug dependence in a working-class community and included a scene in which an eleven-year-old boy tasted heroin to check it was pure.

When asked about the role several years later Jimmy said he didn't think too much about it at first – 'I was drinking a lot at the time' – but as he became more involved, the subject matter left him 'profoundly depressed'. It was, he said, 'the whole idea of how common drugs were to everybody. It was an eye opener how easily available they are. I just hadn't considered that kids under ten could be buying smack. I had ambled along as this guy who had fallen into television, made a load of money, was having a ball and it was a short, sharp shock. It was a bringing back to reality, an awful kind of reality. It brought me right back down to earth. The thought that kids were polluted like that before they had even got out of primary school – didn't enjoy it, it just made me miserable.'

He may have been profoundly shocked at what he experienced but, according to Carol Johnson, it was not enough to put him off recreational cocaine. Despite Jimmy's assertions to the contrary (he declared in the run-up to *Shoot for the Sun* appearing on BBC in 1987, 'The film says all I want to say about drug-taking. If people aren't put off by what they see in it, they're not going to be put off at all. I don't take drugs. I never have done. The strongest drug I've ever taken is Aspirin and vodka') Carol says she witnessed him taking coke.

'We were all into it then,' she said. 'There's no big deal. I don't do it now but we all did it. There's no point in pretending. I did it throughout the eighties because it was the done thing and Jimmy was no exception. The temptations were there, especially when he was wanting to be with the rock and rollers. That went hand in hand with it. You went to a party at Danemede and it was readily available and Jimmy was no exception. He dabbled, he liked it and one night almost died with it and I was there and stopped him taking any more.

'It was after the preview of *Morons From Outer Space* and we all went back to Sue Mensch's house. An actor there had lines of coke the length of a coffee table. Jimmy was keeping up, and it went on and on and on. I was watching and he went a funny colour, he went cross-eyed, his throat started to close because it was so numb, he was having difficulty swallowing. I said, "That's enough, you are getting to dangerous levels now", took him to the kitchen which was downstairs and made him drink four pints of water and said, "No more, Jimmy, I'm taking you home", and I called a cab and we went back to his house and he was very ill. I stayed the night at their place. Miriam was in bed, didn't even hear us come in. He was sweating and in a terrible state. He said, "Carol, thank God you stopped this. God knows what would have happened if you hadn't been there."

Jimmy knew things were getting out of hand. He also knew what lay at the heart of it. The drink. He reflected on his album's failure, on his inability to attract any roles other than thug or screwball, on the strains that alcohol was putting on the fabric of his life. He was approaching thirty-three and he had been drinking since his mid-teens. It was woven into life in Newcastle before he was famous. Whether he was out with his mates, going to football matches or playing in the band, drink was always the prop, the staple diet. He had become famous for playing someone for whom drink played a similar part. Once his career began to take off in various directions in the mid-eighties drink again buoyed him up. Whether it was a long session thrashing out a song or letting off steam after a hard day filming or learning lines or negotiating, drink was always there for him. Jimmy realised he had a problem when it began to interfere with his work, when he began to suspect it of undermining the control of his professional life he so badly needed. In Newcastle there was no danger of that. In London, in the circles he found himself operating in, he recognised it as a hindrance.

Jimmy has never admitted publicly that he was an alcoholic but he alluded to the seriousness of his drink problem in a 1995 interview with the *News of the World* magazine. He said, 'I'm not an alcoholic if it means needing alcohol to get me through the day. I loved the taste of alcohol but it made me act like a fool. But the idea of sharing it, standing up at a meeting of Alcoholics Anonymous and saying, "My name is Jimmy. I am an alcoholic", is not for me. It's fine if it helps, horses for courses, whatever gets you though the night.'

Yet one senior newspaper executive, herself an alcoholic, said she and Nail meet periodically for lunch, occasions at which it is recognised they both suffer from the same condition.

Jimmy's account of his drinking owes more to the macho than the afflicted. 'It did get out of hand, the booze. I realised what a monumental arsehole I was when I was drinking. I think it was about trying to take some control and responsibility for what I was. I just thought, you cannot go into meetings stinking of drink or drunk, or I certainly didn't want to. There was too much resting on the meetings, multi-million pound meetings. They were difficult enough to swing sober and I didn't want to lose them because of the sauce. There are loads of reasons… There was a terrible thing that happened. I used to think if I can get home, get across the threshold, I had made it. So I would lie down on the floor and Miriam would always throw a blanket or a coat on me. Then one day I woke up and said, "Where's the blanket?" and she said, "If you can manage to get across London you can stagger up those stairs. You are not getting any more blankets." So I cut out the drink.'

Control, responsibility on the professional side and perhaps echoes of the distant, ineffective chiding by Laura at his father when he had drunk too much echoed in Miriam's criticisms and finally did it for Jimmy. The formidable willpower he had used to get himself where he was he now turned in on himself. It was time to shape up. He woke up one morning, shortly after his thirty-third birthday, and decided to cut it out of his life.

He reasoned that it was not only the drinking that was undermining his professional effectiveness, it was his general appearance as well. He looked much the same as he did when he first stepped into the audition for Oz. He was scruffy and although he was 6ft 4ins, his sixteen-and-a-half stones did not sit easily on him. Too much indulgence and not enough exercise meant that he was badly out of shape. There was also the not insignificant matter of his nose. A young life of frequent fist fights had left the prominent feature an undulating mess with a knot of cartilage restricting his breathing. Something needed to be done about that too.

His decision was a sudden one but the seeds of unease about his public persona had been germinating for some time.

Carol Johnson remembers in the early days of *Auf Wiedersehen Pet* Jimmy being horrified when he watched a scene in which Oz runs across the German building site wearing only a pair of battered, greying Y-fronts. 'He thought Oz was a beer swilling fat slob and it wasn't him. The scene with him running through the building site with those dirty underpants on mortified him. He is running to go to the toilet. He has his hands over his bollocks and the knickers are flapping in the breeze. It was not a pretty sight and he was horrified. He had a completely different image of himself and he couldn't believe it until he saw it with his own eyes. He thought, Oh my God, is that me?'

By any standards, the transformation was extraordinary. By cutting out the drink, exercising and keeping a rigid control over what he ate, Jimmy lost four stones – twenty-five per cent of his body weight – in just a few months. It didn't end there. He emerged from this purgatory with a fine, new aquiline nose to replace the old bumpy one and a carefully tended hairstyle. He refused to admit that he had had a cosmetic 'nose job', claiming to Carol Johnson that its dramatic re-shaping was the result of an essential operation on blocked sinuses. He also went clothes shopping. His old leather jackets, T-shirts and jeans were out, to be replaced by elegant Paul Smith suits, Comme Des Garçons shirts and expensive shoes.

One old television chum, who had worked closely with him on *Auf Wiedersehen Pet*, remembers getting the shock of his life as he strolled down Hampstead High Street in London one afternoon late in 1987.

'I remember this gaunt, rather distinguished-looking character wearing sunglasses in the middle of winter coming up the street looking like the cover of a pop LP. I was almost level with him before I realised it was Jimmy. He walked off the set of *Auf Wiedersehen Pet* a Geordie thug and came back as this kind of gothic figure.'

Jimmy was not the least bit embarrassed about his change of appearance. Quite the opposite. He proudly informed his dumbfounded friend that he had shed the equivalent of forty-two pats of butter during his physical rehabilitation.

'Drink is a very difficult thing to give up if it is not killing you and he was used to drinking a lot both psychologically and physically,' said the friend by way of tribute to Jimmy's strength of purpose. 'The control thing is interesting. He decided the drink was interfering with his life and resulting in behaviour which was getting in the way of his control.'

This theme is expanded upon by his occasional lunch partner from Fleet Street. Her theory is that men and women alcoholics behave very differently when in denial.

'Recovered men have this mania for absolute control over all areas of their lives. Women are more relaxed about things.'

The strength of mind to forsake alcohol, a drug which had sustained him for half his life, can only be wondered at. Coupled with the decision radically to alter his diet and appearance, the changes he wrought required astonishing strength of purpose. It was the ultimate performance. One manifestation of Jimmy's determination to succeed was his desire to give people what they wanted when he knew it would benefit his career. Thus he played the obnoxious Geordie with spades during the early days of *Auf Wiedersehen* because that is what he thought the powers that be wanted from him. This time he sensed a change was what was needed to give his career the extra impetus he had hitherto felt unable to provide. He was performing now as he had always done, as a means to succeed.

This time, however, he was playing with fire. Not even someone with the iron resolve of Jimmy Nail can effect such a radical change so quickly without extreme dangers. He failed to heed the warning signs, arrogantly convinced he was doing what had to be done. His account of this time gives a glimpse of the turmoil at chez Nail.

'I ended up talking to a shrink because I got so profoundly disturbed by what I felt was the nation's perception of me that I decided to change it. And I changed it so radically that I think I went a bit mad. I completely changed my physical form. It was such a radical re-jig, I don't think I realised what I was embarking on at the time and I think I went a bit mad with it, because I turned into someone else and it is a dangerous thing. I set out trying to be a different person but I think I ended up another person. That was where it went wrong.' His account of this period of his life is uncharacteristically hesitant and vague. He appears to be struggling to understand it himself.

He adds, 'The psychiatrist said I wasn't mad, I was just going a bit crazy after the second series of *Auf Wiedersehen Pet*. I was getting muddled as to who I was and who he [Oz] was. It was becoming a blur and I was finding it difficult to delineate.'

For someone of Jimmy's background, where the male creed is to be tough and self-reliant, this was an enormous admission of his failure to cope. He emerged from the therapy with a clearer picture of what had to be done. He was told he found it difficult to separate himself and Oz. This was not just because the public were confusing the two – you could hardly blame them when Jimmy himself had been playing the role of Oz role since his teens – it was also enormously confusing for him. The part of his personality which had got him into such trouble as a young man also won him fame and fortune. Now, finally, under encouragement from the analyst, he was persuaded it was the time to have the courage to emerge from behind Oz's coat tails and into the spotlight.

Of course, this was far more difficult for Jimmy than it would have been for most people because Jimmy was famous, he would be performing this transformation in front of an audience of millions.

Then there was Miriam. She may have become fed up with Jimmy's drinking, his late-night, unsteady homecomings, his inability to make it up the stairs. She may even have been keen on him losing a bit of weight and smartening up his appearance. But even though she was well aware of her partner's obsessive personality and willpower, she can never have expected the transformation which took place before her eyes. To make matters worse she had given birth to their second son, Freddie, in the middle of it all.

The loud, boozy, forceful character she fell in love with seven years earlier, with whom she had shared her life ever since, the father of her children was literally shrivelling away. The drinking was such a part of Jimmy's life, it influenced the way he behaved so fundamentally, that once he gave it up his whole personality was dramatically altered. It was like living with a different man and Miriam found it very difficult to adjust. Not only did Jimmy look completely different, he began to behave in a way that was nothing like what she was used to. It was as if the man she had chosen had upped and left and a new, strange one taken his place. For her it was the worst time possible for this to happen. The new baby and a demanding two year old were enough of a strain without Jimmy going through his crisis and relying so heavily on her support.

'That can be a very dangerous thing on a lot of levels,' Jimmy admitted. 'Because if you are in a relationship and you change the person you are, the person you change into isn't the person the person you are living with fell for. So that creates its own problems, but you do not realise that until you get to the other end of it.'

He may not have realised the consequences of his personal quest as he was so wrapped up in himself. But Miriam surely did and was forced to work hard to keep everything together. It had all kinds of practical ramifications as well. Jimmy changed overnight from someone who was careless about what kind of food he consumed to an extremely fastidious eater who virtually cut out meat, and based his diet on fish, vegetables and fruit. Typically with Jimmy, he went from the ridiculous to the sublime, from a man who would consume curries or kebabs with relish after a double figures session in the pub to someone who was not embarrassed to question a restaurant waiter closely about which fish on the menu was freshest before making his choice. As always, there were no half measures. Moderation isn't a creed he recognises.

As he gained control over his body, what he fuelled it with and how it looked, he began to direct his energies at controlling his career more closely. His ego continued to demand great things of him. Yet he was desperate for the public's perception of him to change and he also hated the effect on his private life of being so famous. He decided he wanted to explore what lay the other side of the camera. He wanted to get involved more in the business of producing television rather than waiting by the telephone for offers of someone's else's work to come in.

'I decided to get into the production side. I enjoyed business involvement so I thought I would get involved behind the camera, away from the public eye. I could get lost easier. I could duck.'

As this fermented in his mind the thought struck him that it would be even better to take things one stage further. If he could instigate programmes and then go on to star in them, it would represent the ultimate achievement for a man who desired to shape his own career so meticulously.

One is reminded of the observation of his occasional lunch companion from Fleet Street about recovering male alcoholics and their mania for control. That allied to Jimmy's willpower and determination would prove an irresistible combination.

He had had the idea for a detective series for some time, first mentioning it to colleagues at the end of filming the second series of *Auf Wiedersehen Pet* in early 1986. Now he resolved to do something about it.

'I kicked it around and made notes on ideas. I got in touch with La Frenais and I said "I've got this idea." So we met up in London and had dinner and he said I've always wanted to do something up there but he and Dick had never gotten round to it. So Ian and I had this kind of dynamic power dinner and we agreed to work on a script.

'I bumped into Colin Rogers who was a producer at the Beeb at the time and I asked him what he was doing. He said "I'm looking for some drama projects, do you have any?" "Of course, of course. What kind do you want? I've got them coming out of my ears," I lied. He said, "Well, what have you got?" I said, "I've got this idea for a detective" and he said, "That sounds good. Can I read a script?" I got out of the office and thought, What have I got myself into here? The last things I wrote were letters home from prison and they were pretty cack. Colin said just go away and the BBC will risk a script fee. I took Ian's pilot home, counted the pages and basically copied what I thought was the structure. I handed it in and Colin liked it and said you'll have to do some more. And I remember thinking, Oh God, what if I've put every good idea I've ever had into this script?. That's how I got started writing. The *Spender* programme was also an opportunity to completely change the public perception of what I was, which was another reason I wanted to do it. I wanted to completely change.'

Freddie Spender had been fermenting in Jimmy's mind for so long that a very clear picture of the character was lodged there. He has admitted that *Spender* allowed him to explore the moody loner he felt was within him and the hero's sidekick Stick embodied the other facet, the entrepreneurial, mischievous Geordie. Val McLane insists she can see little of her brother in the character apart from his moodiness. Surely it is more the dramatic situation which Spender finds himself in which is an illuminating parallel with Jimmy's life. Spender is a man, like Jimmy, who has escaped Newcastle, his home town, and found refuge in London. Now he comes back and finds himself operating in his old stamping ground. But he is nothing like the people around him. Ian La Frenais – with tongue firmly in cheek – says the success of *Spender* was entirely due to wardrobe. 'He is the only copper to wear Dolce & Gabbana suits and Comme Des Garçons shirts,' is his quip. But there is a serious point here. Spender was wearing the kind of clothes the re-vamped Jimmy was wearing.

Val McLane may not think he was much like her brother but his creator has admitted that he was a projection of a major part of his personality. In other words, the exiled Jimmy was coming home. The brand new, teetotal, slimmed down, serious-minded Jimmy was re-visiting his old haunts. But this time he was prepared to reveal this side of himself in Newcastle, the side he previously kept hidden when he lived there. It was the first big test of Jimmy's transformation. Spender was far more than a fictional detective.

17
SPENDER

It was virtually unheard of for the star and the writer to be one and the same person. But any doubts Colin Rogers may have harboured about this almost unprecedented situation were cast aside by Jimmy. Just as he had grasped the nettle when Rogers asked him if he could write a script around his idea, Jimmy confidently declared himself the only candidate for the central role of Freddie Spender. After all, he had written the series with only one actor in mind – himself. And where else could the BBC find a dour, brooding Geordie who had the screen presence to match the demands of this part?

Rogers commissioned the idea, and it was agreed that Jimmy should be the star. Suddenly he found himself at the decision-making heart of a £2.5 million production. As deviser, writer and star, he was its backbone and he relished the involvement. He knew he was breaking new ground, and that knowledge fired him with a determination that this show he had identified with so closely, would succeed.

Rogers had put a lot of faith in Jimmy. He recognised his talent and star quality and was prepared to back his judgement. What's more he knew Jimmy was bankable material. What he didn't know was how difficult he would prove to work with. There were displays of this in the second *Auf Wiedersehen Pet* series, when the rapidly-learning actor was prepared to throw tantrums over money and argue the toss ad infinitum with established people like Ian La Frenais. But these things had been kept largely in-house. Jimmy had not yet won a reputation as a difficult person throughout the industry. That changed soon enough. Unlike with *Pet*, Jimmy had real power this time, and he made sure he exercised it fully. The first step was hiring a producer and even that quite simple task proved difficult enough.

Several were approached but either they didn't like the terms and conditions laid down by Jimmy or Jimmy didn't like them. Jimmy then suggested the BBC hire his *Pet* producer Martin McKeand. He had proved adept at dealing with Jimmy throughout *Pet*, knew La Frenais and was well-respected as a resourceful and pragmatic producer. Jimmy bumped into him at a London Weekend Television end-of-the-decade awards bash in December 1989 and sounded out his old sparring partner. The response was positive and a week later McKeand received a call from the BBC formally inviting him to produce *Spender*. He agreed. The first hurdle had been negotiated.

Although Jimmy's writing got off to an encouraging start, he was not yet in a position to produce scripts without help. That he could produce them at all with no writing experience was remarkable enough. Consequently Jimmy leaned heavily on La Frenais. The two men got on well, although there was always a tension between them. La Frenais had recognised Jimmy's qualities the moment he clapped eyes on him at the Newcastle audition for *Auf Wiedersehen Pet* back in 1982. He was impressed by the novice's lack of deference to his reputation in the early days, something which continued throughout the two *Pet* series.

In 1989 La Frenais invited Jimmy to stay with him in Los Angeles so that they could work together on the *Spender* scripts. Miriam and the two boys went along too for a few weeks before leaving Jimmy alone to concentrate on the job in hand. He ended up spending nine months there producing the scripts under the watchful eye of La Frenais. Always a quick learner, Jimmy eagerly absorbed the expert tuition he was receiving. He was a diligent pupil, using his ability to pick things up quickly to maximum effect. The notion that not only had he conceived this show, he could now determine exactly the course of the drama was irresistible to him and he was not about to let the opportunity slip. Apart from the pilot script La Frenais wrote one other only. Jimmy did the rest, albeit with a great deal of help and guidance. The decision to go to LA was beneficial to all concerned. It gave Jimmy the peace he needed to devote time to his writing and it allowed the production team to get on with the job of preparing for the shoot without the input of the show's creator which would have undoubtedly slowed the process down.

For a man who wears the north east of England on his sleeve, Jimmy took to Hollywood life. He is nothing if not ambitious and this, for him, was the big time. He was still at the stage where he had to pinch himself that he was a part of this rarefied society. He was star struck when he bumped into Bruce Willis at a supermarket, noticing he looked 'as miserable as me'.

When he returned home early in 1990 ready for shooting he had devised the series, written most of it and was about to star in it. He was the main man and he knew it. He lost no time in letting everyone else know it as well. The problems began immediately. So rare was it for the star of a series to be the writer as well that experienced heads on the production team were shaking knowingly.

One who worked with him on *Auf Wiedersehen Pet*, said, 'Jimmy was certainly a changed man by then. He had very definite ideas on what he wanted done, the way he wanted it done, who he wanted to work with and who he didn't want to work with. It was very much Jimmy's show. He involved himself in all major aspects of it. Sometimes the star actor has an executive producer role, usually with disastrous results, but I honestly don't think there has ever been a case where somebody has been the writer and the star. That was why it was very difficult to find directors who would take the gig on.'

Television series are regarded as near the bottom of the pile by any self-respecting director looking for work. The absolute worst are the soaps, followed by series then serials, one-off TV dramas and then films. It is difficult enough to get top-rate directors for TV series without having to tell them that the writer and star are one and the same person. Still more difficult when that person is Jimmy Nail, who, by now, was acquiring a reputation on the grapevine as not the easiest person to work with. 'A lot of directors wouldn't do series and if they did they didn't want to work in a situation like ours,' said a source. 'But you have to have good directors. We never finished up with a director we didn't want, but it was a long and hard search.'

Eventually they got lucky and persuaded Mary McMurray to come aboard. McMurray is a talented director, articulate and intelligent. What proved to be a bonus was the skill she showed in handling Jimmy, who learned to prize her skills.

'She controlled Jimmy as well as any director,' said an insider. 'Bamford [Roger Bamford] was probably Jimmy's favourite director and is very good, but Mary was a very close second.'

One essential quality when dealing with the great man was pragmatism. Choose your moments to stand your ground and know when to defer to the higher authority. Once during the shooting of the first series, it was deemed necessary that Jimmy and Mary fly out to Los Angeles to consult Ian La Frenais on the scripts. It was while arranging this trip that Jimmy pulled off a coup that went down in BBC folklore and is still talked about with awe by corporation executives.

'He was a brilliant negotiator,' said a source. 'He is pretty well the only actor who has ever got a club class trans-Atlantic seat out of the BBC. The BBC was at its most bureaucratic at the time and that took ages to clear. But Jimmy made the point that he was the only 6ft 4ins writer on their list.'

Unfortunately for Mary Jimmy's skills as a negotiator did not extend as far as procuring her a similar class ticket. Possibly because she isn't 6ft 4ins. This did not deter Jimmy, who accepted his privileged seat without embarrassment and consigned Mary to a lonely, cramped flight in economy. Ever the pragmatist, she did not complain.

Despite the calming influence of McMurray and McKeand, Jimmy proved a handful. If he had been difficult in the past, he was excelling himself now. The root of the trouble was how intensely important the *Spender* series was to him. It represented the confluence of a number of powerful driving forces within him. Firstly – and naturally enough – he was desperate for it to be high quality television. But because the show, and especially the character of Spender, had germinated in his mind for so long, he had intractable views on how things should look and how scenes should be played down to the tiniest detail. To make things worse, what was generally not known was how much *Spender* represented his transformation as a man and how important it was that this return of the new Jimmy to Newcastle – albeit in the fictional drama – be exactly to his liking.

This mania for control and insistence that everything be done his way did not endear himself to the crew or the BBC in general. One senior production member said, 'A major problem on *Spender* was that there was a BBC way of doing things and a lot of people just regarded him as a stroppy actor. Whereas now camper vans and first class travel and all that sort of thing are given to lots of people, he was the first to stand out for it and a lot of people didn't know how to cope with it. I think he had a great desire and need to be taken seriously and that was one of his ways of making sure people took him seriously. If you are making a film you get treated very well indeed but the BBC tends not to treat actors very well. I remember asking a friend of mine, an agent, what he advised all these kids who are making films for nothing. He said if the scripts are good and my client wants to do it I just make sure they get treated well. It doesn't matter if you don't pay them very much as long as you send a car for them in the morning. You can't expect a person to go to the studios by tube then do a day's acting. It's not like sitting behind a computer.'

The point here is that although it may seem to the average person to be the behaviour of a budding prima donna, within the closed world of film and television these fripperies have real meaning. Jimmy was the star now and he was damned well going to have them.

For those who had been present on *Auf Wiedersehen Pet* there was another big difference. The convivial atmosphere of that production had entirely disappeared. Not only was Jimmy proving difficult to work with, he was proving nigh on impossible to socialise with. Those who remember his entertaining antics in the bars at Elstree and Nottingham found it difficult the accept the aloof, superior animal he had become. The phrase 'its all gone to his head' was difficult to resist.

One veteran of both productions said, 'The socialising of *Auf Wiedersehen Pet* had completely disappeared. He socialised very little. Occasionally he'd come and meet people, but he'd stopped drinking so there was no hanging around in bars. He was working very hard, acting during the day and writing at night. It didn't leave a lot of time for socialising but I also thought he didn't particularly welcome the opportunity. If there were plans being made for the evening he would usually say he had to have an early night or he had to work.'

But there were some tantrums it was difficult for even his biggest apologist to excuse. They seemed to be nothing more than his old desire to command centre stage at all times.

'One used to get pissed off when he complained that his camper wagon hadn't been cleaned out properly or there was a dead rose in his vase,' added the same source who defended his demands for status symbols. 'The other thing I got rather impatient with was his hair. His hair could cause very considerable hold-ups. He had very definite ideas of how Spender's hair should be and there were long discussions about it and there was a high turnover in the hairdressing department. The hair had to be just as he wanted it and as it is pretty windy up there we could spend quite a long time making sure the hair was right. It was slightly strange. I don't know why he was so sensitive about this area. He would just say, "It's *Spender*."'

Those who remember the doleful detective in the designer clothes will also recall that his hair looked like it received no attention whatsoever, apart from an occasional buffeting by the north-easter fresh off the Tyne. It was long, lank and hung down in lifeless rivulets, often half obscuring his face, except, of course for the nose, which rose like granite out of the streams of meandering locks. So it may come as something of a shock to learn that this 'look' was not the product of an exposed Newcastle climate but that of hours of debate and skilled preparation. Also that it cost several hairdressers their jobs and sorely tried the patience of senior production crew members who were trying to get on with their task of shooting a television series.

The most extraordinary aspect of this is Jimmy's apparent lack of embarrassment at demanding hours of effort be spent getting his hair right. How this behaviour might have been received at Joe Watson's glass factory or among his old football mates at the Portland Arms can only be wondered at. It shows how much he had abandoned his old self and how obsessed he was with his 'artistic vision' of *Spender*. It also shows what an enormous ego was at work.

It occasionally extended to the comic. Ian La Frenais remembers passing an innocuous remark about the way Jimmy ran in one scene and the response which followed.

'He's quite sensitive. Very sensitive, in fact. I once told him when we watched the first episode of *Spender* that he had a funny way of running, so he got terribly upset. But I noticed that there was never a classic foot chase after that in *Spender*.'

Another foible of Jimmy's which caused huge ructions within the BBC and was harder to explain artistically was his phobia about stills photographs. One of the requirements of a TV series is that stills be taken of the major stars for publicity purposes. Normally this is a routine operation, experienced photographers do the job with a minimum of fuss and the results distributed to the press as part of a publicity package which previews the launch. Jimmy had insisted on a clause in his contract with the BBC which gave him stills approval. He had the right to vet the photographs before they went out and block any he didn't approve of. He took full advantage of this hard-won privilege, offending many a professional snapper. On one occasion a well-respected photographer arrived for the shoot and departed soon after without a frame exposed, such were the demands imposed on him by Jimmy.

A sympathetic explanation for what many would call paranoia comes from one crew member and old friend, 'I think he thinks he looks completely different in stills from on film and there is some truth in it. He's an odd-looking fellow, there's no doubt about it. When his face is still it looks like there's not a lot going on but when he's doing anything – even thinking – there's an animation. It is a difficult face to photograph and he did insist contractually on stills approval which, in those days was less usual than it is now. He certainly exercised it.'

This obsession with vetting photographs of himself is something which has stayed with Jimmy, if anything becoming more intense the more successful he has become. All part of his desire to control as closely as possible the image of him which is presented before the general public. He also insists on approving all photographs to accompany newspaper interviews. Andrew Collins, former editor of *Q* magazine, sent Jimmy seven contact sheets of possible snaps – he sent back one; a shot of himself looking mean, moody and powerful. 'We were used to copy approval with all these swanky stars, but he was the fussiest ever,' said Collins.

Spender was not all pandering to the ego of the star, however.

Jimmy's specific ideas about how he should look, where he should live and what locations should be used were more often than not the correct decisions. Also at this stage of proceedings – the first series – he was still enormously enthused by the project and was as often helpful as he was difficult. One senior crew member recalls being taken on a guided tour of Jimmy's early life via Newcastle locations during a break in filming. But at no time did he feel he was being invited to enquire too closely about the man's past.

'One felt one was not supposed to ask about his early life, I never talked to him about it, I didn't feel one was likely to be told very much if one asked. He showed me the house where he says he was brought up, it looked a fairly normal, tidy, working-class estate, certainly not poverty row. We filmed at Parsons. He was quite keen on going back to various places. He was quite specific – "I had a place in mind when I wrote this" – and nine times out ten you would go there and it would be the ideal location.'

Although there were various problems with the star, they were not of the insurmountable kind, more irritations. By and large Jimmy's demands were compensated for by the enormous enthusiasm, energy and charisma he brought to the project. What's more, by the time it was in the can, it was clear that *Spender* was high quality television: original, fresh and stylish. With its doom-laden atmosphere and dour hero who arrived in Newcastle from London on a mission, it bore more than a passing resemblance to *Get Carter*, the film which had inspired Jimmy twenty years earlier.

One crew member said, 'A lot of people said he was completely impossible – not necessarily the case. He had created Spender so he knew more about him than anyone else.' When the finished product emerged it was clear that Jimmy's vision, however demanding, was vindicated.

18
A FAMILY AFFAIR

James Bradford senior – ex-footballer, ex-boxer, ex-seaman, ex-engineering worker – spent his latter years a lonely, confused man plagued by ill-health.

His life was turned upside down one day when Laura, his wife of forty years, announced she was leaving him. With little more ado, she packed her bags, moved in with their daughter half a mile away and consigned their marriage to history. Separation and divorce didn't happen to people like Jimmy and Laura Bradford. They belonged to a generation which actually believed in the 'for better or worse' part of their wedding vows. They were also seventy years old and had spent more than half a lifetime together. Yet Laura was determined that it should happen. She simply decided she had had enough of her turbulent husband and needed an indefinite rest from him.

Life had never been easy with Jimmy senior. He may have been engaging, friendly and sociable but he was also truculent and volatile, especially when he had been drinking. The Bradford family unit never really recovered from Shelagh's death and almost two decades later the reverberations were still being felt. Also Laura's health was failing. She needed peace and quiet and that wasn't to be found around her husband. What role her children played in her decision is not clear. But just by offering her mother a place to live – and therefore an opportunity to leave – Val, at least to her father, must have appeared to be supporting her mother's decision.

Old Jimmy was not one to weep, tear his hair out, or come knocking at Val's door pleading for his wife back, but her decision was a devastating blow to him nevertheless.

Carol Johnson always had a soft spot for Jimmy's father. She found him amusing and entertaining and she liked his robust attitude to life. She remembers Laura coming round to her home for tea shortly after the separation.

'It was a big step, she was very worried about it but she just decided she had to get away, her health couldn't take it, so she decided she would up and leave and go and live with Val,' she said. 'He was a little lost man without her. He came round to my house and was convinced I was putting Laura up. "You've got my wife in there. I want my bloody wife back." I said, "Come in and see." When he spotted the bar and the stocks behind it and I offered him a bottle of brown ale, his eyes lit up and he stayed. Then he became a regular visitor, much to Jimmy's annoyance. He said, "Don't encourage me Dad. Turn the man away." But he was a canny old feller and I felt sorry for him when he had to knock on doors asking if his wife was there. He was a man lost, he was just floating around looking for anybody.'

He knew that Laura liked to play bingo and he got into the habit of waiting for her to come out of Val's house. When he saw her leave with her friends he would shout across at her calling her a slut and telling her to get herself home. Laura was mortified.

Jimmy senior was alone for the first time in his life. Alone in the house that had been home to his family for many years. He felt his wife and children had conspired against him and he couldn't understand why. He could not work out what he had done wrong. All he knew was that suddenly they had all seemed to abandon him. Inevitably the focus of the family moved from Penfold Close to Val's home on Thropton Avenue. When Jimmy came to visit, it was much easier to go there, especially when he came with Miriam and the boys. A visit to his father invariably meant an argument, as the old man would get straight to the point and chastise his son over what had happened.

Two years later his 'story' appeared across two pages of the *Sun*, some say for a tidy amount of money, others, less kindly, for a night's supply of beer. In it he complained that his famous son hardly ever came to visit him and that he'd never watched an episode of *Auf*

Wiedersehen Pet. 'I'd rather be in the pub,' he explained. 'It's on Friday nights and that's when I like going out. I always make sure there isn't a telly in the pub where I'm going because I'm always very upset if anyone says anything bad about Jimmy. I'd want to punch them in the mouth. I hear he's around from people who spot him in bars and clubs, but he often can't be bothered to see me. When I do hear from him I ask why and he says he didn't have the time to see me. I find that very upsetting. He should find the time to say "Hello" to his old Dad.' He complained he had only seen his one-year-old grandson Tommy once, a few weeks after the birth.

He claims his wife left him because he refused to give up smoking. 'I came downstairs one morning and she said, "I'm leaving you." I thought she was joking and asked her why and she said she couldn't stand my smoking. Jimmy was standing in the room at the time and I said to her that there was no way that I was going to give it up. So she left.'

On reflection this scenario is not as unlikely as it first appears. Jimmy has talked about how his abiding memory of his father is him coughing violently every morning. How he sat on the edge of the bed 'coughing, coughing, coughing. Coughing his guts up.' It is the reason Jimmy has always been such a passionate anti-smoker. By the time he reached seventy, old Jimmy's health was seriously affected by his lifetime of smoking. He suffered emphysema – his lungs were in a terrible state – but he refused to give up cigarettes. Eventually Laura seems to have decided that he was beyond help and left him to his own devices. Jimmy was furious with his father about the article, but his anger was water off a duck's back to the old man.

Jimmy did visit his father occasionally and took Carol along a couple of times. He knew how much she liked him. Once they called without warning and found the house in a dreadful condition, the old man snoozing by the fireside and the plastic coal bucket on the hearth smouldering, thanks to the lighted cigarette he had dropped in it. Jimmy tried to tell his father to be more careful but, according to Carol, all he got in reply was, 'Don't nag, man, it's only a bloody coal bucket.'

Soon after he did set the house on fire. It was only a small one, but the fire brigade had to be called. Val and Jimmy decided that something needed to be done. The old man was drinking heavily, his health was failing. They decided he could no longer look after himself and neither was in a position to look after him. There was no alternative for it. He would have to go into a nursing home. He didn't like it, but eventually gave in to the entreaties of his children. They found a place in a huge converted Victorian house in Jesmond, and Jimmy took care of the cost. His father didn't thank him for it. He hated the place and blamed his son for putting him in it.

However, the old man was no longer a tough, independent figure coping alone, drinking and smoking what he liked. He spent his time in an easy chair, puffed up with cushions and attended to by nurses who allowed him neither tobacco or alcohol. It must have been an incongruous sight to Jimmy. As his father became more feeble and dependent, his anger at being put in the home subsided, he resigned himself to it and he and Jimmy became closer.

The knowledge that he did not have long to live concentrated both men's minds. Although there was no melodramatic reconciliation, they edged closer than they had been throughout Jimmy's adult life – two stubborn, volatile men struggling to find a way to repair the years of damage they had inflicted on their relationship. There was too much ground to make up for a complete reconciliation; too many old wounds on both sides. But things were better between them.

Jimmy Bradford senior went downhill quickly. He developed severe breathing problems and had to be admitted to the city's Freeman Hospital. Pneumonia set in and it was obvious to his family the end was close. Jimmy was shooting *Spender* on location in Newcastle at the time so was able to visit his father regularly. The imminence of death softened both men. They talked.

His father gave him some advice which Jimmy seized upon and invested with great moment. Although the old man simply urged his son to do his best in life, Jimmy saw it as profound. He was in a highly emotional state at the time and he had hardly been overburdened with advice from his father over the years. It was a rare gem to Jimmy and he wasted no time in assimilating it into his life. The irony was not lost on him that the only times in his adult life that he had a real sense of communion with his father were when things were going badly wrong. He recalled the tears streaming down those rugged cheeks when he was locked up. Now because the old man was dying they were talking again.

'In his last days we knew we had a lot to pack in. We knew we had no time for bull, only for truth. I told him I loved him. He told me he loved me.

'He taught me an important lesson as he lay dying. He said, "All you can do, son, is your best. Nothing more, nothing less." It's become a way of life for me, that whole idea that you can't do any more than your best. I believe you owe it to yourself to give no less. It meant a lot to me, what my father said. I try to live by that little tenet.'

James Bradford senior died at the Freeman Hospital on 8 June 1990, from pneumonia and respiratory failure. He was seventy-six. There were no histrionics from Jimmy. He grieved privately. On the day of the funeral he took the morning off from working on *Spender* to attend the service but was back on duty in the afternoon . A few days later Jimmy arranged for his father's ashes to be scattered on the Tyne. Six years of war had left him with a contempt for the Royal Navy but a love of the sea.

It would be wrong to assume from Jimmy's outward calm that his father's death did not affect him. His grief seeped out slowly, mingling with his sense of failure that he did not make an effort to improve things between them until it was too late. He dwelt on this through the remainder of the *Spender* shoot, feeling the need to make amends to his father in some way. He eventually decided he wanted to dedicate the series to the old man and asked producer Martin McKeand to see if he could arrange it with the BBC. When the answer came back from on high that it was a Corporation rule that programmes could only be dedicated to people who died in their making, Jimmy took it surprisingly well, shrugged his shoulders and accepted it. Perhaps he felt it would be in bad taste to kick up a fuss about such an issue.

The desire to recognise his father in his work never left him, however. Eventually, five years later he got his chance and eulogised the old man in the hit song 'Big River'. Yet the pen portrait which appears in the song lyrics is idealised and sentimental. It depicts his father as the tough product of a tough town; a 'working man' who 'earned his living with his hands', and who had 'mouths to feed and bills to pay'. The archetypal tough, uncompromising Geordie man and proud. No mention of the hard-drinking chain smoker who rarely saw eye to eye with his son and who spent the latter years of his life alone, shunned by his family.

The song gave Jimmy a successful single which remains a favourite with Nail fans. In the blurb accompanying his greatest hits album, *The Nail File* (1997) he says, 'I'm very proud of this song… I can't play it live without choking up. Soppy beggar, eh?'

<u>19</u>
LAYING OZ TO REST

With all the obsessive effort that went into the making of *Spender*, one thing appears to have been overlooked. How would the public react to the new Jimmy? They had taken him to their hearts as Oz. Oz was a national celebrity, but Oz was no more. Jimmy's dieting, exercising and change of image had been so complete he now looked like a different person. His weight had dropped from sixteen-and-a-half stones to just twelve-and-a-half, which for a man of 6ft 4ins was approaching beanpole condition. Profile writers talked about his 'pipe cleaner legs' and his arms of 'muscled linguini'.

When he first hit the screen as Spender in January 1991 his audience had to blink to make sure the blurb was correct, that this designer suited figure with the long curly hair and angular face was indeed Jimmy Nail. This was radical stuff. It was certainly no attempt at a spin-off from *Auf Wiedersehen*, no 'Oz joins the police'. This was a bold gamble, but it paid off handsomely. *Spender* was a huge popular success and won a good deal of critical acclaim. Within a month of launch it was attracting around ten million viewers, knocking spots off the ITV rival El C.I.D. Shaun Usher, the *Daily Mail*'s television critic described it as 'Chandleresque'.

'Marlowe's California, flavourful in speech, scene and attitude, is matched for once by *Spender*'s gutsy, sardonic, fierce north east,' he wrote, adding that the detective series gave the 'predictable genre such freshness, depth and style that rivals from both sides of the Atlantic look anaemic.'

In one of the round of interviews he gave after its launch Jimmy said, 'We try to make Newcastle a character and I don't think the programme would work properly anywhere else.'

The BBC was delighted. He may be difficult but he had delivered the goods. *Spender's* success vindicated everything Jimmy had done since the close of *Auf Wiedersehen Pet*. Finally, twenty-four years after being laughed at for suggesting it to a cynical careers adviser, Jimmy was the policeman he wanted to be. He had done it on his own terms. He had revealed to the public the person he felt himself to be. More than anything he succeeded in changing his public persona. He had laid Oz to rest.

Although the programme was totally dominated by Jimmy's presence – he was in just about every scene and everything is viewed through his eyes – *Spender* also gave a platform to new talent, much of it recruited from the north east. Denise Welch, who would later find fame as Natalie Horrocks in *Coronation Street*, got her first big break as Spender's estranged wife and Tony McAnaney, a local musician friend of Jimmy's, also shone on his acting debut as Spender's invalid friend. Jimmy felt everything had been worthwhile. His vision was up there in lights, he had done it his way, he had flown the flag for his home town and he had used local people, not merely bussed in a clutch of actors from London. It was the first major drama to be shot on location in Newcastle since *Get Carter*. Jimmy had never forgotten that. Now he had matched it.

Such was *Spender's* acclaim, plans were laid almost immediately to shoot a second series. The BBC was more than happy to oblige, and, flush with success, most of the crew were tempted to ignore the niggling fears they had about what they saw as Jimmy's growing megalomania, and signed up.

Jimmy was, once again, full of fervour. Fired up by the success of Series I, and never one to rest on his laurels, he began work determined to make the second series even better. Before him lay seven months of six-days-a-week work, but, far from daunted, he was energised by the challenge.

Spender's success had given Jimmy new power and influence.

Television executives were now aware of his ability to deliver quality popular television which struck a chord with the viewing public. What's more, his new look was impressive – there was even talk of a rough kind of sex appeal.

Jimmy knew the time was right to have another stab at his long-standing ambition to carve out a musical career. His chart hit of 1985 seemed ancient history and his ensuing failure to consolidate that breakthrough was still acutely painful to him. Now, however, he was in a position to show them, show the men in suits they were wrong about his musical abilities. The public loved him as an actor, they would love his singing too. Now when he began to put together a proposal to release an album, he found people were more receptive than previously and he was able to secure a deal with Warner Brothers. The plan was to launch on the back of the second *Spender* series to maximise its sales potential.

Meanwhile problems were beginning to emerge on *Spender*. Although Jimmy was ultimately responsible for the scripts, he was still relying heavily on the help and guidance of Ian La Frenais. This proceeded on an unofficial, ad hoc basis with La Frenais, in effect, moonlighting for Jimmy. The arrangement became increasingly difficult as La Frenais came under pressure from his other commitments to end the arrangement.

'I always felt a little bit uneasy that I was stealing Ian away night time and weekends from his and Dick's day job,' said Jimmy.

La Frenais added, 'You feel guilty twice. You feel guilty for short-changing your wife and then guilty for short-changing the mistress. Mistress Nail, who gets very beady.'

One member of the *Spender* crew remembers the whole business coming to a crunch. 'Ian read the scripts as Jimmy wrote them and Jimmy consulted him quite a lot until Ian ran into quite a lot of problems with his partners – he wasn't supposed to be doing this at all. I believe there was a considerable falling out between them all. He had to stop being available. So Jimmy was on his own. It didn't worry him too much though, by that time he had got the bit between his teeth.'

It may not have worried him but Jimmy inevitably missed his friend's help. La Frenais provided an experienced second eye. Jimmy trusted his judgement. It was another responsibility on the shoulders of a man who was already taking on more than was considered wise.

The loss of La Frenais was only one setback. The relationship between Jimmy and the crew was seriously deteriorating. They were beginning to tire of what they saw as his increasing obsession with control, his constant insistence on re-takes in an impossible quest for perfection. His increasingly bizarre behaviour was also getting under people's skins. They began to feel he was getting too big for his boots. This breakdown was partly due to a clash of cultures between Jimmy, whose only experience had been with independent crews and the BBC team he was now working with who were grooved in the well-established customs and practices of the Corporation. Jimmy hated the bureaucracy and the more he tried to cut through it, the more the crew – all experienced and talented technicians – dug their heels in. Often the day was only saved by the mediation of the pragmatic McKeand and McMurray, who were generally able to mollify Jimmy and retain the respect of the crew.

One incident which sent eyebrows rising and heads shaking was a tantrum by Jimmy during a scene being shot in a seaside hotel in the north east. A technician present remembers it well.

'The filming was taking place on the first floor of a hotel and Jimmy said he wanted some people cleared from the pavement on the other side of the road because they were looking at him. He said he couldn't have them in his eyeline. That made things very difficult.' The day was saved by the sagacity of Martin McKeand. 'Rather than have half an hour's argument with Jimmy, he went outside and asked them very nicely if they wouldn't mind moving a bit to the side,' said the technician.

Another time the long-suffering McKeand was called in to mediate when Jimmy refused to continue after an argument with the director during a scene being shot on Newcastle's Quayside. Luckily the producer had just returned from London where he showed the *Spender* footage to the BBC who were very impressed. This news had a dramatic effect on Jimmy's mood and suddenly everything was all right again, the row forgotten.

McKeand soon realised he had to do something fast if the show was to meet its deadline. It was already running well behind schedule and, with no sign of any inclination on the part of the crew to make the time up or any relaxation of the driven star's attitude, he knew things were unlikely to improve.

As one senior production figure explained, 'There was a point when we got seriously behind. We were doing eighteen-hour days and it didn't seem there was any way out. A normal eight- to nine-hour day had become eighteen to nineteen hours. It was horrific. This was before there was any independent production going on and you had to use BBC people. I'm not saying there is anything wrong with BBC crews. Under certain circumstances they are the finest in the world, but in this particular situation with this particular group of people, the chemistry was disastrous.'

McKeand decided to bring in David McDonald, who had worked throughout *Auf Wiedersehen Pet*, as floor manager. McDonald was not a BBC man and was more used to meeting tight deadlines. He was also more used to working with Jimmy. BBC bureaucracy meant McKeand had to move heaven and earth to get the go-ahead to hire him but he persevered, convinced it was the only solution. The effect was instantaneous. One actor remembers it well. 'The day he joined we were shooting in Jarrow. As most of the crew were still making their way to location carrying their coffee and buns and all the things crew carry with them, we had actually finished the first shot.

'They were met by this new assistant director whose first words to them were, "Right, on to the next location." Within a week they were saying that there wasn't any overtime anymore.'

One person who could not get away from overtime was Jimmy. He drove himself relentlessly throughout the shoot, obsessed with achieving perfection by controlling all aspects of the filming process. Also, since La Frenais was forced to stand aside, the scriptwriting had been entirely his responsibility. Often he would work twelve hour days on location then go home and burn the midnight oil putting the final touches to scripts. Other writers were commissioned to help, but often this was counterproductive as Jimmy could be hyper-critical of what was produced. When he read one such script he insisted on such a radical re-write that the author demanded his name be taken off the credits. Jimmy was his own worst enemy. His over-involvement was constipating the show, yet he felt it would suffer if he neglected any part of it.

The shoot eventually limped to completion. The lost time was made up partly by McDonald's efficiency and partly by a punishing schedule of long days. It had been difficult and fractious. In many ways it paralleled the making of *Auf Wiedersehen Pet*, where a relatively trouble-free first shoot was followed by a problematic second. The main players were exhausted and dispirited. The long association between Jimmy and Martin McKeand was at an end. They parted on friendly terms but have not worked together since.

Spender 2 was another popular success even if some critics felt there was a little too much designer grit, that Spender was not a credible character and the series was more a vehicle for Jimmy Nail than anything else. Despite their misgivings, it was adored by the general public with whom he seemed to strike a chord.

As was becoming the norm with Jimmy, there was no time to take a breather. As soon as one exhausting project was over he was obliged to hurl himself headlong into another at the same time as making arrangements for the one after. The most pressing demand was his album deal. *Spender 2* was to be launched in January 1992 and the plan was to release the album the following month. The idea was that it would take a few episodes of *Spender* to raise Jimmy's public profile once again and put people in the right frame of mind to go out and buy his music.

Once again things went more than according to plan. The album, appropriately called *Growing Up In Public*, was a success and the spin-off single, 'Ain't No Doubt', exceeded all expectations. Jimmy was sitting with his mother in Tim Spall's kitchen when they heard on the radio it had reached number one in the charts. Although 'Love Don't Live Here Anymore' had made number three in 1985 and had been his first hit, 'Ain't No Doubt' was the one that gave him most satisfaction. Not just because he had co-written it but also because he knew this was not going to be a one-hit wonder like the last time. He was in a position to make sure of that now. He had been the driving force behind his musical resurrection, using his hard-won experience in the entertainment world to secure himself a solid foundation. Of course, it all depended on the public buying his records, but now they had shown they liked him he knew he could sustain things.

He had come an extraordinarily long way since he auditioned for *Auf Wiedersehen Pet* ten years earlier, rising to every challenge he set himself with apparent ease. He became an actor, then he became a singer, then he became a scriptwriter. He operated in the top echelon of each discipline without any previous experience and possessed the energy to continue with all three simultaneously. One feature of his career has been his ability to impress talented and influential people. From that first, extraordinary audition he branded his mark on Clement and La Frenais' consciousness, going on to become a close friend of the latter. This was not based on fawning respect by Jimmy for the more established man. Quite the reverse. He treated him like an equal almost from the word go and La Frenais recognised some quality in Jimmy which he respected.

Jimmy had the ability to project himself on to the highest stage and not be found wanting, yet it is difficult to pinpoint what exactly he excels at. He is the Kenneth Branagh of popular culture. He once made the comparison himself then added the rider, 'but he doesn't sing'. He tends to identify most closely with people from working-class backgrounds who have made it and remains deeply suspicious of the middle classes. This helps to explain his legendary reputation for being difficult. One never hears someone like La Frenais say he is difficult except in an affectionate way, yet many members of Middle England who have worked with him regard him with deep suspicion.

'Television is a very middle-class environment. I still feel like the renegade who slipped through, like I'm representing the guy on the street, that I'm their man on the inside,' he once said.

As such, he never really joined the cosy club, remaining the outsider. 'The periphery is a good place to lob grenades from. I don't like all the sausage-on-a-cocktail-stick areas of the job.'

This suspicion partly explains his need to be top dog, to prove that he is better than these apparently complacent, spoon-fed people around him. Yet although he liked to emphasise he wasn't one of them, he still needed to impress them at their own game. Hence the designer suits, the acquired love of good food. (Nail the working-class warrior made a point of sampling all Newcastle's best restaurants one by one when filming *Spender* there.) A regular dining companion said, 'He likes good food and expensive restaurants. He is fastidious in his eating habits. I don't think he is vegetarian but he's not a steak and chips man, and I believe he's becoming more so. People have told me sometimes he eats a bowl of peas and that's it for the day.'

Once while having lunch in Soho with a television executive, he saw Mark Tully, the former India correspondent for the BBC, dining at a nearby table. 'He walked up to him and said, "You don't know me. My name is Jimmy Nail and I'm a huge fan of yours and I'd like to shake your hand." It never occurred to me that Jimmy would even know who Mark Tully was, and it must have puzzled Mark Tully because he certainly didn't know Jimmy Nail,' remembers his dining companion.

All the time it was important to Jimmy that he did not let the joins show, that he never admitted to weakness or fallibility. Therefore while everyone was complaining about the monumentally long hours worked on *Spender*, Jimmy remained aloof and got on with it even though, by working on scripts at nights, he was doing more than anyone.

He says now that the workload almost overwhelmed him. 'I'm harder on myself than anyone else. There were times I became literally delirious with fatigue and I'd ask myself why I was doing it. I think it's to do with coming from nothing and getting this far. I know I've been lucky and it would be wrong to piss that away. You have to get out every day and do it, no matter what.'

The rollercoaster ran on and on. Once again there was no time to bask in the warmth of the acclaim for 'Ain't No Doubt' and *Growing Up In Public*. The shoot for *Spender 3* was upon him.

Only this time it was different.

Jimmy, for his part, was determined that the problems he had encountered on series two should not be repeated in series three. He and his agent Duncan Heath formed a plan which, if they could pull it off, would break new ground in television production. They decided to propose to the BBC that it allow the show to be produced independently, with Jimmy as executive producer. This would mean they could hire their own crew and have greater control over the production process. The idea also appealed to Jimmy's desire for total control over what he lovingly regarded as his creation. The BBC wasn't exactly bowled over by the proposal, but then Jimmy knew it wouldn't be. He was prepared for that and brought all his formidable and intimidating negotiating skills into play. He only needed those skills in part. He was such a bankable asset by now and had proved himself so capable of conceiving and delivering high-grade popular television that he held a very strong bargaining hand. The BBC was not about to risk losing this prize asset, so eventually he got his way. The show was farmed out to the independent production company, Initial.

'More than anything it was the need to find out if I could carry it alone, rather than just be part of it,' Jimmy said.

It was a phenomenal responsibility. But, by this stage Jimmy had enjoyed such a long, unbroken line of television and musical success that he felt invincible. He was gradually freeing himself from the checks and balances which had previously existed. As he grew more powerful, so those around him lost the ability to influence him. He was careering forward powered by the considerable head of steam his energy and ambition generated. Yet there were ominous warning signs. Martin McKeand – the rock on which so much of the previous two *Spender* series depended – was to be absent this time and would be sorely missed. The generally-held view among seasoned TV producers is that when actors indulge themselves as executive producers, it all ends in tears. *Spender 3* was to prove no exception.

Jimmy hired his old friend from *Auf Wiedersehen*, Francesco Reidy, to be assistant director. Reidy still regarded himself a personal friend and was delighted to team up with his old sparring partner again. He was soon to regret it.

Reidy offers this account of what it was like to work under Jimmy.

'By the time I started work on pre-production in London, Jimmy was working hard on writing scripts but was also heavily involved in music work as he was just about to release a single. Jimmy was completely absent during the preparation period in Newcastle as he was having a big number one hit at the time. As far as the working production team was concerned, if you wanted to see Jimmy you had to watch Top of the Pops.

'During this period on any production, many decisions are made which cost money and commit the production to a course of action. The director will be chosing locations with the locations manager and designer. Once selected, a contract will be issued and a deal done, a date set. The location may require altering in some way by the designer, the interior may need re-decorating in which case plans have to be drawn, colour schemes agreed, materials purchased, signs made and so on. The costume department will liaise with design to make sure that the costumes don't clash with the set. The director of photography will decide what equipment is needed to light the set. The police may have to be informed of our coming. All of this work and literally hundreds upon hundreds of other things have to be considered for each and every set/location. As a producer on the series, Jimmy had every right to express an opinion on any aspect of the shoot. But he was not there. When all this was going on, he simply was not there. Furthermore he had hand-picked some of the best people available. The director of photography was Ernest Day, who, amongst other things had shot films like *Lawrence of Arabia* and *Ryan's Daughter* with David Lean.

'By the time Jimmy arrived in Newcastle we were very close to the first day of shooting. The fact that we were on target to have the schedule finalised and ready for production was a minor miracle considering the lateness of the scripts and the demands of the stories. Jimmy descended like a black cloud and began to make changes. From the moment he arrived there was an uncomfortable atmosphere. Suddenly we would find that he had rejected locations which had taken weeks to organise.

'Most importantly, the normal system of leadership on a production, whereby the director can approve anything within reason, disappeared because pretty quickly people realised that unless Jimmy liked it or at least was consulted, the chances were it might be rejected. The director's authority was gone. What was the point of the director saying to the prop buyer, "I think he should drive a Rover in scene ten if Jimmy, as he often did, insisted on casting the cars personally, often down to the paint finish. He wanted complete control.

'Working in public places was a nightmare. Jimmy has a hatred of people taking his photograph. Me and my team were under instructions to prevent members of the public taking pictures. We would have to pounce and beg them not to, very often leaving them unhappy or angry. Jimmy would simply stop working if he spotted a camera, even in the middle of a take which was going well. If we failed to stop the happy snapper, then Jimmy would and did leave the set. I have worked with some of the most respected actors in the world and never seen anything like this.

'The general level of organisation which went into keeping Jimmy happy and avoiding his anger was the kind I would expect from a member of a Royal family or perhaps more appropriately a Mafia boss. Doors flew open as he approached. Cars arrived with precision timing to carry him a hundred yards to the set. His clothes would be laid out in a particular way with the shirt buttons undone, as on one occasion he had handed a shirt back to a costume girl which had been given to him with the buttons done up.

'Messages would fly through the airwaves on the unit walkie talkies – "Jimmy's stepping out of make-up", or "Jimmy is ten-one hundred" [a code meaning in the toilet]. Of course various people were fired by him along the way for minor transgressions, although he did not do the firing himself as I recall.

'On one of our rare days off my team told me they had been at a roundabout where Jimmy had been involved in a minor traffic accident. The lads went to assist and found him in his car, steaming. He got out of the car and simply walked away, leaving them to deal with it.

'I received a call from a worried designer late one night because she had learned that I knew Jimmy's house very well and wanted to know exactly how his kitchen was decorated so that she could try to design a kitchen for a set which was in keeping with his style. Every department had tales of woe. Costume people told of how Jimmy would not wear anything other than well-known designer clothes and how they were often forced to sew designer labels into ordinary clothing. I was assured that on at least one occasion he accepted one such item which he had previously rejected because of its label.

'Some time before Jimmy had arrived in Newcastle, Brian Binns – my trusted second assistant – and I had interviewed about two thousand would-be extras from the local area who had responded to adverts in the local press over the previous weeks. We ended up with a book of many hundreds of enthusiasts most of whom had little or no experience. In the main they were a great bunch. Some wanted to do it for the money, others for the "crack", as they say in Newcastle, and others because they were devoted *Spender* or Jimmy Nail fans. I remember two young people, mad keen to work on the show. I decided to use them in a bicycle shop scene. I placed them in the background with the approval of the director. Jimmy arrived on set and we prepared to rehearse. He pointed at the two extras and said, "What are they doing?" I explained. He shook his head and said, "Get rid of them." When they left they did so saying how sad they were that the man they had so admired turned out to be a "heartless, rude, bastard" and they would never watch the show again.

'Perhaps the most uncomfortable thing of all was Jimmy being critical of how Ernest Day used to light a set. Jimmy had no understanding of film stock, exposure, filtration and the millions of factors which can contribute to correctly exposing an image or creating a mood with light. In short, if it was bright on the set he seemed to think that that was what it was going to be like on the end product. This can be the only explanation for him continually complaining about a light being too bright or in his eyes, or asking Ernest Day – a man of legend in the world of feature film – to reduce the light on set. You could see the confusion in Ernie's face. Like many, Ernest Day didn't stick it out very long. He was gone after two episodes.

'By now I was in a state of shock. I was surrounded by frightened individuals who were simply trying to keep their heads down and stay out of the firing line. I felt the wheels were coming off and we were going to crash.'

Reidy soon joined Day and producer Paul Raphael and resigned. A few small press reports pointed to 'artistic differences' as the reason for their departure. Reidy insists he was presented with no option but to quit.

'Over the last few years I have heard literally hundreds of people in the business telling tales of how they hated working with Jimmy and what a pain he can be. From actors to unit drivers, it's the same story.'

The consensus was no one had ever known one person holding so much power on a show. But there was no telling Jimmy by this stage. He regarded *Spender* as his own creation and its continued success as a vindication of his vision. His answer to any complaint was that it was his vision that had propelled the show far and the more input he had the better the prospects of continued success. The resignations and reports of trouble on set sent huge shock waves through Initial. It was the last thing they wanted given that they had just taken over the production from the BBC. But Jimmy appeared unaffected by all the controversy going on around him. He simply re-focused and got on with his various jobs, which now included hiring replacements for the missing men.

Ironically, in the middle of this furore, the past leapt out and nipped Jimmy's ankles. Central Television approached him with what it thought would be good news. It was planning to re-run all twenty-six episodes of *Auf Wiedersehen Pet* and because it was officially 'out of time' as far as standard repeat fees were concerned, the actors were free to negotiate their own figure. A sum of around £180,000 had been mooted. A lot of money for old rope. Or so Central executives assumed. They assumed wrong in Jimmy's case.

One colleague said, 'He did try quite energetically to stop AWP being repeated. He attempted to take out injunctions and I don't think it was just about the money.'

It certainly wasn't a matter of money. It was a question of something far more important to Jimmy. He had lots of money by now and the means to earn much more. He was suddenly faced with the quite appalling prospect of his old self appearing on the nation's television screens at the same time as the new streamlined version in *Spender 3*. Quite naturally, his former colleagues were perfectly happy for the old series to go on air. They would get a shot of publicity and earn a considerable sum of money for doing exactly nothing. Jimmy, stubborn as ever, held out and eventually succeeded in blocking the re-runs until after his *Spender* series had finished. He got the best of both worlds that way.

Although, once again, the third series was successful in terms of audience ratings, it was not well received by the critics. Jimmy could live with that. He was used to their sneering. More hurtful was the general view from within the profession that the quality of his latest offering fell a long way short of the first two series.

One senior producer said, 'I personally think the third series was nothing like as good as the first two. I think it really fell apart. This could have been because Jimmy had total control of the third; he felt he didn't need anybody else's contribution.'

Jimmy knew there were lots of people waiting for him to fall flat on his face, not just in the media, but in the BBC and even in Initial. He had been extraordinarily successful and careless about who he fell out with on the way up. The ructions on the last *Spender* shoot had been an embarrassment at Initial and had persuaded some they did not need the hassle of working on it again. An indication of the speed of the falling off can be gained from the word as late as December 1992 that plans were still very much on track for a fourth series and even a film version of the Geordie detective. A month later Jimmy announced that *Spender* was no more, that all the ambitious plans – alive and kicking four weeks earlier – were now shelved. His explanation that he needed a new challenge – 'I want to do something that stretches me more' -must have provoked knowing smiles from many a television executive and technician at the same time as sending shivers down their spines in anticipation of what that something might involve.

20
LOVE DON'T LIVE HERE ANYMORE

The relationship between Jimmy and Miriam has always been a mysterious one, even to some of their close friends. They appear to be so different. The large, loud, aggressive, hard-living working-class man and the quiet, reserved, petite middle-class woman. By and large, appearances are all anybody gets with Jimmy and Miriam, they are not a couple given to washing their dirty linen in public. And this is the key to understanding the success and longevity of their relationship. For although they appear to be polar opposites they in fact share many fundamental values.

There seems to be a rare depth of understanding between them which was apparent even in their early years together. They are very much a partnership, yet are careful to allow each other space. In those early days, Miriam accepted Jimmy for what he was. Although he credits her with changing him, whatever influence she brought to bear was administered gradually. There was certainly no preaching. She was self-contained and content when Jimmy had an intense need to prove himself to the world. In the early eighties when he was banging on the world's door – at pubs and clubs and parties – she seemed to know when to be with him and when to leave him to his own devices. There was never a 'Jimmy, don't you think it's time to go home' speech from Miriam. If she had had enough, she would go home alone and leave Jimmy to it.

When Jimmy made it, their lives changed dramatically. Jimmy was suddenly wealthy and famous and his life was in the public domain. Miriam didn't change. She was as unfazed by the showbusiness glamour as she had been unbothered by the gritty obscurity of their early Newcastle years. Then Jimmy changed again. Completely. This time the upheaval did take its toll on Miriam but she coped, adapted to life with the new teetotal, fastidious, slimline, designer-clad, driven Jimmy.

It would be quite wrong to assume that this kind of compliance is a sign of weakness. It is clear that Jimmy does not get on with shrinking violets. To have any kind of relationship with him you need to be strong, you need to be able to stand toe to toe and slug it out if necessary. One of the reasons Carol Johnson and Jimmy got on so well is that, although very different from Miriam, she wasn't afraid of him. Miriam exuded the confidence of someone who knows what they want. She, unlike Jimmy, did not crave the limelight, she did not feel the need to prove herself to anybody. She was serene, content and calm and Jimmy was always impressed by this inner strength.

The relationship was based on mutual respect as much as love. When Jimmy started misbehaving at a party Miriam didn't leave because she would be ashamed or embarrassed by what was to follow but because she had no taste for it, while at the same time recognising it was somehow necessary for her partner at that time.

They never married even though they have both long become used to referring to each other as husband and wife. Jimmy was very keen to, especially after the children arrived, and according to Carol Johnson, implored Miriam to become his wife many times. She would have none of it. She kept her own surname and also insisted that the boys were Joneses too.

'Miriam Jones wanted to stay Miriam Jones,' said Carol. 'He said he'd asked her often, including when they were in America, but she wouldn't hear of it and it made no difference when the boys came along.'

Tommy and Freddie were born in the mid-eighties just as their father's career really began to take off. The change of image in 1987 heralded a decade in which Jimmy drove himself relentlessly towards a goal which could be summed up as 'I'll show 'em.' Whenever asked about his family during this time he always went to great lengths to press home two points; that they were not up for discussion with journalists and that the two boys and Miriam were central to his life. He is fond of stressing how the boys changed him, how he wouldn't drive himself so hard if it wasn't for the need to provide for them. Addressing the flip side of him seldom being around to be involved in their growing up because of his need to feather the nest, he answered, somewhat piously, 'I hope to God they understand. They seem to.'

The paradox of being away from your family for long periods in order to look after them was doubtless not lost on Miriam. Once the *Spender* project was being dovetailed with Jimmy's musical career, there really weren't enough hours in the day. Often as many as eighteen would be given over to work – song- and script-writing, acting and the numerous meetings that were part and parcel of Jimmy's other life, that of the executive producer.

Always proud of her Welsh background, Miriam had made sure the boys grew up bilingual. They were sent to a special primary school in London for 'ex-pat' children where all lessons are conducted in Welsh. In 1991 she persuaded Jimmy that the family should move its base from London to north Wales. If he was going to be away for so much of the time, she reasoned, it made sense for her and the boys to be close to her family on Anglesey. Also the peace and security of rural Wales would provide him with a tranquil retreat from his increasingly hectic life.

The following year, Jimmy spent just ten weeks with his boys. It was coming to the point where they were seeing more of him on television than at home. Jimmy's work kept him in London for long stretches. As well as the business meetings, there was also time-consuming location work and the demands of his musical ambitions. Miriam was as stoical as usual but she was becoming increasingly worried that her sons were growing up – they were now seven and five – seeing far too little of their father. Things came to a head in 1993 when, just a few weeks after declaring the third series of *Spender* would be the last, and there was a prospect of a rest from his relentless schedule, Jimmy was persuaded to make a feature length version based in the south of France. Ever the perfectionist, he decided he needed to go and live there to soak up the atmosphere of the place while he was writing the script. This meant he was away from home for ten weeks which was followed by a three month location shoot so that the show could be broadcast at Christmas.

This coincided with a decision by Jimmy to base himself once again in London. He bought a £400,000 home in Alma Square, in prestigious St John's Wood and declared himself bored with rural life. What Miriam felt about the situation is not recorded but soon after the tensions that had fizzled between them for more than a year sparked into the open.

Early in 1995, the stories began circulating that Jimmy and Miriam had split up. That she had stayed in north Wales with the boys while he returned to London. Those closest to the couple believe 'split' is not accurate, more that it was a formal recognition of the direction their relationship had been travelling over the previous two years. Nevertheless it was a traumatic time for both – they had been together fourteen years; these were the kind of problems other people in showbusiness suffered, not Jimmy and Miriam.

It didn't last long. Jimmy quickly realised that he did not want to live without his partner and the boys. He promised he would reduce his workload and make more time for family life. They decided to get back together and Miriam and the boys moved back to London. In July, Val McLane confirmed the couple were together and claimed in a newspaper article, 'As far as he [Jimmy] is concerned there was no separation.'

Promising to take things easier is one thing. Carrying out that promise quite another. Especially when you are Jimmy Nail and are constantly driven to achieve. He was in the middle of a major new drama project over which he held unheard of power. Power meant hard work which in turn meant little time to spend at home. His career was rushing along at such a pace that even Jimmy seemed powerless to slow it down.

Once again Jimmy and Miriam tried to put their lives into some kind of perspective by moving to the tranquillity of north Wales. They rented a converted barn near the village of Rhostryfan near Caernarfon. Once again, Miriam was close to her family. But Jimmy was only there a few weeks before he was off back to London.

Arwen Roberts, a photographer who lives in the neighbouring

village of Rhosgadfan, said, 'They moved here around May 1995. Jimmy Nail left during the summer. The rumour was they had split up and he had gone back to London.'

A celebrity in such a small community is bound to attract gossip and it is easy to see how Jimmy's prolonged absence could give rise to rumours that they had separated a second time. Tommy and Freddie attended the local school in Bontnewydd a mile away, but Miriam did not mix with the local people.

'She kept herself very much to herself,' said Roberts. 'They spent a lot of time visiting her family on Anglesey.'

Seven months after their sudden arrival, Miriam and her two sons left for London. By now there was an added problem in her life, one which was going to take all her formidable strength of character to cope with. It had begun years earlier when she started suffering pain and stiffness in the joints of her hands. Over the years the problem grew steadily worse and affected other joints until doctors diagnosed severe arthritis. During 1995 she needed several stays in hospital for treatment.

A source close to the family said, 'Unfortunately, Miriam has got severe arthritis and has regularly been hospitalised recently because of this.' Arthritis can be treated with modern drugs, but there is no cure. The pain and restrictions on movement mean that Miriam leads an ever more secluded life.

In 1997 Jimmy and Miriam bought a grand £800,000 house overlooking Golders Hill Park in north-west London. The area is not as ostentatiously fashionable as neighbouring Hampstead, but discreet and sophisticated nonetheless. A perfect urban bolthole. Despite Miriam's condition, there seems to be no change in their rather unusual domestic arrangements. Although both were happy to be listed on the electoral register for their home in Cricklewood a few years earlier, Jimmy does not appear on the voters' list for the Golders Hill Park house. Miriam is the only adult listed as living there. Jimmy has a mansion block flat in Maida Vale, a couple of miles away, making their domestic arrangements unclear. Jimmy often needs to have a place he can retreat to for absolute peace when he is writing and his flat would be ideal for that. It is possible that a man as busy as he is has simply forgotten the mundane chore of electoral registers. Yet if Miriam found time to register her name, why not include her partner's as well?

Carol Johnson says rumours are circulating that the couple are once again estranged. Whatever the truth, and however idiosyncratic their relationship has become, Carol is sure they will be together- in one form or another – for life.

'I can't see him with anyone else but Miriam,' she said. 'I can't imagine them not being together, as much as they are the most unlikely pairing they are the most compatible in a bizarre way. Also he couldn't bear to think of another man taking his place, he couldn't accept that. I think that would send him loopy. She will always play a big part in his life. she is the mother of his kids, and that's it in his book. He dotes on his boys. They are the highest priority in his life.

Miriam is a lot like Jimmy's mother, she puts up with things like Laura did. I used to feel sorry for Miriam. I don't think she is stupid and soft, I think she has got it fairly sussed. Her idea of doing her own thing is having peace and quiet, her kids, doing her little courses and visiting her family in Wales. She is not so daft. She has got it sussed, so it suits them both. But it takes a very strong woman to do that and make it last.'

21
CROCODILE SHOES

Like *Spender*, *Crocodile Shoes* had a lengthy conception. It was swirling around in Jimmy's fertile mind during the great self-discovery period of 1982 when he finally began to believe that all things were possible. He had *Auf Wiedersehen Pet* scripts by Clement and La Frenais in his hands all the time, so he was familiar with the format. He decided to have a bash himself and wrote a prototype *Crocodile Shoes* script during breaks in filming on location in Germany. Much later, back in Britain – and only after he and La Frenais had become friends – Jimmy plucked up the courage to show his first ever written work to the great writer.

'He read through it and finished it after about half an hour,' said Jimmy. 'There was silence in the house. I said. "Well, is it any good?" "No!" he said. Just no, that was all. I thought, well he knows better than me and just threw them in a drawer.'

Once again, the dramatic scenario was highly autobiographical. Jimmy was at that time just beginning to turn his thoughts towards forging a musical career on the back of his *Pet* celebrity and the idea of having a Geordie musician plucked from obscurity was too tempting. With La Frenais' damning verdict ringing in his ears, however, Jimmy put thoughts of writing to the back of his mind and concentrated on ensuring a real-life Geordie be plucked from musical obscurity to national acclaim. Once he had accomplished that, and devised, written and starred in three series of a major hit television drama, the idea of doing something with *Crocodile Shoes* returned to him.

There were two major motivational factors at work here. By the end of 1992 it was clear that *Spender* was struggling to stay alive. Jimmy sensed he needed to draw a line under the increasingly troubled show and start afresh. Also his rollercoaster struggles to make it as a musician – his success in 1985 followed by his subsequent rejection then ultimate triumph – had left him with a healthy dislike of the music business in general and he wanted to expose it for the corrupt entity he felt it to be.

The idea had begun to gather momentum during 1992 when he was working on the third *Spender* series. But, as ever, it was not only an artistic vision which motivated him, it was a business objective too. Towards the end of *Spender* his relationship with Initial had begun to cool and this nurtured the idea that he could go it alone, form his own production company, and therefore be completely responsible for the whole. The other great incentive was that it would give him the chance to combine acting and singing. His mind buzzed with the commercial and artistic potential this offered. The prospect of a hit television series dovetailed with a hit album was the stuff of dreams for Jimmy both as a performer and businessman.

Eleven years after writing a prototype script for *Crocodile Shoes*, Jimmy set about doing it for real. No longer the tentative novice, he produced a pilot script which had a Geordie lathe operator and part-time tunesmith Jed Sheppard dreaming of stardom and desperate London record producer Ade Lynn searching for a new star. The scene was set for a fable of wish fulfilment. It was not just a case of writing scripts. Jed – like Jimmy – was to be a singer/songwriter. A soundtrack was needed. Jimmy wanted to make the music 'organic' and decided to use composers from the north east wherever possible.

One of his mainstays was Paddy McAloon of Prefab Sprout. Jimmy approached him at an opportune time. McAloon was in a rut after abandoning an incredibly ambitious attempt to chart the history of the human heart in a series of chanting, mantra-like stanzas. It had taken him two years to get from Eve in Paradise to Kennedy's assassination in 1963. Then he got stuck. While he was pondering his next move Jimmy came along with a request which must have sounded like a breath of fresh air. Could he write some lyrics for his forthcoming soundtrack? He was happy to accept the commission. A bit of commercial pop was just what he needed. Another contributor was Tony McAnaney, who had made his acting debut courtesy of Jimmy in *Spender*, but who had spent most of his life as a musician. Ten years earlier, when Jimmy was just beginning to carve out a musical career, McAnaney sent him the demo tape of a song he had composed, wondering if he could make use of it. At the time Jimmy couldn't, and it gathered dust in a drawer until the two men agreed to resurrect it for *Crocodile Shoes*. The result was the infectiously catchy song that became the theme tune for the series and a top-selling single in its own right.

Jimmy's track record, negotiating skills and sheer energy meant he was well placed to go it alone. He set up his own production company, housed it in a suite of swish Soho offices and called it Big Boy ('Well, I am a big boy, aren't I?') Big Boy could not go it completely alone at this tender stage of life, however. It needed financial backing. It got it in the shape of one of the hottest television production companies of the time. Red Rooster films, founded by Linda James in 1982 when she was just twenty-three years old, had grown into a major concern and James had gained a reputation as one of the most shrewd and formidable operators in the television business. They negotiated a deal whereby Red Rooster 'umbrella'd' Big Boy to produce *Crocodile Shoes* with James as executive producer. The financial deals done, Jimmy set about hiring his team.

The actors were relatively easy to recruit. After all, Jimmy knew how to make popular, successful drama. Chances were they would be involved in big league series. Melanie Hill, actress wife of Sean Bean won the role of Jed's sister and James Wilby took a step downmarket from his Merchant Ivory work to play the role of Ade Lynn. The behind-the-scenes people were more difficult to recruit. Eventually he signed up the experienced team of Peter Wolfes as producer and Malcolm Mowbray to direct. The show was on the road and the shoot, which was in Newcastle, London, Nashville and New York, got underway in May 1994.

The by now familiar scenario did not take long to develop. Wolfes produced and Mowbray directed as they saw fit. The trouble was

Jimmy saw things differently and was not backward in telling them. *Crocodile Shoes* was, if anything, more pure Nail vision even than *Spender* and once again he simply could not stand anyone else's creative input. As far as he was concerned the producer, director and others were there to implement his grand design for the series and not to get in the way with impertinent ideas of their own. Around halfway through the shoot both were sacked. The BBC issued statements that there had been no bust-up or animosity, but its claim was unconvincing.

Wolfes now realises he should have listened to the many warnings he got at the time from colleagues about the wisdom of working with Jimmy.

'When I was approached to produce it, it was quite apparent that they had had difficulty in choosing who they wanted. They actually had interviewed every producer, director and goodness knows who else in the country because that is the way he is. He likes to have a very long list to choose from.

'We tried to get on but we were chalk and cheese and in the end, as I was warned, it was inevitable that we parted company, because that is inevitably what happens in most cases with Jimmy. I was very keen to steer him away from his *Spender* image. But he doesn't like people to really start to influence him or control him in any way. In my case it was just a question of control. He ultimately wanted to control everything. You have to ask the question, Why did you hire me in the first place?'

Part of Wolfes seems to understand the agonies of watching your grand vision altered by putting it through the collaborative medium of television production.

'That happens a lot in our industry. There are people who want ultimate control. If you've devised something of your own, if you've got the talent to do that as he has done in the past, I can understand why he wants to hold onto his own view. Because the one thing which happens a lot on film and television is that the view you hold gets corrupted by other people joining the project. That is when it becomes extremely difficult professionally and in the end he wanted to do it all himself. He would try and direct it and that can't be done, it is just physically impossible as well as mentally. There are very few people who could write, direct and produce at the same time. He does have extraordinary energy in terms of working long hours, but he puts around him a little fiefdom of people who are there to help him at every corner. Loyal subjects who organise his day and are there for his bidding. I just think that with him everything is on his own terms and when you can't have a conversation that is open and honest because you are afraid of saying the wrong thing, then you have got a problem.

'Good luck to him. He knows his market, he know his appeal and in the end he gets his way. He's backed by a very good agent in Duncan Heath and by a very good record company in East West, who obviously know how to market him. He just demands control. That's the way he is. It goes way back. I think he has got deep-rooted problems which go back to his childhood. It is not about deprivation. It is much more deep-rooted than that.'

The lurid tone of Wolfes' remarks is surprising coming from a respected television producer not normally given to such melodrama. It reflects his utter bewilderment over his treatment at the hands of this unfathomable employer

Another crew member said, 'As a character he is very light and dark. We didn't get on. I learned a lesson of sorts. I was warned by many people not to work with him and I chose to go ahead because I was quite interested in the project. I consider myself professional enough to treat it as water under the bridge. As for Malcolm Mowbray, some felt that he was sacked for doing his job, which supposedly was to direct.'

The tone of the criticisms levelled at Jimmy here is reminiscent of those he aroused during the making of *Spender 3*. The more successful he became the more difficult he found it to relate to those around him. As a younger man, he had always been good at impressing his elders or those with bigger reputations than himself. He had the knack of presuming to treat people like Dick Clement, Ian La Frenais and Martin McKeand as equals. When he became famous in his own right their relationships were based on mutual respect and therefore able to survive his not infrequent tantrums. None of these people was present on *Crocodile Shoes*. He had no one with whom he went back any length of time to rely on or who could tactfully manoeuvre him when his ego and obsessive nature were threatening to send things off the rails. Add to that his mindset that he genuinely felt he could – perhaps should – do everything himself. He increasingly saw that as the only way his vision would make it to the nation's television screen intact. Any protest from senior production people was ignored or treated with contempt. It is not surprising therefore that no one present either could or felt inclined to try to look behind the bluster and bad temper, the obsessive demand for control , for any key to help deal with it. They demonised him.

The huge fissures in the production team allied to the enormous workload Jimmy had taken on were bound to have their effect. Once again – just like *Spender* – it became a race against time to complete the series. His workload may have been immense, but Jimmy took on two more roles before the show was ready. He decided that the film editing and re-dubbing of the sound could not be trusted to anyone else so he did them himself, even though his refusal to delegate was already making the show seriously late.

An indication of how close to the wire *Crocodile Shoes* came was that it was the only one of the batch of autumn dramas from both the BBC and the ITV network not to have a press launch. This wasn't a decision of Jimmy's to snub the media critics he despised so much, it was simply because no episodes were ready in time.

Despite all the crises, sackings, overrunning of schedules and general angst that accompanied it, *Crocodile Shoes* was finally completed just in time for its launch on 10 November 1994, a prime time Thursday evening slot. But had it been worth all the effort, was it any good and most importantly of all, would the public like it? The critics did their best to discourage viewer enthusiasm. They were suspicious of what they saw as megalomania at work. A. A. Gill of the *Sunday Times* was probably the most damning. Reviewing the first episode he wrote, '*Crocodile Shoes* was execrable. Watching Jimmy Nail is like watching a skip rust. I'm sorry, but what a joyless, self-regarding old actor, singer, writer, producer he is... I kept losing control of my eyelids.'

Even some of the more favourable could not resist a dig at what was perceived as Jimmy enjoying a massive ego trip. Marcus Berkmann of the *Mail on Sunday* was generally impressed. '*Crocodile Shoes* works because it's full of heart. There's a distinctive tone coming through in

Nail's writing these days – humorous, strong, very masculine, but fundamentally benevolent and optimistic.'

This did not stop him pointing out what he thought were the show's weaknesses. 'Londoners are all weak and superficial and are constantly leaping into bed with each other... Geordies, by contrast, are a strong, honest people, broad of mind and big of heart, and always there when you need them.'

And, of course, the megalomania.

'Jimmy Nail as actor, writer, musician and executive producer, has certainly made sure that everything in his series is geared his way. Writer Nail has decreed that songwriter Nail has a remarkable talent. Writer Nail has given actor Nail all the best lines and sole access to the moral highground. Executive producer Nail has respected writer Nail's work. And writer Nail and executive producer Nail have even laid on an attractive American country singer for Nail to smooch with in forthcoming episodes. Don't you like to be in control?'

First reactions were generally better than more considered views. A month into the series Joe Steeples, in the *Sunday Mirror*, re-iterated the suspicions felt by many about Jimmy's all-powerful position. 'In four weeks *Crocodile Shoes* has gone from fairly average to worse than worse. I've always quite liked Jimmy Nail, but obviously not half as much as he does. He created the series, he stars in it, wrote the script, composed the songs and sang them, and it was made by his own production company. Unless it shows a marked improvement soon he's in danger of making up most of the audience as well. Jed's story – Geordie lathe operator turned country singer – is spoiled by Nail's blind admiration for his own work. Lousy lines that should have been cut or re-written stick out like rotten teeth.'

Mixed reviews. And despite a carefully orchestrated promotional strategy which had Jimmy singing the theme song on *Top of the Pops*, audience response was favourable but not ecstatic. The first episode attracted a worthy 7.63 million viewers, putting it number twenty-four in the week's ratings for BBC programmes. Jimmy needn't have worried. The single, 'Crocodile Shoes', and the album of the same name, sold like hot cakes, both achieving Top Ten status, despite a pasting from the critics, one of whom described the latter as 'dreary in the extreme' and likened two tracks, 'Angel' and 'Don't Wanna Go Home', to rejects from a Fleetwood Mac album.

It was a triumph for Jimmy's business acumen as much as his artistic skills. It was the ultimate package and proved beyond doubt he had not lost his Midas touch. Lynne Truss of the *Times* summed it up as well as anyone when she complained about being manipulated while unable to resist 'caterwauling' the title track and described the series as a 'seven hour pop video'. Elyse Taylor, marketing director of East West admitted the television exposure was the extra element which allowed the music to 'lift off into the stratosphere'.

'I haven't even tried to calculate what would have been the cost to us of guaranteeing that amount of peak-time publicity for the LP but, suffice to say, it would be way beyond any budget we might have to spend,' she said.

The phenomenal success of the *Crocodile Shoes* music (the album reached number two at Christmas) meant that it proved more financially lucrative than the television series which spawned it. Industry estimates put Jimmy's earnings from the album and single at around £500,000, which was enough to convince that shrewd business brain of his that he should devote his immediate future to music. It also persuaded him the time was right to fulfil a long standing ambition of his, one he had secretly nurtured since his days playing the Newcastle pub scene.

The prospect of putting together a band and touring Britain excited Jimmy like nothing had done since he cut his first album three years earlier. The radical change of direction was enough to re-charge the batteries, as after the rigours of producing two hit television series, even his stamina and enthusiasm was flagging. Touring was another huge challenge, one that would test his credibility as a musician and singer. It was the part of his repertoire that he was most sensitive about and the most anxious for recognition. For while he would admit to being an inexperienced actor and a writer who still had the L-plates on, questions about his credentials as a singer met with an indignant response to the effect that he had served his time at the grass roots of the music business for many years before he was famous. This, of course, was misleading. It implied years striving for musical success, which was not the case. When he released 'Love Don't Live Here Anymore' back in 1985, he displayed his sensitivity on the subject. 'I realise people might think that anybody can be made to sound good in a recording studio, and that's true. But when I do some live shows, and people come to see if I fall flat on my face, then I'll show them.'

So at the grand old age of forty, Jimmy began to plan for his debut tour. He had not played live – apart from appearances on Top of the Pops – since his days with the King Crabs, and then only in front of a semi-interested audience who often only wandered in from the bar to see what the racket in the adjoining room was all about. So much for his half a lifetime of experience. But this was Jimmy Nail. The man who had stepped effortlessly into acting, writing and music. He thrived on challenges like this.

Once more, Jimmy's sharp business brain did not miss a trick. Although he had a number one single and a successful album behind him, he realised that the current perception of him was as a country singer thanks to the huge success of *Crocodile Shoes*. He tailored his tour accordingly, hiring Nashville-based country singer Deana Carter as support. 'He was looking for a female singer from Nashville to complement his music and I fit the bill,' she explained. Then, offering a small insight which must have raised a few eyebrows in the television world, she added, 'Jimmy is a scream and we have had lots of fun together in rehearsals. We have a similar sense of humour.'

The tour was a four-week long, twenty-date tour of medium-sized sized venues in towns around Britain, culminating with two dates at Newcastle City Hall and two at the Hammersmith Apollo in west London. His appearance at Newcastle was particularly moving for him and he tried hard to get his new single, 'Big River', a tribute to his father and home town, ready for the concerts, but was unable to finish it.

By the time Jimmy came to London the tour was being described as 'highly successful' by reviewers. Jimmy was at pains to hammer home the point to his audiences by way of an introduction that he was no actor riding on a spot of commercial success but that he was a serious musician who had been playing on and off for twenty-five years. Paddy McAloon's compositions were praised as the highlights while Jimmy's cover versions were described as shaky. Even though generally complimentary, Alan Jackson of the *Times* fell into the by now familiar patronising tone favoured by the critics. Reviewing the first Apollo concert, he said Jimmy resorted to 'a more high-budget version of the sort of music favoured by competent bar and club bands everywhere from Texas to Tyne and Wear.' Another, Ian McCann in the *Telegraph*, commenting on the final gig, wondered how 'the actor had travelled this far on such modest musical talent'. These broadsides were part of a now-familiar pattern. What the critics scorned the punters lapped up enthusiastically. It simply served to increase Jimmy's distrust of the chattering classes.

Jimmy backed up his first tour with another hot on its heels, but this time at arena-size venues. He was keen to be perceived as a major musical player and after the success of the debut tour he was confident he could fill the larger halls. He had to move fast because negotiations were drawing to a satisfactory conclusion which would tie him up for the whole of 1996. Having done touring for the time being, Jimmy was preparing to meet yet another challenge – Hollywood.

The deal was finalised in the autumn. Jimmy had won a support role opposite Madonna, Jonathan Pryce and Antonio Banderas in the £60 million film musical *Evita*. Once again it was a radical change of direction. The big fish was going from the relatively small pond of British television to the stormy, piranha-infested waters of American movie-making. There was much private speculation about how his legendary tantrums would be viewed over there, especially as he wasn't the star but a supporting player.

For Jimmy it was a golden opportunity to make a name for himself in Hollywood. His film experience was limited but he was not a complete novice, having appeared in a number of low-budget British releases in the mid-eighties. The type-casting he suffered – always the villain or buffoon – was one reason he grew tired of the medium, deciding to create interesting roles for himself rather than wait for someone else to take him seriously. But he was growing weary of television, he was beginning to tire of all the problems which go with making TV drama – the tight time schedules, the financial constraints, and in his case the rows with his colleagues. When his agent told him about *Evita* he was extremely keen. The film was unusual in the sense that there was no dialogue. The 'script' was purely a musical score. In a way this suited Jimmy fine. He was confident his voice was good enough, and he knew there were no outstanding vocal talents among the main players against whom he would suffer in comparison. The director was to be Alan Parker, a tough Englishman with a reputation for knowing his own mind and delivering the goods as his previous credits (*Bugsy Malone*, *Midnight Express*, *Angel Heart* and *The Commitments* among them) testified. Above all, the grandeur of the production seduced him. A £60 million budget, huge sets, shooting in Europe and Argentina. After the claustrophobic atmosphere of British television, it would be an adventure. By the time Jimmy joined the cast, planning was well-advanced and the shoot was due to begin in January 1996. That left him with the task of completing his new album, *Big River*, and the single of the same name, before packing his bags for South America.

Ironically *Big River* was better received by the critics than some of Jimmy's other releases, but was less successful in the charts, reaching respectable Top 40 positions and platinum status, but not scaling the heights of the million-selling *Crocodile Shoes*. Likewise the single – a favourite of Jimmy's and many of his fans and a popular part of his concert repertoire – was solid rather than spectacular. It is an intensely personal song, which took Jimmy a long time to compose. In it he encapsulates his feelings for his home town and pays tribute to a man who was spawned by it – his father. The lyrics lack Paddy McAloon's elegance and are downright clumsy and clichéd in places, but the tune is infectious and the delivery intense and sincere enough to rescue it from sentimentality.

Jimmy finished 1995 on a high. His musical projects complete, he took Christmas off and prepared himself for the challenge of the New Year, the challenge of working with someone who was, by all accounts, the biggest control freak and perfectionist of all. Someone who made his attempts at re-inventing himself look like small beer indeed. Someone who could match his ego, his drive, his will to succeed. He would be locking horns with one of the most famous women on earth – Madonna.

22
WHEN JIMMY
MET MELVYN

The most surprising thing was that Jimmy said yes. The South Bank Show was none too optimistic when it approached him with a view to compiling an in-depth profile for its Sunday evening show. His reputation for being difficult with the media preceded him. However it held a trump card. Its considerable gravitas. Jimmy just could not resist the idea of a top quality, serious arts programme devoting an entire show to a study of his career.

Whether he would have made the same decision at the end of 1995 as he looked forward to working on *Evita* is open to question. By then he had had time to digest the various unpleasant ramifications that the screening of the programme – in October – had generated. When he was approached, more than six months earlier, he could not have foreseen them. He was concerned only about whether he could bear the show's researchers dissecting his life and, most of all, if he could stomach the prospect of being grilled for forty-five minutes by the presenter Melvyn Bragg. Jimmy had always hated being interviewed.

Once he agreed he was obliged to provide researchers with information, contact telephone numbers of people close to him, even photographs. It was not something he was easy with, it went against the grain, but he complied with as much good grace as he could muster. The interview – the centrepiece of the programme – took place in a cavernous deserted warehouse in Newcastle. As they were about to start Bragg asked an ill at ease-looking Jimmy if he was OK. 'Oh yes, Melvyn, can't you tell?' came the ironic reply. Then, 'I'll be alright once we get going.'

The interview was interspersed with footage of a very cool-looking Jimmy walking around his old Newcastle haunts wearing a designer suit and trendy sunglasses to a score of pounding electric guitars. It was not well-received by a number of Jimmy's former colleagues, who suspected Jimmy's force of personality and desire for control may have unduly influenced the programme-makers.

Peter Wolfes said, 'All you got at the end of the day was a kind of stereotypical, ad-land view of Newcastle with long shots of the bridge and with him interviewed in a warehouse looking very trendy and media and powerful. But there was no substance, absolutely no substance. Melvyn Bragg did not have a clue how to open the door. I bet Jimmy did it on his own terms.'

A TV producer who worked closely with Jimmy said, 'I thought the South Bank Show was appalling. It was obviously done very much on Jimmy's terms. It seemed like he was calling the shots, including the camera angles.'

One thing he had no control over was the effect of this programme on his family. One of the contact numbers he had provided researchers with was that of his sister, Val. She was probably the person who knew most about Jimmy. She was also an experienced actress with a deep knowledge of the world her famous younger brother was operating in. A must, one would have thought, for a serious profile.

Wrong. Val was interviewed for two hours, but the footage remained on the cutting room floor. Instead editor Susan Shaw chose to use Ian La Frenais and feminist writer Bea Campbell as the 'talking heads'.

When Val saw the finished programme she was 'distressed' that her contribution had been left out. To make matters worse, Jimmy had made no mention of the role she had played in getting him an audition on *Auf Wiedersehen Pet* nor the subsequent coaching she provided. She made her feelings clear to her brother who assured her he had no part in the decision to cut her out of the show.

'I would like to know from the producers the real reason for doing that,' she said. 'It was the first time I had spoken at all. I told the truth. They made some kind of editorial decision to omit me altogether, and who made that decision I don't know, but I know it definitely wasn't my brother. I am absolutely clear about that. He said he didn't have anything to do with it.'

Val's suspicions are justified. Her absence from the programme had nothing to do with damaged film. It was an editorial decision to leave out her contribution. A senior source on the show said, 'We did not use the Val McLane interview because we felt her view of Jimmy Nail was distorted by her own career. We felt she gave too much prominence to her own role in launching Jimmy's career.'

Although no one has spelled this out to Val, she almost certainly suspected the reason. Nearly eleven years older than Jimmy, she was an established actress when he was languishing in prison. She helped to get him an opportunity and he struck gold with it. He was famous overnight, something she has not achieved in thirty years in the business. Whereas once she was known as Val McLane the actress, more and more people began referring to her as Val McLane, sister of Jimmy Nail.

Val and Jimmy are alike in many ways. They share the same robust nature. Neither is afraid to speak their mind whatever the consequences. She loves her baby brother and doesn't resent his success. She was and is delighted for him. But she did feel that her name had somehow been unfairly erased from the Jimmy Nail story.

Some say that Jimmy was not keen to put the story about that there was already an actor in the family who was able to give him a helping hand. They say he preferred people to think he did it all by himself, in spite of his humble beginnings not with a lift from someone who was supposed to be a part of them.

Although there was never any serious bad blood between them, there was friction. And normally it was acting that brought it to the surface. The day Val worked alongside Jimmy on *Auf Wiedersehen 2*, Roger Bamford remembered as one of the worst of the whole shoot. This kind of tension, and Val's lingering sense of being unfairly treated, explains her anger at the content of the South Bank Show profile.

Things went from bad to worse. Rumours that Val was angry over the way she was left out began to circulate and soon reached the press. The *Sunday People* approached her and she spoke to one of its journalists. The resulting story was splashed across the front page under the headline 'Jimmy Nailed By Sister'. According to Carol Johnson, Jimmy was apoplectic. He felt betrayed.

23
DON'T CRY FOR ME

Those who expected Jimmy to get his comeuppance on *Evita* were disappointed. It was a reasonable hope. They knew how difficult he could be. They knew all about Madonna's reputation as the queen of egos. And they knew what a tough taskmaster Alan Parker was. All the raw material was there.

One former television colleague said, 'I would have loved to have seen them together as Alan is tiny and aggressive and very much wants things done his way.'

Any such wishes lingering in the hearts of bruised television executives as Jimmy flew out to Buenos Aires to begin the six month shoot were to be dashed. They had failed to remember an important aspect of his character, the aspect that led Ian La Frenais to describe him as stubborn but not arrogant. His great desire to learn and advance.

It first surfaced on the set of *Auf Wiedersehen Pet* when the novice Nail absorbed the requirements of television acting extraordinarily quickly. Then it was evident during his film debut on *Morons*, where he was known as 'one-take-Jimmy'. Now he knew full well that he was stepping on to a much bigger stage than he was used to. He also knew that, if all went well, it could be the vital stepping stone to the real big time of movie stardom. He was a novice again, albeit one who had learned how to handle himself a little better than the last time he was in such a position thirteen years ago.

He and Parker got on. Parker left nobody on the set in any doubt who was boss and Jimmy respected that. What was more, it soon became apparent that the director had a very clear vision of the way he wanted the film to be done. That was something that Jimmy could relate to because it was the way he had worked on *Spender* and *Crocodile Shoes*.

The other characteristic which would stand him in good stead was his ability not to be overawed by celebrity, that knack, which he demonstrated from the beginning, of being able to breathe easily in a more rarefied air than he was used to. Instinctively he knew that he would have to stand up to Madonna. His role as Augustin Magaldi, a club singer who becomes Eva's first lover, meant that they would be playing opposite each other in the early part of the film, so it was vital the chemistry was right between them.

The early exchanges between the two were spectacular and gave rise to rumours that things were less than cordial between them. John Gallagher, one of three American assistant directors on the shoot, remembers the crew looking forward each morning to the banter which would ensue when they came together.

'The first thing I was struck by was how often Jimmy was getting struck by Madonna with a suitcase during the rehearsal,' he said. 'I can see that perhaps any rumours were generated because of their antics. There was nothing but good nature, kidding between them. Both are tough, street-raised, shoot from the hip, no holds barred kind of people.'

It was not all fun and games, however. There was a real tension there, which often spilled over into boisterous humour, but occasionally in the early days into acrimony.

Jimmy blames this on the pressure both actors were under. 'Things were pretty tense at the beginning,' he admitted. 'That job was so important to all of us involved that there were bound to be a few stressful moments. Madonna was under enormous pressure to prove herself. She knew all eyes were on her and she had to get it right. It was nerves mostly – certainly on my part.'

Gallagher had never worked with Madonna before and had little experience of British actors. His general impression of them was the one many Americans have – genteel, middle class, technically skilled.

He was surprised to find that this 'Brit' was, in fact, very similar to the sassy lady he was playing opposite.

'I came in with a bunch of preconceptions about Madonna – none of them were really positive – and I had heard stuff about Jimmy, but he certainly did not live up to it on *Evita* and neither did Madonna. It was a goal she had set for herself and she is a goal-oriented person, an extremely hard worker and a perfectionist. She wasn't any tougher on anybody than she was on herself. She raised everybody's game. I think that's why they got on so well. They would make fun of each other and give each other a hard time, all good-natured. It made for good spectator entertainment as well. They would do it on the set. We'd all be standing round, they'd go at it and we'd say who was going to get who the worst. Then they would wind up having Thai food that night for dinner.

'Jimmy was good fun, a good guy, I liked him. He is a city boy like I am, no mincing words, no fluff, all substance. She got a kick out of him probably for the same reason I did. He was no nonsense, say what was on his mind. I thought that was an endearing quality. He definitely has a certain unique quality, a rough edge. One of the guys from the streets.'

Goal-oriented person, hard worker, perfectionist, tougher on herself than anyone else. Gallagher could have been talking about Jimmy. Madonna no doubt also quickly realised that she and her screen lover were in fact very much alike. Although Jimmy made it abundantly clear that he was not going to be overawed by Madonna, he had the intelligence to convey to her early in their relationship that he was not trying to compete with her either. She was the star, he knew that, and was not arrogant enough to presume he could or should in any way upstage her.

'I said to her one day, "Think of this movie as an apartment block we're trying to build. I'm down in the foundations supporting the block while you're right at the top. You're the penthouse. So if we get the foundations right you'll look good and you'll sell the whole block." She smiled at me but I'm not sure she had any idea what I was going on about.'

You can bet Madonna, even if she affected otherwise, knew exactly what Jimmy was saying and took the message onboard. As filming progressed and Jimmy and Madonna gained a deeper understanding of one another, the verbal jousting became less frequent. It was no longer required.

According to Gallagher and others, Jimmy was the model professional throughout – punctual, efficient, hard working and easy to get on with. It wasn't his show, of course. He was a hired actor. All the programmes he created problems on were his responsibility, he was the one charged with making them as good as possible. Even on *Pet 2*, where he first began to emerge as a thorny customer, most who were on the receiving end were convinced it arose out of a sense of loyalty to the show. Now he knew the picture was in good hands. Alan Parker made it very clear that he was in charge and would brook no argument. Jimmy had confidence in his abilities as a director and respected his decisiveness. He was happy to be as good as he could be and leave the rest to others.

One aspect of *Evita* which amused observers in Britain who had worked with Jimmy on *Spender*, was the way he looked. *Evita* was a film which depended on its visual authenticity and Alan Parker set great store by striving for a documentary feel by matching the actors as closely as possible physically with their real life counterparts. Consequently Jimmy was required to have a pencil moustache and his hair slicked back tight to his head every day. Those who remember how fussy he was over his hairstyle on *Spender* were amazed to see him so altered.

Chief hairstylist Martyn Samuel was the man in charge of the coiffure. Samuel knew his job. He is highly respected in the business and a personal friend of Alan Parker for twenty-five years. Despite his experience he was nervous about dealing with Jimmy because of warnings he had received about his temperament.

He said, 'We had all been warned that he was going to give us a hard time. We thought, "Oh my goodness." And he was just the perfect gentleman and we became very good friends. He was very into it. We went through everything, but he was so co-operative. It was very easy to do, his hair was perfect for the look we were creating. He had it slicked down every day and trimmed once a week.

'He was absolutely fantastic to Madonna. They got on extremely well. He was just amazing. He kept her totally under control. She kept going off the loose end quite a lot. It became more and more demanding. She gets irate very quickly and it was a tremendously long arduous shoot for her. She worked every day for months. He helped her by being patient and always making her laugh.'

Patient, considerate, co-operative. What was going on?

Gallagher confirms the sense of awe in which Parker was held, even by Madonna. He was a man who would stand no nonsense and was particularly intolerant of the kind of artistic tantrums actors are prone to from time to time. 'Anybody who was trying to veer Alan Parker off his set course was in for some rough seas. He knew exactly what he wanted and that is a quality of good directors to make sure everybody else knows he knows what he is doing. Madonna didn't get away with anything, she had to pick her battles carefully, because Alan was no easy opponent. It was pretty much established early on that this was an Alan Parker film. There were no clashes between Jimmy and Alan Parker, but when a guy knows what he is doing to that extent you don't argue.

'It was Alan Parker's vision. The script was the movie. He had pretty much directed the script when he wrote it. We shot it image for image, line by line. Anybody who thinks he made it in the editing room is dead wrong. His vision was there on paper before we had even started. He was very clear about what he wanted and he runs a tight ship and everybody got on board with that.'

Parker sounds like a man after Jimmy's own heart.

Jimmy was not such an experienced showbusiness man not to have a few stars in his eyes. He loved the grand scale on which everything operated, something which served to heighten his sense of the limitations of television. And, although he would never show it, he was excited at working with some of the biggest stars in cinema. He was the new kid on the block once again. He was new to film-making on this scale and new to most of the cast and the largely American crew he was working with. He was out to impress and he succeeded.

The shoot proceeded with an intensity that Jimmy was familiar with. As Gallagher said, it was a tight ship. It needed to be as a huge amount of work had to be crammed into the six months available. The scale of the scenes being shot and the documentary detail Parker insisted upon meant that thousands of extras were employed, all of whom had to be organised and made up before any shooting could begin. It was not unusual for Gallagher to wake with an alarm call at 3 a.m. and work through well into the evening six days a week.

The schedule meant there was no room for error or hold-ups, everything had to run smoothly to meet the deadline. Parker managed to create a sense of togetherness and camaraderie rare on film sets, but which was vital in oiling the wheels. Jimmy must have looked on in envy, it was something he had never managed when in charge himself.

'You work on demanding movies and you get your pay cheque,' said Gallagher. 'But there was a different sense on that movie. Everyone felt they were a part of an important project and even though I was exhausted I was anxious to get to work in the morning. A lot of it was recreating these actual historical events. Like the funeral of Eva. It is amazing to what extent we tried to recreate that down to every detail. We tried to match the people pulling the gun wagon with the casket on it to the way the actual people looked like in the photographs. There was a "We're all in this together" thing, let's drop rank. You do not often get that feeling, the sense of being on something important.'

The shoot moved from the major location shots in Argentina to Budapest where scenes which were impossible to recreate in the hugely modernised Buenos Aires were filmed. After that the team limped into London for the final batch of scenes at Shepperton Studios. Everyone had worked their socks off to meet the tight deadlines and they had just about managed it. Ironically once they decamped to the relative comfort of the studio they began to lose time. Jimmy, of course, was not required constantly, and had enough spare time on his hands – especially in Budapest – to turn his thoughts to the forthcoming *Crocodile Shoes 2* shoot which was planned for the late summer and autumn. With *Evita* showing signs that it might run over he was becoming increasingly concerned. He had already written 'Country Boy', which turned out to be the title song on the new series, during breaks in filming in Argentina. Now he was having to spend almost all his free time preparing the ground for the new show as it was becoming increasingly clear to him he would have very little time for that after *Evita* finished. There was little socialising on the *Evita* shoot. No one had the energy after the incredibly long days. This suited Jimmy, who invariably retreated to his hotel room in the evening to burn the midnight oil on *Crocodile Shoes 2*. However hard he pushed himself, however, he made sure his fatigue didn't show.

Gallagher declares himself extremely impressed with this unusual 'Brit' who seemed to know how to handle himself and Madonna into the bargain and is happy to forecast a bright future for him in Hollywood, although not as a leading man.

'I think it was a great casting coup and he did a fantastic job with it and he showed a lot of talent. He has got a great comic sensibility. It's hard to work within the framework of a musical and communicate subtleties like that. His singing was not supposed to sweep you off your feet, not supposed to pull on your emotional strings at all, but it stood up very very well.

'Presence? Yes, absolutely. I am surprised nobody over here has exploited it to date. I am not going to be surprised if I see him round the campus over here. Look at him, he has got a very unique look. He would play great supporting role, villain kind of guy, certainly he is not going to carry a movie as a lead, at least in any conventional story that I can think of right now, but it is all those unique qualities about him. That accent – bringing an accent to the States is upping your value, even an accent like Jimmy's.

'I would love to see him again. I expect that eventually some smart guy over here will introduce him to the American public on a broader scale. He has an appeal for us. It has got to be the right role but I think he has all the material.'

It is one of the great myths of the acting profession, the idea that doing bedroom scenes is somehow sexy, a thing to be envied. Ask any actor if 'giving passion' in an austere studio in a bed surrounded by numerous technicians and a director issuing instructions is in any way a turn-on. They will reply it requires professionalism, a sense of humour and a certain rapport with the other participant. But sexy? Not since Cary Grant and Sophia Loren.

Jimmy and Madonna's bedroom scene was pretty tame stuff. In fact, Magaldi woke up with the most famous woman on the planet wearing a vest Oz would have been proud of. Nevertheless the sobriquet stuck. Not only was Jimmy cracking Hollywood, he was to be 'in bed with Madonna'. The subject inevitably kept cropping up during the publicity interviews, the Geordie 'bit of rough' who gets to share a bed with one of the most desirable women in the world. The Jimmy of a few years earlier would have bridled at the clichés being thrown at him. He had never been entirely comfortable with sex scenes. In *Spender* he admitted feeling uneasy about writing them for his character because he was worried he would be seen to be abusing his all-powerful position. It was not until the third series that he allowed himself a lover. The more mature Jimmy attempted to take the hoo-hah in his stride and even attempted to use the situation. 'I'd be a liar if I said it wasn't fun,' he lied to one reporter.

The scene was shot at Shepperton near the end of the schedule. By that time Madonna had hit Jimmy with enough suitcases and the two had exchanged enough robust insults to have forged something of a working friendship. Madonna liked this big, unusually uncouth Brit and Jimmy found he was comfortable with her heart-on-the-sleeve style.

'Fortunately the bed scene came right at the end of the film so by then we had got to know each other pretty well. It would have been awful if we'd only just met and then found ourselves in the sack together. We talked about it and it went without a hitch,' he said.

According to Jimmy he had budgeted for a six week recuperation period between the end of *Evita* and the beginning of the *Crocodile Shoes* shoot. Gallagher insists the film ran over by just a week which, if true, suggests that Jimmy made dangerously little allowance for the vagaries of film production. He was forced to start shooting his new television series the day after filming on *Evita* ended at Shepperton. What made things worse, *Evita* had been an extraordinarily tough schedule and although Jimmy wasn't required every day of the six months the work lasted for, he had been very busy during the final phase of shooting. Gallagher admitted he had been 'running on fumes' for the last few weeks, such was the effort he had put in. Once back home in New York, 'it was two months before I would even put the phone back on the hook'.

Jimmy had no such luxury. Exhausted, he dragged himself onto the *Crocodile Shoes* shoot. To make matters worse, his plans to spend some time with Miriam and the boys in between the two shoots had to be scrapped. Once again, he couldn't deliver on his promise to them to be around more often, even though his absence had already almost destroyed their relationship.

'I finished *Evita* on the Thursday evening and began the second *Crocodile Shoes* series on the Friday morning,' he told a journalist. 'That was madness. For the first two or three weeks, I was calling everyone the wrong names.'

The schedule was extremely tight. Filming began in June for a series which was to be screened from 14 November. To make matters worse the spin-off album, *Crocodile Shoes 2*, was due for release four days later. Once again, Jimmy had sole responsibility for the production as well as being star, scriptwriter and songwriter, not to mention editing the series once it was in the can. Days which began at 5.30 a.m. and did not finish until two the following morning were not unusual as Jimmy juggled his various tasks. He kept going, did not let it show, but the truth was he was utterly exhausted.

One other manifestation of Jimmy's obsession with control was that he insisted on doing as many of his own stunts as possible. Exhausted or not, that practice continued on *Crocodile Shoes 2* with disastrous results. They were filming a scene in the North Sea in which Jimmy's character had to fall overboard from a trawler. Such moments are always very tense even when experienced stuntmen are involved. When it is the star of the show who is about to plunge into a freezing sea a whole gamut of potential disasters will run through the mind of the director, even though he has placed a team of experienced divers in the water ready to act if anything goes wrong.

If the director had known about Jimmy's talent for physical calamity he would have been even more worried. The old knack did not desert him. It did all go wrong, so badly wrong that – as everyone said afterwards – a few more seconds and he would have been a gonner.

Jimmy went overboard and the scene was shot to satisfaction. Then the crew realised the star was nowhere to be seen. There followed a few seconds of mayhem on board while the divers went into action. After what seemed like an age he was spotted, floating face down, apparently unconscious. The divers fished him out and, to general relief, he came round, coughing and spluttering. Jimmy had kicked for the surface but lost his bearings underwater and cracked his head against the underside of the trawler as he came up. He was conscious but obviously badly affected by the blow. Filming was halted for the day as Jimmy was rushed to hospital where he had a precautionary brain scan and X-rays which revealed a depressed fracture of the skull. The doctors advised him to rest for several days at least. Jimmy arrived on set first thing the next morning.

He had been working like Superman since he became famous, driven on by his desire to prove people wrong, and sustained by remarkable powers of endurance. There were signs that his reserves of stamina were coming to an end and while the accident was not a turning point it brought home to everyone his human frailty. Although he worked on, Jimmy was plagued by severe headaches as a result of his accident and the schedule he had set himself became an increasing burden. The *Crocodile Shoes 2* project – TV series and album – limped to completion.

Jimmy was falling out of love with television. The man who had imposed upon himself the most demanding workload possible began to complain that schedules were too tight, ignoring the possibility of delegation as a solution. Part of the problem was that he had gone from the grand scale of movie-making Hollywood style to the confines of a BBC series. What's more, he had been free of the responsibilities of production for six months then suddenly constrained by them again.

'I found it incredibly refreshing simply to be the actor for hire, to go in and be told what to do by somebody I greatly respect,' he told a one journalist. 'If Alan [Parker] doesn't like something he tells you why, you do it again and then you leave and go home. It was tremendous. I hadn't done that since *Auf Wiedersehen*.'

But that wasn't the only factor. He was tired. As John Gallagher might say, he was running on fumes. He was beginning to feel that television was no longer worth it. He summed up his feelings at this time almost a year later.

'I felt I'd got really stale and I didn't have anything really special to give. I'm not interested in doing it just for the sake of working in television. Everything's so pared down financially, there's no adventure, no magic ... the schedules are becoming almost impossible.'

It showed. Whether it was because Jimmy had taken on more than he could handle, or that the creative juices had run dry, or that he had simply worked himself to a standstill, *Crocodile Shoes 2* was a pale imitation of its predecessor. The critics hated it wholeheartedly, with none of the equivocation that had accompanied reviews of previous Nail offerings.

Tony Purnell, in the *Daily Mirror*, said, 'Jimmy Nail created it, wrote it and starred in it so now he can take the blame for it. *Crocodile Shoes* was a load of old codswallop and a classic example of what happens when an actor gets ideas above his station. He gave himself all the rope and well and truly hanged himself.'

A. A. Gill was equally caustic in the *Sunday Times*: 'Jimmy Nail's vast ego has finally landed, crashed and burned. This second series about the dull, ugly Geordie, who inexplicably comes from Alabama when he sings, was proof that a hugely inflated opinion of oneself isn't enough to keep a cretinous script and remedial direction aloft. Jed Thing has become a rock legend, but he has problems – not enough to make a plot, mind, just enough to make you snigger. Nature has followed art: Nail isn't acting an old, soft, ambling, sad rocker, he's become one.'

The album was not much better received either by the critics or the public. Sales were modest, nowhere near the million selling first series spin-off, nor even up there with the *Big River* album. Neil McCormack, in the *Daily Telegraph* at least attempted to do Jimmy justice.

'As a singer and songwriter, he trades in the same tough but tender paradox that fuels his acting career: He is a big, ugly, macho man with a sensitive, romantic soul. Although his melodies and arrangements are relentlessly obvious, Nail infuses the songs with character.'

Evita was released at the end of the year accompanied by all the usual razzmatazz – premieres in London and Los Angeles and numerous press conferences. Jimmy's distaste for this side of the business was tempered by the fact that little was required of him other than to turn up and accept the acclaim. No one was really interested in him, or in Jonathan Pryce, Antonio Banderas or Alan Parker for that matter. All eyes were on Madonna. The 3,000-strong crowd who gathered outside the Empire cinema in London's Leicester Square for what was described as 'the starriest premiere of the year' did not come to see Jimmy or Andrew Lloyd Webber, the Duchess of York or even Rod Stewart. They came to chant Madonna's name, wave photographs of her in the air and, if they were lucky, catch a glimpse of the star. For once, Jimmy didn't mind being upstaged. He was enjoying this rarefied air and the relative anonymity of moving around in Madonna's slipstream.

Once all the fuss had died down, the cold facts were that *Evita* was not rapturously received in Britain. The critics generally disliked the all-music, pop-opera format, complaining that it needed dialogue. Tom Shone, in the *Sunday Times*, summed up the general dissatisfaction. 'Sitting through the wall-to-wall warbling of *Evita* ... is like watching a news programme that's all headlines; you hunger for the tiniest sliver of real dramatic meat, for the cast to stop emptying their lungs in song and start breathing life into their parts.'

Most of the criticism was directed at the failure of the format, not the performances of the cast. Jimmy won moderate praise for playing his cameo role perfectly competently. Nevertheless he must have been galled by the criticism of something he had worked so hard on and had been personally ecstatic about when Parker showed him the finished article for the first time.

John Gallagher reflects the general disappointment at the film's reception. 'I wish it had been better received than it was. It was a rough year. There was always the doubt in everybody's mind whether that medium – a musical one hundred per cent through – was going to sit well. It had that polarising effect on people, they either loved it or they were turned off by it totally. It is tough to get close to the characters in that kind of genre. In hindsight people were saying it would have been so much better if they had broken it up and allowed people to actually speak with each other to give it just a little air but I don't think that was possible. There were a lot of different strings to that project. I don't think it was possible for it to be altered to that extent.'

The most arduous year of Jimmy's professional life was over and what had he got to show for it? A television series that was derided, a mediocre album and a film that failed to punch its considerable weight, albeit through no fault of his own. He was physically exhausted and plagued by recurring headaches after his aquatic collision. He was approaching his forty-third birthday and had been driving himself relentlessly now for almost fifteen years. The demands he was placing upon himself had begun to worry those who knew him best. His sister had already voiced her concern. 'He has an obsessive personality. The fact that he drank far too much, then decided to give it up completely and throw himself 120 per cent into his work, producing, directing writing – he has to do everything. I don't understand this compulsion to do absolutely everything, because I worry that he's going to wear himself out. He's only in his early forties now, I want him to get to his late forties.'

In the past his Herculean efforts had always reaped just rewards. Each successful product, be it television series, album or concert tour, gave him the impetus to extend the boundaries of his career still further. *Crocodile Shoes 2* was the first project not to inspire him to continue. With mixed reviews for *Evita* following hard on the heels, he could be forgiven for losing heart. Yet it was not all doom and gloom by any means. One advantage of *Evita* being released in the middle of *Crocodile Shoes* was that it deflected the critical attention. Instead of being associated with a dubious TV series, he was part of a Hollywood blockbuster, grand in design, if flawed in format. And his personal performance was not criticised. He had acquitted himself well. With no obvious 'next project', he decided it was time to take stock, spend some time with his family, and maybe even to explore the exotic waters of Hollywood a little more closely to see what treasure could be found.

24
STILL CRAZY

The Royal Albert Hall, London. 22 April 1998. An early evening chill and the threat of rain means there is no loitering. The crowds walk briskly along Kensington Road, hunched against the wind that is blowing large, dark clouds across Hyde Park. Others dart from Queen's Gate into Prince Consort Road and Albert Court where the tall, discreetly well-tended mansion blocks lining the narrow streets offer some shelter. The huge, circular building has entrances splayed around its circumference and as soon as they become visible – the doorways silhouetted by the lights within them – the people quicken their pace.

The audience making its way along these well-trodden paths is not that of a typical rock or classical music concert. In fact, these people are rather nondescript, difficult to categorise. They are in early middle age, largely, with very few over fifty and just about no one under twenty-five. Most are dressed in a smart-casual manner. Jeans – but not denims – stiff-looking new leather jackets, quite a few floral frocks. The prevailing accent is working-class London, albeit somewhat refined. There are more women than men. Quite a few groups of them, in fact. Lots of couples too. Generally the women look more enthusiastic than their partners, as if they have persuaded them to come along, persuaded them that Jimmy Nail is worth listening to.

They file through the entrance doors and up a flight of stairs to the circular corridor which surrounds the concert hall. Here there are a couple of bars and a foyer where Jimmy Nail paraphernalia is on display and for sale. There is a large souvenir booklet with nearly every one of its twenty-four pages containing huge photographs of Jimmy arranged around a potted biography of his showbusiness career. There are T-shirts with the concert tour logo, 'On The Boards 1998' displayed on the front.

The chatter in the corridor mingles with the sound of a harp and many decide to go inside the auditorium to hear the support act, Irish singer Ursula Burns. Soon it is time for the moment they have been waiting for. The stragglers find their seats, the hall is almost full...

Jimmy Nail steps out onto the most famous concert stage in the country wearing an expensive-looking dark grey suit and carrying a guitar. His six-piece band take their positions while their leader begins his preamble. It is none too fluent at first. Soon, however, he is into his stride, and a sort of earthy, folksy, man-of-the people charm emerges which makes him sound rather like a Geordie Henry Cooper. He enjoys a similar kind of popularity as the old boxer too. The impression he creates is of a man who has made it but who has remained unspoiled and loyal to his roots. He is quickly into his repertoire. Jimmy's singing voice is nothing like his exterior. It is surprisingly high-pitched, soulful and expressive. His music is relentlessly middle of the road pop (Virgin was right in its assessment) with a streak of sentimentality which he is unashamed of and which his fans clearly love. The big man with the harsh exterior and the soft centre.

He has sex appeal too. Especially, it seems, to a certain type of middle-aged woman. By and large, the audience are restrained but one bold lady shouts 'Get your kit off, Jimmy' at him and he pauses a moment before replying that once you turn forty it is better to keep your clothes on in public.

He plays for two hours – good value for the £22.50 it cost to get in – and makes sure he includes all his most popular tunes. England are playing football against Portugal at Wembley and Jimmy provides regular updates for his audience. The final score is 3–0 to England which he relays to them with a shout of triumph. At the end he calls his younger son Freddie out of the audience to join him on stage and holds the boy's hand when he seems a little bit overawed. When his final encore is over the band departs but Jimmy stays to thank the audience once again, telling them: 'It's nights like this that make this the best job in the world.' He seems to mean it, too.

Jimmy Nail has a lot to be happy about. The musical career he worked so hard to establish has borne rich fruit. It earns him considerably more money now than his acting or writing. Just about all of his releases – albums and singles – have sold well. He plays live regularly too, as he loves the chance to 'communicate' with his huge following this way. He is still phenomenally busy. The Albert Hall concert is the culmination of an intense, thirty-eight-date nationwide tour in which he deliberately played smaller, town hall-sized venues which itself followed hard on the heels of shooting his latest film, *Still Crazy*, about a seventies rock band which re-unites twenty years later. After the tour he begins work on his new studio album. Yet there is the sense that he has eased off the throttle, that his white knuckle ride through the eighties and most of the nineties has slowed to a more enjoyable pace.

It wasn't so long ago – just three years – that he told Melvyn Bragg that he was incapable of enjoying anything, that there never seemed to be the time for that kind of indulgence. Now he appears to have come through the period in his life during which he felt compelled to prove himself to the world. He succeeded in that, emerging as an arresting if not brilliant actor and a more than competent writer and a singer who has the knack of producing stylish and commercially successful music. He is the classic all-rounder, a man who always fancies having a go and will not rest until he has mastered all challenges placed before him.

The critics still enjoy sneering at Jimmy Nail. The recurring theme tends to be that he lacks real talent in any of his various disciplines, that he is more a product of slick marketing than a performer of any real substance. Part of this critical unease stems from the difficulty in classifying him. His frenetic energy over the last fifteen years has established him on so many different fronts that there is no one to compare him with. Also it is true that feeling the desire to succeed in so many areas must lead to the conclusion that he is more concerned in promoting himself than fully exploring his potential in any single art form.

But not even his severest critics can deny him the scale of his achievement. He got there the hard way, driven by a profound insecurity, a deep-seated fear that it could all turn to dust and he was just one failure away from installing panes of glass and singing in pubs again. He didn't spare anyone either, allowing nothing and no one to get in his way. Never afraid to speak his mind, this led to as many verbal confrontations in his middle years as there were physical ones in his youth. Just as he bears the scars of those early battles, so he must live with the less tangible consequences of his often belligerent nature. Friendships won with his great charm have subsequently foundered on the ruthlessness of his march ever onwards and upwards.

He has achieved fame and fortune. Always shrewd with money, he has become a wealthy man over the years, largely from his lucrative musical career. He is famous and well loved in Britain, possessed of a folksy quality that seems to strike a chord with the public. But there is an altogether harder edge to the private man, which has cost him friends, like Francesco Reidy, over the years. Even Carol Johnson – divorced from her rock star husband for nine years and divorced from the celebrity lifestyle after a financial crisis – now feels the real friendship between them is at an end. They have seen little of each other in recent times. Yet, she is nostalgic for the man she remembers. 'There is a place in my heart for Jimmy Nail. He will always be special. But the person I first met is not there anymore. I miss that old Jimmy, the out of control, overweight, hard-drinking Jimmy. He was more himself then,' she says.

There is no doubt he has great charisma. The light is brighter and the darkness deeper when he is around. No one who comes into contact with Jimmy Nail can remain indifferent to him.

Also he has had to suffer long periods apart from his family. The man who so dotes on his two sons has missed large chunks of their formative years, omissions that no amount of fame and money can make up for. Then there is the strained relationship with his sister.

He now appears to be at a crossroads in his remarkable life. The last couple of years have seen him – by his standards only – treading water. Consolidating. Busy, but not breaking new ground. He has done a lot of thinking during this time. At forty-four, he is no longer a young man, and there are signs of a new maturity. Ever since his time with Ian La Frenais in Hollywood, he has been captivated by the place. Yet, after *Evita* there was not the headlong rush to conquer it that might have taken place had the role come, say, a decade earlier. The signs are that the mature Nail is a more balanced, even a more secure creature. But it would be a mistake to suggest complacency. America is still very much in his sights, as an actor and musician. He has grown a little big for Britain.

One senior TV man who worked closely with Jimmy for years admitted still not being able to decide how much real talent he possessed. He then added, 'I think his greatest achievement is himself, to have come from being a Geordie tearaway to what he now is. He is not a superstar but he would like to be and possibly he will be. It is very difficult to categorise him. Anything could happen in his career. I will watch with some affection and great interest.'

ILLUSTRATIONS

The author and publishers are grateful to the following for use of photographic material:

The Bradford's home in Longbenton; Joseph Watson's glazing firm on the Walker Industrial Estate (© Propix)

Jimmy Bradford snr (© the *Sun*)

Jimmy at Carol and Brian Johnson's fancy dress party; Jimmy, Tim Healy and Carol having lunch; two pictures of Jimmy with Carol Johnson at her home, Danemede; Jimmy and Miriam in London; Jimmy with a dog at Danemede; Jimmy trying out his musical skills; Jimmy on the set of *Morons from Outer Space*; Jimmy meeting his match on the Newcastle Quayside (courtesy of Carol Johnson)

Jimmy with Kevin Whately and Timothy Spall on the *Auf Wiedersehen Pet* set (© Mirror Syndication International)

Jimmy in full *Morons from Outer Space* costume (© Scope Features)

Shoot for the Sun publicity still (© Universal Pictorial Press & Agency Ltd)

Jimmy with Miriam and their two sons (© Mirror Syndication International)

Jimmy with Miriam at the *Evita* premiere (© Fred Duval/Famous)

Jimmy with Madonna and Antonio Banderas at the *Evita* premiere (© Capital Pictures)

If any copyright holders have inadvertently been overlooked, the publishers will be pleased to make the necessary arrangement at the earliest opportunity.